THE MODERN THEORY OF PRESIDENTIAL POWER

Recent Titles in
Contributions in Political Science

THE MODERN THEORY OF PRESIDENTIAL POWER

Alexander Hamilton and the Corwin Thesis

RICHARD LOSS

CONTRIBUTIONS IN POLITICAL SCIENCE, NUMBER 253
Bernard K. Johnpoll, *Series Editor*

Greenwood Press
New York • Westport, Connecticut • London

Library of Congress Cataloging-in-Publication Data

Loss, Richard.
    The modern theory of presidential power : Alexander Hamilton and
the Corwin thesis / Richard Loss.
      p.   cm.—(Contributions in political science, ISSN 0147-1066
; no. 253)
    Includes bibliographical references (p.   ).
    ISBN 0-313-26751-0 (lib. bdg. : alk. paper)
    1. Presidents—United States—History. 2. Executive power—United
States—History. 3. Hamilton, Alexander, 1757–1804—Political and
social views. 4. Corwin, Edward S., 1878–1963—Political and social
views. I. Title. II. Series.
JK511.L67   1990
353.03'22—dc20   89-27372

British Library Cataloguing in Publication Data is available.

Library of Congress Catalog Card Number: 89-27372
ISBN: 0-313-26751-0
ISSN: 0147-1066

First published in 1990

Greenwood Press, 88 Post Road West, Westport, Connecticut 06881
An imprint of Greenwood Publishing Group, Inc.

Printed in the United States of America

The paper used in this book complies with the
Permanent Paper Standard issued by the National
Information Standards Organization (Z39.48-1984).

10 9 8 7 6 5 4 3 2 1

For my mother, Mary T. Jones, Kathy Loss, Tom and Andrea Loss, and Nadine Martin

Except for my immediate obligations to my family, this book would have been dedicated to C. Herman Pritchett and in memory of Alpheus T. Mason and Herbert J. Storing.

Whatsoever things are true, whatsoever things are honest, whatsoever things are just, whatsoever things are pure, whatsoever things are lovely, whatsoever things are of good report; if there be any virtue; and if there be any praise, think on these things.

Phillipians iv, 8

Yet all these ought not to discourage us from exertion, for . . . I believe no effort in favor of virtue is lost, and all good men ought to struggle both by their counsel and example.

John Adams

The natural progress of things is for liberty to yield and government to gain ground.

Thomas Jefferson

The executive branch of the government was eternally in action; it was ever awake; it never slept; its action was continuous and unceasing, like the tides of some mighty river, which continued flowing and flowing on, swelling, and deepening, and widening, in its onward progress, till it swept away every impediment, and broke down and removed every frail obstacle which might be set up to impede its course.

Henry Clay

Contents

Preface

One opinion teaches that the Vietnam War under Democratic and Republican presidents, the Watergate crimes, the Nixon administration's
enemies list and the Reagan administration's Iran–*Contra* affair have
shaken confidence in the strength of the limitations on presidential
power. Such doubts have indirectly led to skepticism about the fashionable doctrines of presidential power, the Constitution and political morality. Representative Lee Hamilton's closing statement in the Iran–
Contra investigation implied the desirability of again consulting Edward
S. Corwin's understanding of the presidency. With Corwin's aid, this
book attempts to identify the intellectual problem of presidential power
on the premise that understanding should precede action. My main
subject is the relationship of the teachings of Alexander Hamilton to the
modern theory of presidential power.

   Proceeding from the premise that the unequal treatment of unequals
is consistent with justice, this book emphasizes presidents according to
their contribution to our understanding. Beyond all presidents Washington had the incentive, capacity and opportunity to think comprehensively and fruitfully about the moral ends of the American political
community and the constitutional means of presidential power. The
other presidents discussed in this book often contented themselves with
thin rationalizations, comparable to a bus ticket good for one ride only,
of their intentions or deeds. Hence public explanation of the relationship
between the ends and presidential means of the regime deteriorated.
Perhaps the qualitative change since Hamilton and Washington in the
understanding and explanation of presidential power will shock or upset
some readers. If so, I pray that these readers will charitably avoid blaming

the messenger, myself, for bearing bad news. I have neither invented nor concealed the qualitative change of subsequent thought. Certainly all readers are entitled to be concerned about the narrowing of presidential understanding. Readers seeking an overview of presidential interpretation of presidential power might begin with works such as those by Norman Small and Arthur Tourtellot listed in the Selected Bibliography. These readers should be aware of the complacent assumption of a steadily advancing constitutional progress found in some of the older works.

The Institute for Educational Affairs supported my research. Thomas Engeman read and criticized the chapter on Hamilton; Professor Engeman bears no responsibility for the chapter's contents. I thank the editors of *The Political Science Reviewer*, *Presidential Studies Quarterly* and Scholars' Facsimiles and Reprints for their permission to reprint.

R. L.

Introduction

Edward S. Corwin, the most eminent commentator on the Constitution and the presidency of the twentieth century, concluded that "the modern theory of presidential power" is "the contribution primarily of Alexander Hamilton."[1] Corwin also identified as the goal for modern presidents "the kind of President George Washington was, or as close an approximation thereto as [a modern president's] character and abilities enable ...him to be."[2] I have discovered no writing of Corwin's that demonstrates these two theses, but emerging as they did after a lifetime of reflection on the presidency, Corwin's theses deserve our attention.[3]

Clinton Rossiter attempted to elaborate Corwin's Hamilton thesis. Article II of the Constitution, said Rossiter, is "thoroughly Hamiltonian today."[4] In agreeing with Corwin's thesis, Rossiter directed attention to two of Hamilton's writings: Hamilton read Article II "grandly and creatively as Publius, Pacificus, and Secretary of the Treasury." The documentary evidence for Rossiter's elaboration of Corwin's thesis is Hamilton's *Federalist* papers on the presidency and his Pacificus Letters. Rossiter continued that subsequent responses to "mighty events" by presidents and subsequent constitutional interpretations "have been, in one sense, merely an elaboration of the principle he first announced as Pacificus: 'that the *executive power* of the nation is vested in the President; subject only to the *exceptions* and *qualifications* which are expressed in the instrument.' " Rossiter, then, found the Pacificus Letters to be of crucial importance for the modern theory of presidential power. He concluded that "the 'Stewardship Theory' of Theodore Roosevelt expresses the realities of presidential power in a government committed to vast responsibilities at home and abroad, and that theory may be traced back *in unbroken line* to Hamilton's teachings."[5] In sum, two leading scholars of the Constitution and the presidency stressed the continuity between Hamilton's teachings and the modern theory of presidential power. The acceptance of Corwin's Hamiton thesis and praise of Washington by political scientists, law teachers and historians has important consequences for the understanding of American constitutional and political development and for the direction in which changes of the presidency are sought.

Part I of this study explains how Hamilton and Washington understood the American regime, what sets the tone, what the political community venerates and how this is reflected in the distribution of power and honors. Part I also examines how Hamilton and Washington understood the presidency. Part II explains what happened to Hamilton's teachings in the thought of key makers of the modern presidency, Abraham Lincoln, Theodore Roosevelt, Woodrow Wilson and Franklin D. Roosevelt. Part II also explains what happened to Hamilton's teachings in the scholarship of men who molded public expectations of the modern presidency, Corwin himself, Clinton Rossiter and Richard Neustadt. The Epilogue states my general argument and attempts to discern the possible direction of the presidency.

Corwin's theses on Hamilton and Washington imply that a return to their teachings, prudently adapted to our circumstances, is possible, necessary and desirable. I am aware that I am writing about Washington shortly after James Flexner observed that "the current attitude toward Washington ... is often hostile."[6] Flexner persuasively counterattacked: "In being ourselves untrue to *the highest teaching of the American tradition*, we of this generation ... have discarded an invaluable heritage. We are blinding our eyes to stars that lead to the very ideals many of us most admire."[7]

Aristotle identified four themes of political inquiry: the best regime, the best regime under actual conditions, the origin and preservation of a given inferior regime and the most practicable regime.[8] Hamilton and Washington were not political philosophers investigating the best regime or even the best regime under actual conditions. They were active statesmen concerned with the origin and preservation of the United States of America. Yet their attention to how virtue might prolong American liberty and republicanism surely elevates them above their lesser rivals.

NOTES

1. Edward S. Corwin, ed., *The Constitution of the United States of America: Analysis and Interpretation*, Sen. Doc. 170, 82nd Cong., 2nd Sess., at 381 (1953).
2. Edward S. Corwin, *Presidential Power and the Constitution: Essays, by Edward*

S. Corwin, Richard Loss, ed. (Ithaca, N.Y.: Cornell University Press, 1976), p. 174.

3. The titles of multi-volume works cited in the footnotes of this book will be preceded by the volume number and followed by the page number where appropriate. Edward S. Corwin, 1 *Corwin on the Constitution*, Richard Loss, ed. (Ithaca, N.Y.: Cornell University Press, 1981); 2 *Corwin on the Constitution*, Loss, ed. (Ithaca, N.Y.: Cornell University Press, 1987); 3 *Corwin on the Constitution*, Loss, ed. (Ithaca, N.Y.: Cornell University Press, 1988).

4. Clinton Rossiter, *Alexander Hamilton and the Constitution* (New York: Harcourt, Brace and World, 1964), p. 248.

5. Ibid., p. 248, italics added. A version of the Hamilton continuity thesis also appears in Jacob E. Cooke, *Alexander Hamilton* (New York: Charles Scribner's Sons, 1982), pp. 128–129: "Hamilton's view of presidential power [in the Pacificus Letters] has served as a model for strong chief executives, particularly in wartime, from his day to our own. . . . Hamilton's prescription of presidential power became an incalculably important precedent." Even a critic of expanded presidential power, C. Perry Patterson, misstates Hamilton's theory of presidential power by deleting Hamilton's requirement in the Pacificus Letters that presidential power must be subordinated to the principles of "free government." Patterson then concludes that Pacificus's theory "was the theory of presidential powers held by Theodore Roosevelt, Woodrow Wilson, and Franklin D. Roosevelt." C. Perry Patterson, *Presidential Government in the United States: The Unwritten Constitution* (Chapel Hill: University of North Carolina, 1947), pp. 132–133. See also James MacGregor Burns, *Presidential Government: The Crucible of Leadership* (Boston: Houghton Mifflin, 1965).

6. James T. Flexner, *Washington: The Indispensable Man* (Boston: Little, Brown, 1974), p. xvi.

7. Ibid., p. xvi, italics added.

8. Aristotle, *Politics*, Ernest Barker, trans. (Oxford: Clarendon Press, 1948), p. 155.

Part I

HAMILTON AND WASHINGTON

1

Alexander Hamilton's Understanding of the American Regime and the Presidency

That he possessed intellectual powers of the first order, and the
moral qualifications of integrity and honor in a captivating degree,
has been decreed to him by a suffrage now universal.
                    Alexander Hamilton, according to James Madison

This chapter discusses Hamilton's teaching on the principles of human
conduct and political power before taking up his understanding of the
republican regime. The chapter then delves into Hamilton's understanding of the executive prior to the Constitutional Convention, his speech
of June 18, 1787 in the Convention and his defense of the Constitution
in the New York ratifying convention. Then I consider the design of
the presidency, Hamilton's understanding of presidential "energy" in
Federalist 67–77, his architectonic advice to President Washington, his
understanding of presidential "power" in his Pacificus Letters and the
objections to Pacificus's argument by James Madison. Finally, the chapter
attempts to establish the rank of the Pacificus Letters over *Federalist* 67–
77 in Hamilton's teaching on the presidency.

To employ a non-Hamiltonian distinction, Hamilton's thought may
be divided for our present purpose into moral and institutional reflections. One criticism sometimes made of the Founders, including Hamilton, is that they neglected the formation of human character in their
eagerness to devise institutional solutions to the political problem. This
criticism gains plausibility from Hamilton's praise of ancient over modern political science in *Federalist* 9. He there contends that modern political science better understands the effects of certain principles than

did the ancients.[1] These principles are institutions, such as legislative balances and checks, not ethical principles.

Yet from the first Hamilton also proceeded on the assumption that men with the proper character, the proper philosophical and religious principles, will act rightly in political matters, including the quarrel between the colonies and Great Britain. Ideas about right conduct, not institutions, are Hamilton's weapons against his adversary in "The Farmer Refuted," which attempts to vindicate American rights against Great Britain. This remarkable essay combined an appeal to natural law with a criticism of the modern philospher Thomas Hobbes, who held that "moral obligation . . . is derived from the introduction of civil society; and *there is no virtue*, but what is purely artificial, the mere contrivance of politicians for the maintenance of social intercourse."[2] Hamilton traced Hobbes's "absurd and impious doctrine" to Hobbes's rejection of "an intelligent superintending principle, who is the governor, and will be the final judge, of the universe."[3] He quoted Blackstone on the law of nature "dictated by God himself," which is "binding all over the globe, in all countries, and at all times."[4] Hamilton derived the natural rights of mankind from the creation of man by a Supreme Being and the endowment of man with reason to pursue his duty and interest.[5] The relations between a colony and the mother country are governed by compact and "more especially by the law of nature" and the "supreme law of every society—its own happiness."

"The Farmer Refuted" is Hamilton's most philosophic writing. The less frequent references to natural law and Christianity in Hamilton's later writings do not mean that he abandoned his initial understanding of the ultimate standards governing human conduct and political power and his rejection of Hobbesianism. Hamilton's later writings dealt with a more normal range of situations than that prevailing in the pre-revolutionary America of 1775, and he was not compelled to state the ultimate grounds of right political action, virtue, Christianity and natural law. Virtue understood in a pre-Hobbesian and pre-modern sense, Christianity and natural law are thus the tacit framework for Hamilton's more concrete analyses in his later writings.

Hamilton's moral reflections are distinguished not only by a defense of American freedom grounded in ultimate principles but by a manly defense of moderation in rulers. He opposed Plutarch, who said a ruler must not give up his authority. "A false sentiment; it would often be praiseworthy in a prince to relinquish part of an excessive prerogative to establish a more moderate government, better adapted to the happiness or temper of his people!"[6] Consider further Hamilton's maxims: "That honesty is still the best policy; that justice and moderation are the surest supports of every government, are maxims, which however they may be called trite, [are] at all times true, though too seldom regarded, but rarely neglected with impunity."[7] Hamilton argued from the examples of Augustus and Queen Elizabeth that moderation promoted stability.[8]

"Our governments hitherto have no habits," wrote Hamilton in the "Second Letter from Phocion."[9] "If we set out with justice, moderation, liberality, and a scrupulous regard to the constitution, the government will acquire a spirit and tone, productive of permanent blessings to the community." According to Hamilton's son, Hamilton stood for "free, vigorous, yet moderate government."[10] "To him nothing was more distasteful than an irregular and unnecessary exercise of power. Order working by its proper means to secure and enlarge the sphere of order, was all his favorite thought—*Moderation in the selection and use of means, his favorite practice*."[11] Hamilton's son omitted parts of Hamilton's teaching, especially on virtue, that are of crucial importance, but his summary is satisfactory as far as it goes, and it is particularly valuable for the emphasis on Hamilton's moderation. John Hamilton showed that his father had a complex understanding of government in which vigor was only one, and not the controlling, element.

Hamilton's letters are brimming with reflections on American character that influenced the direction in which he sought an amelioration of the political situation. "It is not safe to trust to the virtue of any people."[12] "My dear Laurens," he confided to his intimate friend, "our countrymen have all the folly of the ass and all the passiveness of the sheep.... They are determined not to be free and they can neither be frightened, discouraged nor persuaded to change their resolution. If we are saved France and Spain must save us."[13] Hamilton concluded that even a young Demosthenes would be unable to rouse Americans from "the lethargy of volup[tuous] indolence, or dissolve the fascinating cha[racter] of self interest" to inspire them with the "wisdom" of legislators and the enthusiasm of republicans: "Every [hope] of this kind my friend is an idle dream; every [—will] convince you that there is no virtue [in] America—that commerce which preside[d over] the birth and education of these states has [fitted] their inhabitants for the chain, and that the only condition they sincerely desire is that it may be a golden one."[14] Hamilton understood virtue in a pre-modern sense in opposition to the Lockean acquisitiveness of the golden chain, which he denied was compatible with republicanism or political liberty. Without naming Locke, Hamilton touched upon the important question of the compatibility of Lockean acquisitiveness and patriotism.[15]

Clearly, Hamilton identified virtue as the controlling or highest principle. "The *worst* of evils seems to be coming upon us—*a loss of our virtue*."[16] Even ambition in the service of fame failed to qualify for Hamilton as the highest principle. He warned Lafayette in 1789 to "be virtuous amidst the seductions of ambition."[17] It is reported that after resigning as secretary of the treasury Hamilton entered a room in the presidential mansion: "Glancing his eye upon a small book that lay on the table, he took it up and observed: 'Ah, this is the Constitution. Now, mark my words: So long as we are a young and *virtuous* people, this instrument will bind us in mutual interests, mutual welfare, and mutual happiness; but when we become old and corrupt it will bind us no longer.' "[18] Even if this report is apocryphal, its dominant emphasis on virtue shows that this part of the Hamilton legend is consistent with Hamilton's own principles.

For Hamilton the spirit of virtue resembled Aristotle's teaching that the virtue of a horse is running well, of a knife cutting well and of a man acting well in accordance with reason. This means that for Hamilton virtue was inegalitarian. Hamilton's writings referred to Aristotle, which was consistent with his education.[19] Samuel Eliot Morison has written that "the fathers of our Revolution, the framers of our federal and state constitutions," including Alexander Hamilton, "were steeped in Roman and Greek history.... They were closer to the ancients in spirit, Americans as they were, than we are to them."[20] In addition to experience in self-government and the influence of Christianity, "the amazing success" of the American republic was "partly" "due to the classical training of her leaders."[21] Not "courses in civics, sociology, and psychology" but Plutarch's *Lives* and the orations of Cicero and Demosthenes prepared these statesmen for their tasks: "a study of classical culture ... broadened their mental horizon, sharpened their intellectual powers, stressed *virtus* and promoted *areté*, the civic qualities appropriate to a Republican."[22]

At King's College, now Columbia University, Hamilton "found one of the most complete classical curricula offered in America during the second half of the eighteenth century."[23] Among the ancients studied when Hamilton attended King's College were Plato, Aristotle, Xenephon and Thucydides. In the two years that Hamilton attended King's College "his college education was primarily centered around this [classical] curriculum."[24]

In these authors and in Plutarch's *Lives* and the orations of Demosthenes, which Hamilton quoted, he "could find fine examples of statesmanship, lofty political ethos, and remarkable precedents; and there he could enrich his knowledge with the experience of the political failures and successes of the ancients."[25] Perhaps also Hamilton learned from the ancients the connection between morals and government, as in his saying: "It is an axiom that governments form manners [i.e., morals], as well as manners [i.e., morals] form governments."[26] Hamilton's point about the relationship of morals and government was more clearly stated by James Wilson: "as excellent laws improve the virtue of the citizens, so the virtue of the citizens has a reciprocal and benign energy in heightening the excellence of the law."[27]

According to Stuart Gerry Brown, "Hamilton, like Aristotle, thought of government as itself the prime moral agent. In this he was a classicist. ... he was certainly familiar with the *Politics* as a part of the corpus of political philosophy he read both as a young student and later on when he was preparing himself for a role in the Constitutional Convention."[28] Gilbert Lycan concluded that "in his *Federalist* essays, in his speeches on the Constitution, and even in his personal correspondence we can almost see ancient Greece living again."[29] "Hamilton's mature philosophy on the subject of the basic factors underlying men's actions ... is, that men are guided by selfish interests and by their virtues."[30] "Most of his essays in the public press would have made no sense at all had he not been appealing to the noble qualities of the minds of his contemporaries."[31]

More generally, Hamilton understood the passions and interest in light of virtue, the lower in terms of the higher. One of the basest passions for Hamilton was greed. His noble contempt for greed is found in his statement to his intimate friend: "My Dr. Laurens in perfect confidence I whisper a word in your ear. *I hate money making men.*"[32] Hamilton, who has been called "the first American business man," held that "when avarice takes the lead in a state, it is commonly the forerunner of its fall. How shocking it is to discover among ourselves ... the strongest symptoms of this fatal disease?"[33]

Hamilton's argument distinguished between the necessary and sufficient conditions for the survival of republican government and freedom; he denied that the satisfaction of the passions, especially greed, was a sufficient condition. Generally, Hamilton's position on greed is compatible with Aristotle's teaching that money getting unregulated by moderation is a disease and disorder of the human soul because it reverses the hierarchy of reason over the appetite. Accordingly, the audience and passions addressed by Hamilton's economic writings, such as the "Report on Manufactures," are far from representing Hamilton's understanding of the highest form of human character.

According to Helene Johnson Looze, Hamilton's diplomacy "very probably relied ... upon principles gleaned from the Greek and Roman classics."[34] There was a "remarkably similar" resemblance between classical principles and Hamilton's decisions and explanations of them. In sum: virtue is the highest or controlling principle for Hamilton, and he understood virtue in an inegalitarian Aristotelian fashion. He may have come to this understanding of virtue naturally and through his education in the classics. There is no labored argument for this understanding of virtue in Hamilton's writings, for to demonstrate virtue to the virtuous is redundant, and to demonstrate virtue to the unvirtuous is impossible. What induces an active statesman to identify with or respond to a specific teaching in political philosophy is not necessarily a logical demonstration. It is reported, for example, that a friend once lent Winston S. Churchill

"Welldon's translation of Aristotle's *Ethics*, with a particular request that he should carefully study what that friend (rightly or wrongly) believed to be the greatest book in the world. Winston read it (or read part of it) and is reported to have said that he thought it very good. 'But,' he added, 'it is extraordinary how much of it I had already thought out for myself.' "[35] Hamilton may have come in part naturally to Aristotelian virtue as Churchill did to the teaching of the *Ethics*.

In addition to virtue, moderation and natural law, Christianity as a basis of moral rights and duties was a key principle for Hamilton. He proposed the formation of a Christian Constitutional Society, a measure that was in part an exercise in civil religion.[36] Hamilton also vigorously opposed stigmatizing the Christian religion and government as abuses.[37] He opposed "opinions...which threaten the foundations of religion, morality and society."[38] He defended Christian revelation, the existence of "a Deity," the duty of piety, the immortality of the soul and the doctrine of a future state of rewards and punishments in opposition to "natural religion."[39]

Hamilton's criticism of "natural religion," together with the strong influence on Hamilton certain scholars attribute to the modern philosopher David Hume, recalls Hume's *Dialogues Concerning Natural Religion*. What did Hume teach on religion, and how likely is it that these teachings molded Hamilton's thought? The term *natural religion* in Hume's title was used by eighteenth-century writers "as opposed to 'revealed religion.' "[40] Norman Kemp Smith held that Hume "certainly did not picture himself...as recasting, or even merely delimiting, the essentials of religious belief. He is consciously, and deliberately, attacking 'the religious hypothesis,' and through it religion as such."[41]

"But," Kemp Smith continued, "it is in his *Dialogues Concerning Natural Religion* that the problem of expressing his mind freely, *while yet not too greatly violating the established code*, meets Hume in its most difficult form. For in the *Dialogues* he is doing precisely *what was above all else forbidden, namely, to make a direct attack on the whole theistic position*."[42] Hume's advice on Rousseau's writing shows how Hume understood the relationship between persecution and the art of philosophic writing:

When I came to peruse that passage of M. Rousseau's Treatise [*Émile*] which has occasioned all the persecution against him, I was not in the least surprised that it gave offense. *He has not had the precaution to throw any veil over his sentiments*; and as he scorns to *dissemble his contempt of established opinions*, he could not wonder that all the zealots were in arms against him. The liberty of the press is not so secured in *any* country, *scarce even in this*, as not to render such an open attack of the popular prejudices *somewhat dangerous*.[43]

Hume's rule of cautious writing is that since liberty of the press exists neither in France nor England it is "somewhat dangerous" to philosophize against or openly attack the "popular prejudices" without the "pre-caution" of throwing a "veil" over the philosopher's teaching.

Hume himself said of his *Dialogues*: "I find that *nothing can be more cautiously and more artfully written.*"[44] Hume's caution was such that he used "devices" to "mask . . . his batteries, that they may be the more effectively brought into action in demolishing" religion and theism.[45] One such device is Hume's use of a distinction for the purpose of "tempering for the ordinary reader the force and proper scope of the sceptical objections" in the *Dialogues*.[46] Kemp Smith reasonably distinguished the "ordinary reader" from the "attentive reader" of the *Dialogues*.[47] The "attentive reader" would be more likely to detect Hume's masking of his argument and conclusion and to identify which character spoke for the conclusions most congenial to Hume. In discussing a possible division of labor for writing the *Dialogues*, Hume said that if someone else had written the arguments for the character Cleanthes, "I should have taken on me the character of Philo, in the Dialogue, *which you'll own I could have supported naturally enough.*"[48] Hume's admission suggests that Philo is "naturally" closer to Hume's position than Cleanthes. Speaking again of the character Philo, Hume said: "I there introduce a Sceptic, who is indeed refuted. . . . yet before he is *silenced*, he advances several topics, which will give umbrage, and will be deemed very bold and free, as well as much out of the common road."[49] Philo is "refuted" by silencing him, in other words is not truly refuted.

Hume told his publisher that the *Dialogues Concerning Natural Religion* "will be much less obnoxious to the law, and not more exposed to popular clamour" than his *Enquiry Concerning Human Understanding*.[50] Hume's will left instructions for the posthumous publication of the *Dialogues*, and he enjoined his publisher to "keep an entire silence on this subject."[51] Hume expressed "a particular partiality" for the *Dialogues* and so took pains to avoid having them suppressed after his death.[52] After Hume's death his friend Adam Smith refused in any way to have his name associated with the publication of the *Dialogues*, and they were printed in 1779 with no publisher's name given.[53] The editors of two separate editions of the *Dialogues*, Henry Aiken and Kemp Smith, identified the conclusion of the *Dialogues* in the skeptical character Philo's summation: "The whole of natural theology" affords "no inference that affects human life, or can be the source of any action or forbearance."[54] Hume's conclusion eliminated God from human conduct.

Nor was Hume's destructiveness to religion limited to the *Dialogues*. In the *Natural History of Religion* Hume identified the "origin of religion" as "the active imagination of men." In a chapter of this work entitled "General Corollary" Hume announced that "*ignorance is the mother of* [religious] *devotion.* . . . The whole is a riddle, an enigma, an inexplicable mystery."[55] Hume's unpublished essay on "The Immortality of the Soul" contended that "in reality, it is the gospel, and the gospel *alone*, that has brought life and immortality to light."[56] "The *physical* arguments from the analogy of nature are strong for the mortality of the soul: and these are really the *only* philosophical arguments, which ought to be admitted with regard to this question, or indeed any question of fact."[57] Hence Hume found no rational evidence for the immortality of the soul.

Hume assaulted the doctrine of miracles. "A miracle may be accurately defined" as "a transgression of a law of nature by a particular volition of the Deity, or by the interposition of some invisible agent."[58] "A miracle is a violation of the laws of nature; and as a firm and unalterable experience has established these laws, the proof against a miracle . . . is as entire as any argument from experience can possibly be imagined."[59] "No human testimony can have such force as to prove a miracle, and make it a just foundation of *any* such system of religion."[60] Hume pronounced the "miracles, related in Scripture" to be "the production of a mere human writer and historian."[61] He wrote of accomplishing "an entire annihilation" of "all popular religions."[62] After attempting to demolish miracles, Hume ironically concluded that

the Christian religion not only was at first attended with miracles, but even at this day cannot be believed by any reasonable person without one. Mere reason is insufficient to convince us of its veracity: And whoever is moved by faith to assent to it, is conscious of a continued miracle in his own person, which subverts all the principles of his understanding, and gives him a determination to believe what is most contrary to custom and experience."[63]

Hume put an argument against miracles to a Jesuit who, said Hume, "observed to me, that it was impossible for that argument to have any solidity, because it operated equally against the Gospel as the Catholic miracles;—which observation I thought proper to admit as a sufficient answer."[64]

Hume even stamped his irreligion on his *History of England*, though he acted somewhat differently there than in his philosophical writings. He asserted that "there is no passage in the *History* which strikes in the least at revelation. But as I run over all the sects successively, and speak of each of them with some mark of disregard, the reader, putting the whole together, concludes that I am of no sect; which to him will appear the same thing as the being of no religion."[65] Hume offered no defense against the inferences of the careful reader who put the "whole together," which is to say he authorized the soundness of this way of reading his *History*.

Hume's reply to the charge of "infidel" was to point to his "many" volumes on history, literature, politics, trade and morals, "which in that particular at least, are entirely inoffensive."[66] "I could wish your friend had not denominated me an infidel writer, on account of ten or twelve pages which seem to him to have that tendency.... Is a man to be called a drunkard, because he has been seen fuddled once in his lifetime?" Hume's misleading reply reduces to the invalid argument that his "many" inoffensive volumes on other subjects disprove that he wrote infidel philosophy for "ten or twelve pages." Hume's apparent denial of the charge of writing "infidel" philosophy actually concedes the objection.

Hume reported an instructive definition of atheism that is of interest for comparison with his own position: "You know (or ought to know) that Plato says there are three kinds of atheists. The first who deny a Deity, the second who deny his Providence, the third who assert, that he is uninfluenced by prayers or sacrifices."[67] The teaching of "natural theology" of the *Dialogues* denies in effect a Deity, his Providence and the utility of prayers and sacrifices, making Hume's teaching atheistic in light of the definitions Hume attributed to Plato. Hume further observed that "a man...may have his heart perfectly well disposed...yet from this circumstance of the *invisibility and incomprehensibility of the Deity* may feel no affection toward him."[68] Whether we consult Hume's *Dialogues Concerning Natural Religion*, his *Natural History of Religion*, his arguments against the immortality of the soul and miracles, his ill-defended denial that he wrote "infidel" philosophy, the correspondence between his teaching and the definition of atheism he attributed to Plato or his jocular explanation of why men may feel no affection toward an invisible, incomprehensible God, Hume is a subverter of Christianity and all "popular religion."

The gulf between Alexander Hamilton's Christianity and David Hume's "natural religion" is complete and unbridgeable. Thus Forrest McDonald most mistakenly argued that "Hume was a doubter and Hamilton was a Christian."[69] McDonald attempted to minimize Hume's antireligion to save the thesis of Hume's influence on Hamilton. But David Hume wasn't in any doubt; he was an enemy of Christianity. Moreover, it is conceivable that Hamilton aimed his criticism of "natural religion" against Hume, which could scarcely be an argument in favor of Hume's influence on Hamilton. Hamilton clearly understood the issues and stakes between revealed religion and Hume's "natural religion." Hamilton was a Christian, an opponent of "natural religion" and no ally of Hume's energetic efforts to undermine revealed religion. Thus the Humean influence thesis fails in the important area of Hamilton's religion and his principle of Christianity as a basis of moral rights and duties.

Hamilton judged the standards that should govern human conduct and political power in the light of eternity. "There are principles," he wrote, "eternally true and which apply to all situations," such as "those eternal principles of social justice [that] forbid the inflicting [of] punishment upon citizens...without conviction of some specific offense by regular trial and condemnation."[70] In short, "the government . . . is the mere creature of the constitution."[71] At the same time Hamilton seems to deny that the republican regime is the only legitimate regime: "I hold with *Montesquieu* that a government must be fitted to a nation as much as a coat to the individual, and consequently that what may be good at Philadelphia may be bad at Paris and ridiculous at Petersburgh."[72] This maxim implied a large role for the statesman's prudence to adjust what is desirable to circumstances.

Hamilton's "own political creed" or understanding of republicanism was given "with the utmost sincerity" to Edward Carrington: "I am *affectionately* attached to the republican theory."[73] "This is the real language of my heart which I open to you in the sincerity of friendship."[74] "I desire *above all things* to see the *equality* of political rights exclusive of all *hereditary* distinction firmly established by a practical demonstration of its being consistent with the order and happiness of society."[75] "But in candor I ought also to add that I am far from being without doubts. I consider its success as yet a problem. . . . On the whole, the only enemy which republicanism has to fear in this country is in the spirit of faction and anarchy."[76] This letter is the *locus classicus* of Hamilton's understanding of republicanism. His understanding of the American regime will also emerge in our discussion of the New York ratifying convention.

The enslavement of Americans by acquisitiveness and the lack of virtue predisposed Hamilton to expect less of the generality as he inspected governmental institutions in order to improve them. He noted the deficiencies of the New York constitution: "That there is a want of vigor in the executive, I believe will be found true. To determine the qualifications proper for the chief executive Magistrate requires the deliberate wisdom of a select assembly, and cannot be safely lodged with the people at large."[77] He observed of the congressional boards that acted in the place of an executive: "Another defect in our system is want of method and energy in the administration."[78] Hamilton mentioned the "want of a proper executive," which should consist in part of a single man in each department. This solution would give a "chance of more knowledge, more activity, more responsibility and of course more zeal and attention."[79] Already, then, before the Constitutional Convention of 1787 Hamilton was groping for the solution to the problems of the executive in state and national government.

Hamilton's speech of June 18, 1787 overplays the executive theme, just as his speeches before the New York ratifying convention underplay the executive theme.[80] In the Constitutional Convention Hamilton found the "source of government" in the "unreasonableness of the people— separate interests—debtors and creditors."[81] He stated the objectives of his plan for an executive serving during good behavior: "we ought to go as far in order to attain stability and permanence, as republican principles will admit."[82] "As to the Executive," Hamilton said, "it seemed to be admitted that no good one could be established on republican principles. Was not this giving up the merits of the question: for can there be a good government without a good executive. The English model was the only good one on this subject."[83] Hamilton's plan attracted no support in the Convention.

In the New York ratifying convention Hamilton spoke in a more subdued vein, scarcely mentioning the executive directly.[84] Instead he dwelled on the meaning of republicanism and the conditions of political leadership in America that would influence the executive. "It is our duty," he argued, "to draw from nature, from reason, from examples, the justest principles of policy, and to pursue and apply them in the formation of our government."[85] "There are two objects in forming systems of government—safety for the people, and energy in the administration."[86] "We must," said Hamilton, "submit to this idea, that the true principle of a republic is, that the people should choose whom they please to govern them."[87] Enlarging upon government and the popular will, he argued that "there are certain conjunctures, when it may be necessary and proper to disregard the opinions which the majority of the people have formed: But in the general course of things, the popular views and even prejudices will direct the actions of the rulers."[88] Although the people in every country desire its prosperity, "it is equally unquestionable, that they do not possess the discernment and stability necessary for systematic government." Misinformation and passion "frequently" lead the people into the "grossest errors." A community "will ever be incompetent" to administer foreign affairs.[89] "These truths are not often held up in public assemblies—but they cannot be unknown to any who hear me."[90]

In the New York ratifying convention Hamilton returned to the problem of virtue. "Where does virtue predominate? The difference indeed consists, not in the quantity but kind of vices, which are incident to the various classes; and here the advantage of character belongs to the wealthy. Their vices are probably more favorable to the prosperity of the state, than those of the indigent; and partake less of moral depravity."[91] Hamilton distinguished two senses of the term aristocracy: "1st. The best men who have most virtue and goodness of heart 2d. An independent body of men not depending on the choice of the people— We have none such."[92]

Not only was virtue in slight evidence in any class, Hamilton predicted that *"the tendency of things will be to depart from the republican standard*. This is the real disposition of human nature" because of the concentration of wealth, the prevailing of "luxury" and the likelihood that "virtue will be in a greater degree considered as only a graceful appendage of wealth."[93] Hamilton's speeches in the ratifying convention are credited with securing the approval of the Constitution in New York. They also lowered expectations of political leadership and posed the clear alternative of either republican government sustained by virtue or an inevitable departure from the republican standard. Hamilton adopted a fatalism, as though the die were cast, toward the departure from the republican standard, informing his listeners that "it is what, neither the honorable member [Melancton Smith] nor myself can correct. It is a common misfortune, that awaits our state constitution, as well as *all* others." Thus for Hamilton the overriding condition of political leadership was that virtue predominated in no class in America and that although the vices of the wealthy might favor to some degree the purely economic prosperity of the regime, without virtue among the active and potential statesmen the departure from the republican standard and the sinking of freedom were guaranteed. Hamilton, transcending completely the self-applause inherent in accepting the idea of progress, persuasively argued that the national path ran downward because it was impossible to form a good whole out of bad or vicious parts or individual characters. Ruling out in effect a condition of static preservation, he argued that the alternatives were either the diffusion and authority of virtue or decline. Moreover, Hamilton argued this matter with a clarity and range that justifies the observation of his friend Chancellor Kent that Hamilton might have been a philosopher had his life not ended when it did.

Perhaps one reason why Hamilton's elevated speeches in the ratifying convention are almost silent on the executive is that institutional design is no substitute for the lack of virtue. He identified the basis of the Constitution in a speech to the Philadelphia Convention of 1787: "the government must be so constituted as to offer strong motives. In short, to interest all the *passions* of individuals. And turn them into that channel."[94] The Constitution, then, seeks to channel the passions of the statesmen and the people, but this is a second best solution of the political problem, and no solution at all to the lack of virtue, which Hamilton understood as the sustaining energy of republicanism. Hamilton's peroration in the New York ratifying convention artfully "forgets" his earlier criticism of the lack of virtue in America: "Sir, when you have divided and nicely balanced the departments of government; when you have strongly connected the virtue of your rulers with their interest; when, in short, you have rendered your system as perfect as human forms can be; you must place confidence; you must give power."[95] Hamilton's great contribution in the ratifying convention was to demonstrate that, the design of institutions and the executive to the contrary notwithstanding, the Constitution, government and regime lacked the means to perpetuate themselves according to the republican standard. This daring and shocking conclusion was coupled with soothing praises of the Constitution as the most eligible solution for the actual political conditions in America. Hamilton was disposed to "adopt a system, whose principles have been sanctioned by experience; adapt it to the real state of our country; and depend on probable reasonings for its operation and result."[96]

Thus the first part of my reply to the Corwin–Rossiter thesis is that Hamilton reflects on the standards that should regulate human conduct and political power and on the American regime. America is a republican regime grounded in inegalitarian virtue, natural law, Christianity as a basis of moral rights and duties, an extensive system of Christian principles including the immortality of the soul and rewards and punishments in the hereafter, moderation, honesty, justice and liberality. Hamilton's political or civil doctrine of Christianity opposed the irreligion and anti-religion of David Hume, the philosopher scholars often mention as the chief influence on Hamilton. Hamilton's reflections on conduct, political power and the regime are a prelude to his institutional reflections on the presidency. Let us turn to Hamilton's two writings identified in Rossiter's elaboration of the Corwin thesis, Hamilton's *Federalist* papers on the presidency and his Pacificus Letters.

Hamilton's *Federalist* 1 partially stated the subject of the *Federalist* as "the conformity of the proposed Constitution to the true principles of republican government."[97] How in the main did Hamilton understand these "true principles" in the *Federalist*? In *Federalist* 9 Hamilton informed us that "the efficacy of various principles is now well understood, which were either not known at all, or imperfectly known to the ancients."[98] As noted previously, these principles are institutions as distinct from ethical principles. Hamilton listed the following institutions as evidence of the superiority of modern over ancient political science:

The regular distribution of power into distinct departments; the introduction of legislative balances and checks; the institution of courts composed of judges, holding their offices during good behavior; the representation of the people in the legislature by deputies of their own election—these are either wholly new discoveries or have made their principal progress towards perfection in modern times. They are means, and powerful means, by which the excellencies of republican government may be retained and its imperfections lessened or avoided.

To these institutions that "tend to the amelioration of popular systems of civil government," Hamilton added the extended republic.[99]

A parallel appears to exist between Hamilton's unqualified praise of institutions and omission of character in *Federalist* 9 and the political science of David Hume, which is institutional and minimizes the importance of character. "How could *politics* be a science," asked Hume, "if laws and forms of government had not a uniform influence upon society?"[100] Hamilton quoted Hume's essay, "That Politics May Be Reduced to a Science."[101] Hume's argument in "reducing" politics to a science is: "So great is the force of laws, and of particular forms of government, and so little dependence have they on the *humors and tempers of men*, that consequences almost as general and certain may sometimes be deduced from them, as any which the mathematical sciences afford us."[102] By "humors and tempers of men" Hume means character. Republican and free constitutions, he held, make it the "interest, even of bad men, to act for the public good."[103] In comparison to the importance of forms and institutions Hume disparaged character or "the humors and education of particular men."[104] Finally, Hume tried to argue that "public spirit" does not derive from "private virtue."[105] According to Duncan Forbes, Hume's teaching on the primacy of political institutions

and dissociating that from the question of manners and morals throws a question mark over...great commonplaces of British eighteenth century political thought: (1) that without virtue there can be no liberty, and without liberty no virtue—meaning political liberty, free or republican institutions; (2)...that political science is primarily concerned with the manners and morals of a nation, because what is to be done will depend on the state of its moral health, the degree of public spirit or "corruption."[106]

In *Federalist* 9 Hamilton adopted an institutionalism that was consistent with Hume's teaching that political institutions are primary and that the molding of character can be ignored. Hamilton previously did not dissociate morals and government. Nor even in *Federalist* 9 did Hamilton adopt Hume's distinction between public spirit and "private" virtue.

Hamilton generally described the subject of *Federalist* 67–77 as a "survey of the structure and powers of the executive department."[107] He also described the subject as "the intended President" of the United States and "the intended power of the President."[108] He contrasted the "intended power" of the president with the "actual power" of the British king, thus indicating the somewhat hypothetical character of the argument in *Federalist* 67–77.[109] *Federalist* 67–77 maintained a pregnant silence on the first sentence of Article II of the Constitution: it is never quoted or paraphrased, perhaps out of fear of awakening curiosity about the meaning of the "executive power" of the United States. Within the "survey" of the "intended power" of the president the main subject, beginning in *Federalist* 70 and continuing through 77, is the consistency of a vigorous executive with the genius of republican government. Recalling his formulation in the Constitutional Convention, Hamilton remarked that "there is an idea, which is not without its advocates, that a vigorous executive is inconsistent with the genius of republican government."[110] "Energy in the executive is a leading character in the definition of good government." What did Hamilton mean by energy? At a minimum he meant vigor. As a skillful rhetorician Hamilton may also have been aware of the rhetorical significance of "energy." Aristotle's *Rhetoric* III, xi, 2, held that "those words 'set a thing before the eyes,' which describe it in an active state."[111] Aristotle used energy to describe a species of metaphor that calls up a mental picture of something "acting" or moving.[112] Hamilton may have used energy to signify vigor and also as a metaphor to "set the presidency before our eyes" without shocking the state ratifying conventions with a too blunt exposition of the executive power of the United States. Hamilton seems to have preferred the older Aristotelian understanding of energy, denoting activity in contrast to potentiality and a rhetorical metaphor of animation or personification, over the leading definition of energy in Samuel Johnson's popular eighteenth-century *Dictionary of the English Language*, which was "power not exerted in action" and for which the authority was the modern philosopher Francis Bacon.[113]

Hamilton held that executive energy required unity, duration, adequate support and competent powers.[114] "Those qualities in the executive, which are the most necessary ingredients in its composition, [are] vigor and expedition."[115] The ingredients of energy with which Hamilton was chiefly concerned were "competent powers," which were treated from *Federalist* 73 through 77.[116] By naming unity as an ingredient of energy, Hamilton adroitly sidestepped the question, what is the meaning of the "executive power" of the United States? and drew attention instead to the latter part of the first sentence of Article II, which specified that a single executive shall exercise the power. Article II, clause one, is intimated to be a designation of the officer, not a grant of power. More precisely, Hamilton did not explicitly deny that Article II, clause one, was a grant of power. He preserved a lofty silence on the meaning of the phrase "executive power" of the United States. Hamilton's three repetitions of the phrase "executive authority" were perhaps intended to inform the reader that the president's competent powers were in fact his enumerated authority.[117] The *Federalist*, in sum, sets only a part of the intended presidency before our eyes: Article II merely designated the officer, and competent powers were enumerated to avoid offending the state ratifying conventions.

Hamilton's reflections on human nature formed an important part of *Federalist* 67–77 and were designed to create realistic expectations of the presidency. Praising the Electoral College, Hamilton said that even the opponents of the Constitution admitted that the election of the president was "pretty well guarded."[118] Indulging in optimism and exaggeration, Hamilton concluded that "there will be a constant probability of seeing the station filled by characters pre-eminent for ability and virtue."[119] But commenting on the necessity of the Senate sharing the treaty power with the president, Hamilton retracted his earlier optimism: "the history of human conduct does not warrant that exalted opinion of human virtue" that would make it wise to entrust foreign relations solely to the president.[120] Hamilton rejected a hope of "superlative virtue" in those likely to become presidents. Not the love of virtue, he found, but the "love of fame" was the "ruling passion of the noblest minds"; the love of fame remained a passion nevertheless, whether it afflicted noble or ignoble minds.[121] In the absence of virtue Hamilton revised his prediction that the presidency would be occupied by "characters pre-eminent for ability and virtue." The method of appointing the president meant that "there would always be great probability of having the place supplied by a man of abilities, at least respectable."[122] Hamilton concluded his "survey" of presidential authority by observing that the presidency combined "as far as republican principles would admit" energy and responsibility through elections, impeachment, liability to disqualification from office and criminal charges. *Federalist* 67–77, in short, were a selective presentation, not an exhaustive analysis, of the presidency. Hamilton wrote his *Federalist* 67–77 with one eye on the state ratifying conventions and the other on posterity.

For a more candid treatment of presidential "power," we turn to Hamilton's Pacificus Letters after first noting Hamilton's architectonic advice to Washington on the conduct of the presidency. Rossiter's elaboration of the Corwin thesis omitted Hamilton's advice to Washington, but it is important because it shows the moderation that guided Hamilton in advising a president he described as a virtuous man.[123] Hamilton wrote to Washington in 1789 that

the public good requires that the dignity of the office should be supported. . . . Men's minds are prepared for a pretty high tone in the demeanor of the Executive; but I doubt whether for so high a tone as in the abstract might be desirable. The notions of equality are yet in my opinion too general and too strong to admit of such a distance being placed between the President and other branches of government as might even be consistent with a due proportion. The following plan will I think steer clear of extremes.[124]

Hamilton then prescribed rules of presidential etiquette for the reception of visitors and, more important, gave advice about the president's relationship to senators. "I have thought," Hamilton wrote, "that the members of the Senate should also have a right of *individual* access [to the president] on matters relative to the *public administration*. . . . I believe it will be satisfactory to the people to know that there is some body of men in the state who have a right of continual communication with the President. It will be considered as a safeguard against secret combinations to deceive him." The senators, he concluded, were "in a degree his constitutional counsellors and [this] gives them a *peculiar* claim to the right of access."[125]

Hamilton's architectonic advice, after criticizing the idea of equality, actually concluded with moderate recommendations on the Senate. It is necessary to stress this moderation because of the popular notion that Hamilton wished to aggrandize the presidency at the expense of constitutional limitations on the president. Hamilton is also seen by many as a patron of today's presidency, in which many of the limitations have eroded. But his architectonic advice shows that Hamilton urged a fastidious sense of constitutional duty upon a man of Washington's rare virtue.[126] In Hamilton's judgment such constitutional limitations are much more necessary as wholesome precedents and restraints for the unvirtuous presidents who would mostly fill the office. The letter and spirit of Hamilton's advice to Washington are classic expressions of moderation and restraint in presidential conduct, and they contradict the all too familiar blustering invocations of presidential prerogative or the "strong presidency." Hamilton was, above all, a scrupulously constitutional statesman.

The other writing of Hamilton's mentioned in Rossiter's elaboration of the Corwin thesis is the Pacificus Letters. Rossiter was charmed by the Pacificus Letters and noted that Pacificus "placed the President in a position of clear superiority in the field of foreign relations" and was "still one of the most effective shots in the locker of advocates of the strong Presidency," which only reasserts the continuity thesis in other words.[127] We shall examine the argument of Pacificus with some care, because the Pacificus Letters and *Federalist* 67–77 are the mainstay of Rossiter's elaboration of the Corwin thesis.

In April 1793 President Washington issued a declaration of impartiality (the term neutrality was avoided) to keep the United States out of the Franco–British war.[128] Writing as Pacificus, Hamilton defended the declaration, which the partisans of France had criticized as exceeding the president's authority. Out of his study of the constitutionality, prudence and morality of Washington's declaration, Pacificus arrived at general principles of what is constitutional, prudent and moral as such for the president and Congress in foreign relations.

Pacificus replied to four objections: that the proclamation lacks constitutional authority (discussed in Letter I); that the proclamation is contrary to treaty obligations with France (II, III); that the proclamation is contrary to the gratitude owed to France for helping the American Revolution (IV, V, VI); and that the proclamation is imprudent (VII). Pacificus promised a future discussion of a fifth objection, that by not assisting France in the war the United States will harm the cause of liberty. Americanus Letters I and II, originally drafted by Hamilton as the eighth and ninth of the Pacificus series, keep this promise to assess

the "merits" of the French case. The manuscript of Americanus I held
that the proclamation "must derive its defense, from a just construction
of existing treaties and laws. If shown to be consistent with these the
defense is complete."[129] Pacificus I through III therefore are the complete constitutional defense of the proclamation. Why did Pacificus—
Americanus write six additional letters? The additional letters focused
on issues of morality and prudence, which, though technically irrelevant
to the narrowly understood constitutional defense, clarified the beneficial
use of presidential power. In reading Pacificus–Americanus it is a sound
practice to avoid an absolute distinction between constitutionality,
whether power exists, and policy, how power is or ought to be used.
The additional letters also carried the argument into his opponents'
territory and cut off their lines of intellectual retreat.

Unlike *Federalist* 67–77 Pacificus I quoted the first sentence of Article
II: "The executive power shall be vested in a President of the United
States of America." Pacificus I held that Article II is a "general grant"
of power: "The *executive power* of the nation is vested in the president;
subject only to the *exceptions* and *qualifications*, which are expressed in
the instrument," which must be "interpreted in conformity with other
parts of the Constitution, and with the principles of free government."[130]
In elaborating Corwin's thesis Rossiter's quotation from Pacificus I deleted Hamilton's strict requirement that Article II, clause one, be interpreted in "conformity" with the "principles of free government," leaving
the false impression that for Hamilton presidential power was an end
in itself.[131] But to return to Pacificus's argument: the exceptions he
named are the participation of the Senate in appointments and treaties,
the right of Congress to declare war and to grant letters of marque and
reprisal. Pacificus deleted from his published version the provocative
observation that "the Executive indeed cannot control the exercise of
that power [the power of Congress to declare war]—further than by the
exercise of its general right of objecting to all acts of the Legislature;
liable to being overruled by two-thirds of both houses of Congress."[132]

The division of the executive power in the Constitution created a
concurrent executive and congressional authority. For example, the executive power of diplomatic recognition and the interpretation of treaty
obligations added up to "the right of the executive, in certain cases, to
determine the condition of the nation, though it may, in its consequences,
affect the exercise of the power of the legislature to declare war." In
short, the president's initiative in foreign affairs reduced congressional
discretion in declaring war. Finally, Pacificus asserted that he could have
vindicated the president's authority with the clause of the Constitution
that makes it his duty to "take care that the laws be faithfully executed."
Treaties are part of the law of the land, and the president, as law ex-
ecutor, must judge their meaning according to conditions.

Letter II treated the "principal" objection to the proclamation, its alleged inconsistency with the treaties between the United States and France. The United States, said Pacificus, has a defensive alliance with France. France, however, is fighting an offensive war, which releases the United States from an obligation to aid her. Pacificus confesses his unfamiliarity with the argument that the abstract justice of a war obliges a nation to do what its formal obligations don't enjoin. The justice of the war on the French side is problematical: the conduct of France is repugnant to the "true principles of liberty" and a "violation of just and moderate principles." Hence either France is fighting an offensive war or the justice of the French cause is questionable. Both alternatives release the United States from an obligation to aid France.

Letter III declares that the United States' guarantee relates only to the defense and preservation of France's American colonies. France cannot render American naval help useful and cannot prevent the destruction of American trade. This "alone" discharges the United States from any obligation to help France. Pacificus develops his explicit theme, the obligation of treaties, in order to set down a moral principle: "Self preservation is the first duty of a nation." Good faith does not require that the United States risk essential interests or independence for the sake of an objective of limited interest to France.

Letter IV addresses "this very favorite topic of gratitude to France." Faith, justice, and interest, though not gratitude, Pacificus contends, exist between nations. In a passage dear to the realist writers on foreign policy, Pacificus lays down that the rule of morality differs for nations and individuals. "Rulers are only trustees for the happiness and interest of their nation, and cannot, consistently with their trust, follow the suggestions of kindness or humanity towards others, to the prejudice of their constituents." "A policy regulated by their own interest, as far as justice and good faith permit, is, and ought to be, their prevailing one." Enlightened self-interest, not selfishness or treachery, is Pacificus's credo for an American foreign policy.

Letter V uses the framework of IV in explaining French assistance to the American Revolution. France, Pacificus finds, aided the American Revolution to weaken British ascendancy and redress French defeats in the war that ended in 1763. French aid was "magnanimous" but not such as to justify the sacrifice of substantial interests or the safety of the United States. If the United States owes gratitude, it is to Louis XVI rather than to his victorious enemies. Moreover, if Louis acted from reasons of state without regard to the American cause, this destroys the basis of American gratitude to France. Letter VI distinguishes the argument for gratitude, which refers to kind offices received, from the argument that to assist France is to assist the cause of liberty. Pacificus reiterates that the interest of France governed her aid to the American

Revolution. Letter VII repeats and reinforces the "solid answers" already given to objections to the prudence of the proclamation.

Americanus I detects the "fresh appearances of a covert design to embark the United States in the war." Opinion is divided, says Americanus, on whether the cause of France is truly the cause of liberty pursued with justice and humanity and likely to meet with honorable success. If there is even a tolerable case against the cause of France as the cause of true liberty, that is a conclusive argument against the United States' participation. American power and resources offer no hope of rendering material help to France by entering the war: "If France is not in some way or other wanting to herself, she will not stand in need of our assistance; and if she is, our assistance cannot save her." Americanus II details the harmful consequences of engaging with France in the war. War would interrupt the prosperity of the United States, which promises to place "our national rights and interests upon immovable foundations." War would annihilate commerce and make the United States unable to finance her role in the war. It is erroneous to believe, Americanus holds, that the combined powers will attribute to the United States the principles they object to in France: the United States rests on justice, order and law. It is also erroneous to believe that the United States and France have the same principles.[133] The United States took refuge in revolution because of encroachments on rights anciently enjoyed, but France, Americanus hints, pursued new rights and privileges not reconcilable perhaps with any form of regular government. The argument of Pacificus–Americanus, in sum, is a bold yet moderate position in the context of Hamilton's requirement that Article II, though a grant of power, be interpreted in conformity with other parts of the Constitution and with the principles of free government.

"It is fortunate," wrote Edward S. Corwin, "that at the very outset of our national history a debate occurred between the two ablest members of the body which framed the Constitution" bearing on the president's powers in foreign relations "and disclosing its most fundamental issues. This was the debate between 'Pacificus' (Hamilton) and 'Helvidius' (Madison)."[134] Unfortunately, Rossiter's specific elaboration of Corwin's thesis on the Hamiltonian root of the modern theory of presidential power fails to mention that Hamilton's teachings as Pacificus were criticized by James Madison.[135] Rather than assume, as Rossiter did, that Pacificus vanquished Helvidius, let us examine Helvidius's argument before deciding its merit.[136]

Hamilton's argument made Thomas Jefferson implore James Madison with his customary moderation: "Nobody answers him and his doctrines will therefore be taken for confessed. For God's sake, my dear Sir, take up your pen, select the most striking heresies and cut him to pieces in the face of the public. There is nobody else who can and will enter the lists against him."[137] "The interest in the articles was extraordinary," Gaillard Hunt wrote, "because there was no doubt who the real authors were."

In Letter IV Helvidius distinguishes his "defined Constitution" from Pacificus's alleged "prerogative," which Helvidius seems to understand in the Lockean sense of "power to act according to discretion, for the public good, without the prescription of the law, and sometimes even against it."[138] The "basis" of Pacificus's reasoning is the "extraordinary doctrine" that the powers of making war and treaties are executive (Letter I). Helvidius's thesis is that Congress's power to declare war means that the grant of executive power, Article II, does not determine foreign relations. Hence Helvidius denies an executive prerogative and teaches that "the prerogative ... [was] vested in another department," Congress (Letter V). A concurrent discretion in the executive and Congress would be confusing in theory and awkward in practice.

Helvidius dismisses "writers of authority on public law," particularly Locke, whose "chapter on prerogative shows, how the reason of the philosopher was clouded by the royalism of the Englishman." He evaluates Pacificus with other standards: "the quality and operation of the powers to make war [later, to declare war] and treaties" and the Constitution (Letter I). He denies any analogy between the president's power of removal (during the removal debate of 1789 Madison urged that Article II was a general grant of executive power) and the powers of war and treaty. Finally, Helvidius charges that Pacificus borrowed his doctrine of prerogative from the British constitution. Letter II argues that powers of war and treaty are neither executive nor concurrent. Even judging of the obligation to declare war is an exception from the grant of executive power in Article II. Letter III asserts that the executive's power to receive ambassadors merely provides for a particular mode of communication with foreign governments. The treatment of a foreign government as a despotism was not given to so limited an organ of the national will as the executive. Helvidius strongly challenges Pacificus's assertion that the executive may put the legislature under an obligation to declare war.

Letters I through III complete the criticism of the "new and aspiring" doctrine that prerogative allows the executive to judge and decide whether causes of war exist in the obligations of treaties. Letter IV holds that the power to declare war includes the power to judge the causes of war and is fully vested in the legislature. The executive has only the right of "convening and informing Congress, whenever such a question seems to call for a decision." Letter V summarizes the previous argument that the executive has no constitutional right to interfere with any question of a cause of war. Helvidius concludes by examining whether Pacificus has correctly interpreted Washington's proclamation.

Who won the grand debate over executive power? On the merits, Henry Cabot Lodge stated that "Hamilton had the best of the discussion."[139] Irving Brant, Madison's biographer, concluded that "Hamilton, with his main position riddled, said no more."[140] Brant deduced Hamilton's defeat from his silence without mentioning that he fell ill with yellow fever during Madison's rejoinder and that Hamilton extended his Pacificus argument in the Americanus Letters. Madison himself abandoned his intention to meet all of Pacificus's arguments. Madison's reluctance is evident in his letter to Jefferson: "I must resume the task I suppose in relation to the Treaty and gratitude....I shall deliberate whether a considerable postponement at least may not be advisable."[141] Madison had no trouble persuading himself to suspend operations. Moreover, Helvidius declined to argue with Pacificus whether the opening clause of Article II constituted a grant of power. Helvidius's main thesis was that the powers to make war and peace were legislative. Hence Pacificus's central thesis was neither rebutted nor refuted.

Before taking up his quill as Helvidius, Madison wrote that "if an answer to the publication be undertaken, it ought to be both a solid, and a prudent one. None but intelligent readers will enter into such a controversy, and to their minds it ought principally to be accommodated."[142] Madison complained to Jefferson of being "under some difficulties first from my not knowing how far concessions have been made on particular points behind the curtain. Secondly, from my not knowing how far the President considers himself as actually committed with respect to some doctrines. Thirdly, from the want of some light from the law of nations as applicable to the construction of the Treaty. Fourth from my ignorance of some material facts."[143] Madison himself doubted his ability to give prudent advice on foreign relations. His doubt, of course, is far from establishing Hamilton's victory on the constitutional point.

Ralph Ketcham, a judicious commentator on Pacificus and Helvidius, notices that Madison began *ad hominem*.[144] Ketcham concludes that

Madison perceived correctly that the doctrine of implied powers would have hindered the ratification campaign of 1788, and that its subsequent avowal was therefore in some sense an imposition. His narrow construction was also probably closer to the intent of the ratifying conventions than Hamilton's assertion of implied powers. Yet from the standpoint of effective government, on the specific issue of the proclamation of neutrality, Hamilton's arguments seem less exceptionable than Madison's tight, legalistic, almost tortured constructions.[145]

Helvidius's case against Pacificus warrants a Scotch verdict of "not proven," and Hamilton scored both a triumph and a constitutional victory. Unnoticed by the commentators on Helvidius is the crucial inconsistency between Madison's description of the Constitution as a "defined constitution," presumably one of enumerated powers, and Madison's contention that the prerogative, which implies a Constitution of more than enumerated powers, belongs to Congress, not the president.[146] Madison is unclear here on the nature of the Constitution. He expresses indirectly the tension between prerogative, whether held by Congress or the president, and the Constitution. Madison also failed to develop the implications of vesting the prerogative in Congress. Madison's position was weakened by the negativism of Helvidius, his failure to advise an alternative to the proclamation and the narrowness of his criticism.

The reader who sides with Hamilton may ask whether Pacificus's doctrine requires in the president a delicate combination of moderation and assertiveness in pursuit of the national interest. How often is that combination found among typical American presidents since President Washington? If the answer is seldom or rarely, Pacificus may have cut a pattern for the presidency that exceeds the capacities of, and is unsafe for, the common or garden-variety president. What Rossiter and other fans of Pacificus ignore is the possibility that in the wrong hands the arguments of Pacificus not only may be misunderstood but also may be dangerous.

Some commentators have plausibly argued that Pacificus has enjoyed greater historical influence than Helvidius. To Henry Cabot Lodge, "the adoption of the neutrality policy, and the action of Washington in declaring it, are events of the first moment in our history. To thoroughly understand them, and the motives and reasons for them, 'Pacificus' is indispensable and is the best authority."[147] To Louis Hacker, Pacificus "laid out in detail the concept of the national interest as the basis of foreign policy."[148] To Hans Morgenthau, "it illustrates both the depth of the moralistic illusion and the original strength of the opposition to it that the issue between these two opposing conceptions of foreign policy was joined at the very beginning of the history of the United States, was decided in favor of the realistic position and was formulated with unsurpassed simplicity and penetration by Alexander Hamilton...[in] the 'Pacificus, and 'Americanus' articles."[149] To Henry Jones Ford, the Pacificus Letters "are so dignified in style, elevated in thought, acute in analysis, and cogent in reasoning that they have taken classic rank as a treatise on international rights and duties."[150] To Frederick Oliver, "the letters of Pacificus..., apart from their special argument on the facts, will ever remain a classic of wise, illusionless, unprovocative statesmanship."[151] Even if Hamilton and Madison tied in quality of argument, Hamilton's argument has enjoyed the wider influence, including being a main pillar of Chief Justice William Howard Taft's majority opinion in Myers v. United States, 272 U.S. 52, at 138–139 (1926). It remains to be seen, however, whether the modern theory of presidential power, formulated by presidents and scholars, can be traced to Hamilton's teachings.

Another question that Rossiter's elaboration of the Corwin continuity thesis overlooked is the relationship of *Federalist* 67–77 on the presidency and the Pacificus Letters. Rossiter implies that these two teachings add up to a harmonious whole. Yet *Federalist* 67–77 may be in tension with the Pacificus Letters. *Federalist* 77, for example, held that the Senate and the president shared the power of removal. Citing the "decision of 1789" on the removal of the secretary of state, Pacificus I overruled *Federalist* 77, attributing the power of removal to the president alone. The opposition between *Federalist* 77 and Pacificus I raises the more important question of the precedence of *Federalist* 67–77 and the Pacificus Letters. What is the comparative excellence, rank and authority of *Federalist* 67–77 and the Pacificus Letters? Tradition ranks the *Federalist* with the Declaration of Independence, the Articles of Confederation and the Constitution itself as one of the seminal works defining the principles and practices of American politics. Tradition assigns the Pacificus Letters a secondary rank, presumably because they are inferior to the *Federalist* in excellence and authority. Tradition, then, decides the comparison of the *Federalist* and the Pacificus Letters in all respects in favor of the *Federalist*.

The difficulties with the traditional understanding of the *Federalist* are hinted at in Justice Joseph Story's description of the *Federalist*'s character and limitations: "the *Federalist* could do little more than state the objects and general bearing of these powers and functions."[152] Moreover, the *Federalist* was written in important part to influence the ratification of the Constitution. Although Hamilton wrote both *Federalist* 67–77 and the Pacificus Letters, *Federalist* 67–77 of necessity lack complete candor on divisive issues such as the extent of presidential power. The traditional understanding overlooks the possibility that in *Federalist* 67–77 Hamilton accommodated the expression of his ideas on presidential energy to the necessity of rounding up votes for the ratification of the Constitution.

Hamilton was under no such prudential constraints when writing as Pacificus. Pacificus I, as we have seen, amends the *Federalist*'s idea of presidential "energy," which is qualified by considerations of responsibility and safety and by the interpretation of presidential powers as enumerated powers, through the contention that with limited exceptions the entire executive power of the nation is completely lodged in the president. Contrary to the *Federalist*, Pacificus discloses that section 1 of Article II is a general grant of executive power, to be "interpreted in conformity with other parts of the Constitution, and with the principles of free government." Clearly, Pacificus is not simply embroidery or repetition of the teaching on presidential energy in the *Federalist*. The Pacificus Letters are a corrective of the *Federalist*'s concession to the fears of the state ratifying conventions.

Nor did Hamilton dismiss the Pacificus Letters as an occasional writing of no permanent importance in comparison to the *Federalist*. Douglass Adair reminds us that "Hamilton insisted on the republication of his 'Letters of Pacificus' in the 1802 edition of the *Federalist*" itself.[153] Indeed, Hopkins, the publisher of the 1802 edition of the *Federalist*, told Hamilton's son that "the letters of Pacificus were added at your father's suggestion; and corrected with his own hand. He remarked to me, at the time; that 'some of his friends had pronounced them to be his best performance.' "[154] Were the Pacificus Letters a better performance than Hamilton's papers in *Federalist* 67–77? Hopkins related that Hamilton "did not regard" the *Federalist* "with much partiality." "He seemed indeed to doubt" whether a revised edition of the *Federalist* was "desirable."[155] Hamilton's opinion of the *Federalist* is reflected in Hopkins's report that "when Hamilton hesitated his consent [to a revised edition of the *Federalist*], that he remarked to him, '*Heretofore* I have given the people *milk*; hereafter I will give them *meat*;' words indicating his formed purpose— to write a treatise upon government."

Douglass Adair concludes that "Hamilton was intensely proud of Pacificus, not because it was better written than Publius, but because, pragmatically speaking, it had worked to keep the United States neutral in 1793 and could still be used for the same purpose in 1802."[156] An alternative conclusion, supported by the above considerations, is that Hamilton was intensely proud of the Pacificus Letters because they were more profoundly reasoned than the *Federalist*. That is, Hamilton understood the Pacificus Letters to be superior in excellence and authority to *Federalist* 67–77. The Pacificus Letters are a midpoint between the *Federalist* and the unwritten treatise on government that Hamilton saw with his mind's eye. If *Federalist* 67–77 are the antechamber, the Pacificus Letters are the core of Hamilton's teaching on presidential power. In sum, the Pacificus Letters, considered as an exposition of presidential power, take just precedence over *Federalist* 67–77. Yet because the grant of power in Article II is qualified by the interpretive requirement of the principles of free government, Pacificus's argument must be read in light of the fuller exposition of free government in the *Federalist*, or else we risk obscuring presidential moderation and responsibility in the dazzle of presidential power.

Let us consider certain objections to my argument. Against my interpretation that virtue is the highest principle for Hamilton, Douglass Adair advances the thesis that "the desire for fame operated ... as a constant goad in the political behavior of ... Hamilton" and writes of "Hamilton's demonic passion for fame."[157] A more moderate version of Adair's thesis is that "the love of fame, and the belief that creating a viable republican state would win them fame, is *part* of the explanation" of the writing and ratification of the Constitution.[158] What is the remainder of the explanation, which is perhaps the largest "part"? Adair provides a clue in his discussion of the professional motivation of historians as opposed to statesmen such as Washington and Hamilton: "It is this urge to model oneself on the very greatest, to emulate the best, that provides the spur that sets this creative minority apart."[159] Here Adair resorts to standards of excellence, not fame. Why deny the possibility that Hamilton acted with reference to standards of excellence? Adair cites Hamilton's discussion of a member of Congress as a "founder of an empire," as evidence of Hamilton's "demonic passion for fame."[160] Adair overlooks, because he wishes to deprive Hamilton of the possibility of having acted and having urged others to act according to standards of excellence, Hamilton's requirement in this passage that the "founder of an empire" be "a man of virtue and ability."[161] Contrary to Adair's interpretation of it, this passage suggests that Hamilton subordinated the desire for fame to standards of excellence or virtue. To paraphrase Adair, the standard of virtue was married in Hamilton's mind to the problems and opportunities facing the leaders of the American Revolution and the founders of the Constitution.

Gerald Stourzh's *Alexander Hamilton and the Idea of Republican Government* also argues against the importance of virtue for Hamilton. Stourzh, alas, follows Adair in concluding that love of fame was the "ruling passion" of Hamilton's mind.[162] Stourzh closes by saying that Hamilton, in terms of Lincoln's speech on the "Perpetuation of our Political Institutions," belonged to the family of the lion or the tribe of the eagle. That is, Hamilton's ambition transcended the limits of constitutional statesmanship.[163] I have argued that Hamilton's national service generally sets the constitutional example and that Adair and Stourzh ignore or fail to appreciate the importance of virtue as the controlling principle for Hamilton. In Stourzh's case this may be because he sees Hamilton through the eyes of Lincoln, a post-virtue statesman, an egalitarian and a repealer of the Founders' understanding of the Constitution. A more favorable and just assessment of Hamilton's ambition was given by George Washington, who had unparalleled opportunities to observe Hamilton in war and peace: "That he is ambitious I shall readily grant, but it is of that laudable kind which prompts a man to excel in whatever he takes in hand."[164]

When Hamilton resigned as secretary of the treasury President Washington said: "In every relation which you have borne to me, I have found that my confidence in your talents, exertions and integrity, has been well placed. I the more freely render this testimony of my approbation, because I speak from opportunities of information which cannot deceive me, and which furnish satisfactory proof of your title to public regard."[165]

Washington argued in effect that Hamilton subordinated ambition to service and excellence. In 1797 Hamilton instructively explained his reasons for resigning office:

Public office in this country has few attractions.... *The opportunity of doing good* from the jealousy of power and the spirit of faction, is too small in any station to warrant a long continuance of private sacrifices. The enterprises of party had so far succeeded as materially to weaken the necessary influence and energy of the executive authority, and so far diminish *the power of doing good* as greatly to take the motives which a *virtuous* man might have for making sacrifices. The prospect was even bad for gratifying in future the love of fame, *if that passion was to be the spring of action.*[166]

Hamilton stresses the dwindling opportunities of "doing good" and virtue and dismisses the "passion" of love of fame.

One of Hamilton's most succinct criticisms of excessive ambition is that "ambition without principle never was long under the guidance of good sense"; this maxim Hamilton draws from the "experience of all times."[167] A merited and enduring rank as a statesman must be achieved by principle, the love of glory and doing what "good men will approve." In the light of Aristotle's distinction between ambition and magnanimity or great-souledness, Hamilton sought the mean between an excessive and defective pursuit of honor for noble deeds. Aristotle said that such a man "at great honor from good men ... will be moderately pleased, as getting nothing more than his due, or even less; for no honor can be adequate to complete virtue.... But honor from ordinary men and on trivial grounds he will utterly despise; for that is not what he deserves."[168] Great-souled men, Aristotle continued, "seem to look down on everything"; the great-souled man "will not hesitate to say all that he thinks, as he looks down upon mankind."[169]

Much of Hamilton's reputation for allegedly being disloyal to republicanism springs instead from his towering magnanimity. Jefferson, more courteous and perhaps less truthful with the people, seems to enjoy a higher popularity than Hamilton, especially with American youth. Hamilton's popularity suffered because he and Washington approached the body politic much as physicians would approach a patient, and Hamilton's opponents misrepresented his detachment and lack of flattery. Hamilton's detachment and his complete freedom from courting the populace were accompanied by his prodigious efforts to inform the judgment of good men about his and Washington's measures. This form of seeking consent for leadership is immeasurable by Gallup polls. If the level of public explanation has rarely been higher in American political history than in Hamilton's writings, he presented good men with an abundance of opportunities to inform and act upon their judgment, thus satisfying the criterion of the consent of the governed.

Another objection might be that I have paid insufficient attention to Hume's influence on Hamilton. Gerald Stourzh, for example, writes that Hamilton was "profoundly influenced by Hume."[170] Forrest McDonald holds that in the area of governmental problems "Hamilton's master was David Hume."[171] Garry Wills speaks of Hamilton's extensive "debt" to Hume in the *Federalist*.[172] These writers generally assume that Hume's influence was healthy, beneficial and constructive and that it made Hamilton a better statesman than he would have been without Hume. The notion of better statesman is rarely, if ever, spelled out, and no proof is offered that Hume's influence was completely healthy.

The contemporary effort to absorb Hamilton's teaching into the philosophy of David Hume takes off from a 1927 effort by Alex Bein, who counted citations of Hume in Hamilton's writings but who also concluded with a balance rarely found in contemporary discussions of Hamilton that there are "numerous differences" between the philosopher and the statesman.[173] Given the overemphasis in our day on alleged similiarities between Hume and Hamilton, it is prudent and necessary to heed Bein's warning. Hamilton "only" took from Hume what he needed to deal with the practical situations confronting him.[174] Hamilton made a selective use of Hume. Jacob Cooke remarked that "there is no convincing basis for the assertion that as 'Publius' Hamilton was decisively influenced by the Scotsman. His principal guide was his own experience and his extraordinary legal and logical skill in presenting the best possible case for his client, ... the United States Constitution."[175] To return to Bein, as a political philosopher Hume is almost only analytical.[176] Leslie Stephen forcefully stated this point: "The problem which lay before Hume ... was how to make a rope of sand, and to frame a political theory out of theoretical and practical scepticism. Hume's power as a *destroyer* is contrasted with his weakness as a creator, even more conspicuously in his political than in his other writings."[177] As an example of Hume's destructiveness with clear implications for political and moral philosophy and statesmanship, consider Hume's contention that no inference of the ought or ought not may derive from the is or is not.[178] Hume insisted that the separation of the *ought* from the *is* "would subvert all the vulgar systems of morality." If Hume's contention is accepted, the result is that "no valid argument can move from entirely factual premises to any moral or evaluative conclusion."[179] The statesman is then left floundering without guidance.

Another example of Hume's destructiveness for the statesmanship of a republican regime is that he held that "the chief spring or actuating principle of the human mind is pleasure or pain."[180] Accordingly, Hume reduced virtue to pleasure: "We have already observed, that moral distinctions depend *entirely* on certain peculiar sentiments of pain and pleasure, and that whatever mental quality in ourselves gives us a satisfaction

...is of course virtuous; as every thing of this nature, that gives uneasiness, is vicious."[181] More concisely, "every quality of the mind is denominated virtuous, which gives pleasure ... as every quality, which produces pain, is called vicious."[182]

Hume showed his true colors in Paris after meeting Madam Pompadour and Louis XV: "Do you ask me about my course of life? I can only say, that I eat nothing but ambrosia, drink nothing but nectar, breathe nothing but incense, and tread on nothing but flowers."[183] Hume wrote of his doctrine to Francis Hutcheson, professor of moral philosophy at Glasgow University: "What affected me most in your remarks is your observing that *there wants a certain warmth in the cause of virtue....* I must own, this has not happened by chance, but is the effect of a reasoning either good or bad.... To every virtuous action there must be a motive or impelling passion ... and ... virtue can *never* be the sole motive to any action.... *I think there is no proposition more certain or important.*"[184] Hume adds that "final causes ... is a consideration, that appears to me pretty uncertain and unphilosophical."[185] Hume breaks from the moral teaching that held a virtuous action to be choiceworthy for its own sake. He includes among the rejected "final causes" "happiness," "virtue" and man's "Maker"—striking at both classical antiquity and Christianity.

Hume's *Enquiry Concerning the Principles of Morals* asks "But, *useful?* For what? For somebody's *interest,* surely. Whose interest then? Not our own only; for our approbation frequently extends farther."[186] "Why Utility Pleases," the central chapter of the *Enquiry,* apparently holds that "we must renounce the theory, which accounts for every moral sentiment by the principle of self-love."[187] Hume thus apparently urges that we "retain a general standard of vice and virtue, founded chiefly on general usefulness."[188] As an apparent disproof of the self-love theory, he says "we frequently bestow praise on virtuous actions, performed in *very distant ages and remote countries*; where the utmost subtilty of imagination would not discover any appearance of self-interest."[189] Hence the disinterested praise and, presumably, practice of virtue are possible. But Hume argues oppositely to his apparent disproof of self-interest: "There is no necessity, that a generous action, barely mentioned in an *old* history or *remote* gazette, should communicate any strong feelings of applause and admiration. *Virtue, placed at such a distance,* is like a fixed star, which, though to the eye of reason, it may appear as luminous as the sun in his meridian, *is so infinitely removed, as to affect the senses, neither with light nor heat.*"[190] Hume says that virtue must be brought "nearer, by our acquaintance or connection with the persons." Nearer to what? To our "interest" or "self-love." "There are few occasions," said Hume, when "*What is that to me?.... is not pertinent.*"[191] Hume really teaches that the disinterested praise and practice of virtue are impossible. "Usefulness" and "utility" are Hume's euphemisms for "interest" and "self-love." "Utility," in Hume's chapter title, "pleases" more than a shocking teaching of utter selfishness, so Hume accomplishes his goal while pleasing the casual reader.

After stating a traditional way of understanding moral philosophy, to teach duty, praise virtue, condemn vice and "beget correspondent habits," Hume states as a command the destructive alternative to this traditional understanding: "Extinguish all the warm feelings and pre-possessions in favour of virtue, and all disgust or aversion to vice: render men totally indifferent towards these distinctions; and morality is no longer a practical study, nor has any tendency to regulate our lives and actions."[192] Hume's teaching of selfishness was calculated to have such an effect on virtue. Hence we see a further key difference between Hume and Hamilton, who did the opposite of extinguishing virtue. Moreover, Hamilton taught natural law on a non-utilitarian basis. These are two additional reasons for rejecting Hume as a healthy, comprehensive influence on Alexander Hamilton.

Hamilton defended rational liberty. What duty did Hume assign to reason? "We speak not strictly and philosophically when we talk of the combat of passion and of reason. Reason is, and ought only to be the slave of the passions, and can *never* pretend to any other office than to serve and obey them."[193] Hume concedes that "this opinion may appear somewhat extraordinary." In sum: the separation of the *ought* from the *is*, the reduction of virtue to pleasure and selfishness, the prostration of reason as the "slave" of the passions and the rejection of final causes are four striking examples of Hume's destructiveness. Hamilton, on the other hand, was a constructive statesman for whom virtue and reason were infinitely more than pleasure and the service of the passions. What Hamilton called "the great principles of social right, justice and honor" had a foundation on an unchanging moral order discovered but not made by human reason.[194]

As Hamilton put it in counterattacking a certain argument: "Are they not rather to be branded as men who make their passions, prejudices, and interests the sole measure of their own and others rights?"[195] Hum-ean man, judging from the above examples, is a valetudinarian volup-tuary unequal to the rigors of Valley Forge or the disinterested patriotism of founding the Constitution. Hamilton holds that, while we must not blind ourselves to the strength of the passions, reason and virtue should prevail over passions, prejudices and interests in measuring rights. In sum: certain recent commentators on Hamilton have lacked the balance of Alex Bein, who explored the differences between Hamilton and Hume as well as Hume's influence. These differences are more profound than the extent of Hume's influence on Hamilton. On balance Hume was a destructive political philosopher; Hamilton was a constructive statesman, a Christian and an upholder of virtue, reason and natural law in senses incompatible with Hume's teaching. From Hume's perspective Alexander Hamilton supported the vulgar system of morality.

Drew McCoy disagrees with my interpretation in his *The Elusive Republic*.[196] McCoy's Hamilton, "perhaps more so than any of his countrymen . . . had succeeded in discarding the traditional republican heritage."[197] "He came to accept the commercialization of society as not only inevitable but fundamentally salutary as well," a conclusion that ill agrees with Hamilton's criticism of the enslaving golden chain of acquisitiveness.[198]

J.G.A. Pocock holds that "Hamilton can be said to have [shown] that if virtue is the principle of republics, interest is that of empires, so that a nonclassical federalism is necessary if the republic is to be also an empire."[199] Speaking generally but also of Hamilton, Pocock concludes that "the decline of virtue had as its logical corollary the rise of interest."[200] Relying largely on the secondary literature instead of Hamilton's writings, Pocock asserts that Hamilton "declared specifically . . . that the virtue of the individual was no longer a necessary foundation of free government."[201] Pocock's assertion is unwarranted by his analysis or his single quotation from Hamilton's speech in the New York ratifying convention. In brief, the decline of virtue that Hamilton predicted for the United States meant for him also the decline of republican government and freedom. A necessary corrective of Pocock's overemphasis of interest is Hamilton's maxim that "opinion, whether well or ill founded, is the governing principle of human affairs."[202] Another formulation of this maxim reads: "Men are governed by opinion; this opinion is as much influenced by appearances as by realities."[203] These maxims show that Hamilton stressed opinion more than interest as "the governing principle of human affairs."

Another objection to my understanding of Hamilton is Adrienne Koch's emphasis on "Hamilton's own paramount preoccupation with power" in alleged isolation from more important moral ends.[204] "Hamilton's normal outlook," she writes condescendingly, "is . . . not bathed in the open light of larger human and spiritual ideals."[205] Hence she finds "little in a Hamiltonian tradition to withstand the appeals of totalitarian 'efficiency' " or the Marxist critique depicting the powerful state as "nothing more than the police arm of the capitalist class."[206] Professor Koch has unfortunately ignored almost the entirety of Hamilton's political thought in fabricating this caricature of his teachings.

Finally, Roland Mulford might object that I have paid insufficient attention to the importance of liberty for Hamilton: "Liberty was to Hamilton the main object of government, as it was of society."[207] For Hamilton liberty by itself was a questionable principle, for liberty could lead to evil as well as good. Mulford might have seen this if he had understood the priority of virtue and reason for Hamilton.

In summary and conclusion, this chapter explored Hamilton's thought on conduct, political power, the American regime and presidential power to begin to assess Corwin's thesis on the continuity of Hamilton's teachings and the modern theory of presidential power. Hamilton's moral reflections stressed natural law, Christianity, the immortality of the soul and rewards and punishments in a future life, honesty, justice, liberality, moderation and virtue. These moral reflections undergird Hamilton's understanding of character, conduct, political power and the American republic. Though a parallel exists between Hume's teaching on political institutions and the institutionalism of Hamilton's *Federalist* 9, the differences between Hume's philosophy and Hamilton's stand are ultimately more important than Hamilton's selective use of Hume.

Hamilton had appraised American virtue before defending the institutionalism that neglects the formation of human character. His speech in the Constitutional Convention of 1787 held that men's passions had to be channeled and their interests attached to the Constitution. The Federalists, according to the late Herbert Storing, admitted that the attachment of the people to the Constitution "was not sufficiently assured by narrow self interest."[208] But the "Federalists regarded this as a somewhat peripheral problem . . . to be dealt with by avoiding certain kinds of mistakes and providing auxiliary institutions, such as judicial review."

Some of the evidence points to the conclusion that Hamilton belongs with those Federalists described by Herbert Storing who saw the inadequacy of narrow self-interest but who did not attempt to transcend it by providing for virtue and character. Yet Hamilton's institutionalism and doctrine of interest represent a statesman bowing to circumstances he is powerless to change over the short run, namely, the prevailing lack of virtue in America. In contrast to certain Federalists described by Herbert Storing, Hamilton saw the lack of virtue as a central, rather than a "somewhat peripheral," problem. Virtue remained for Hamilton the touchstone even though virtue was conspicuous by its absence from America. Hamilton somewhat provided for virtue by defending it on important occasions, and he took a limited step toward spreading Christianity as a civil religion with his Christian Constitutional Society. For these reasons Hamilton is in a class by himself rather than with those Federalists described by Herbert Storing.

Hamilton's *Paybook* quotes Plutarch's *Lives* of Theseus, Romulus, Lycurgus and Numa Pompilius. Because Numa neglected "that cement which should have kept all together, education," "Numa's whole design and aim . . . on his death vanished with him."[209] Plutarch ascribed the "permanence" of Lycurgus's laws to the "unity of the common model of virtue" he established.[210] Though he neglected the "cement" of education for the United States, Hamilton's search for virtue kept it alive as the standard for judging the American political experiment. Hamilton did more than Numa but less than Lycurgus to perpetuate the regime through the "unity of the common model of virtue."

Hamilton presented two teachings on the presidency, dealing respectively with presidential "energy" and presidential "power," in *Federalist* 67–77 and the Pacificus Letters. The *Federalist* qualifies presidential "energy" with the principles of safety and responsibility. Presidential powers are enumerated ones, and Hamilton interpreted the first sentence of Article II of the Constitution as a designation of the office rather than a grant of power. The *Federalist* steers a prudent course between the fears of the state ratifying conventions and the degree of candor necessary for the guidance of posterity and potential presidents. *Federalist* 67–77 are a triumph of rhetoric, but they lack complete candor on the dimensions of the presidency. Hamilton focuses the Pacificus Letters on presidential "power" and gives a more candid treatment of the office than the *Federalist*. He interprets the first sentence of Article II as a grant of power and qualifies the president's power by the requirement that it be compatible with other parts of the Constitution and with the principles of free government. Hamilton was far too wise to detach presidential "power" from constitutional and extra-constitutional limitations even after the ratification of the Constitution.

What is the legacy of Alexander Hamilton? In his eulogy Fisher Ames, the noted Federalist orator, spoke of Hamilton's standing and rank with the people: "As long as virtue . . . is ever respectable when distinctly seen, they cannot withhold and they will not stint their admiration."[211] The legacy of Hamilton derived from the fact that "the most substantial glory of a country is in its virtuous great men; its prosperity will depend on its docility to learn from their example."[212] Hamilton warned his countrymen about the danger of their lack of virtue, and he left them an example of virtue that, "when distinctly seen," may rouse citizens to practice the classical virtue that was Hamilton's standard for judging America. In that event Hamilton might say: "I anticipate with you that the country will ere long assume an attitude correspondent with its great destinies, majestic, efficient and operative of great things. A noble career lies before it."[213]

After President Washington's death Hamilton wrote: "I have been much indebted to the kindness of the General, and he was an Aegis very essential to me."[214] Aegis here signifies a shield or protection. "I cannot say in how many ways the continuance of that confidence and friendship was necessary to me in future relations."[215] Alexander Hamilton was the brilliant second of George Washington. Hamilton and the other Founders developed their ideas of the presidency in light of Washington's character and the likelihood that he would be the first president. What did Washington stand for? We turn to his political thought and conduct as president and Hamilton's superior.

NOTES

1. Alexander Hamilton, John Jay, and James Madison, *The Federalist*, Jacob Cooke, ed. (Middletown: Wesleyan University Press, 1961), p. 51. Unless otherwise stated, all references are to this edition of the *Federalist*. The premise of Hamilton's observation was what he called "the improvement of moral science in modern times." Hamilton, "The Defense No. XX" (1795), in Alexander Hamilton, 19 *The Papers of Alexander Hamilton* 333, Harold Syrett, ed. (New York: Columbia University Press, 1961–1987); hereafter cited as *Papers*, preceded by the volume number and followed by the page number.

2. Hamilton, "The Farmer Refuted" (1775), 1 *Papers* 87, italics added.

3. Ibid.

4. Ibid.

5. Ibid., pp. 87–88; for the supreme law of every society, see 1 *Papers* 90.

6. Hamilton's Pay Book (1777), 1 *Papers* 396.

7. "First Letter from Phocion" (1784), 3 *Papers* 495.

8. Ibid., p. 496.

9. 3 *Papers* 556.

10. "Historical Notice," in Hamilton, Jay, and Madison, *The Federalist* cxxxvii, John C. Hamilton, ed. (Philadelphia: J. B. Lippincott, 1892).

11. Ibid., p. xxix, italics added.

12. To John Jay, November 26, 1775, 1 *Papers* 177: see the requirement of moderation.

13. To Lt. Col. John Laurens, June 30, 1780, 2 *Papers* 347.

14. To Lt. Col. John Laurens, Sept. 11, 1779, 2 *Papers* 167.

15. Secretary of the Treasury Hamilton tried to make an advantage out of the fact that his countrymen were tethered by a golden chain of acquisitiveness. He declared that the goals of the nation were "prosperity and greatness." Hamilton, "Final Version of the Report on the Subject of Manufactures" (1791) 10 *Papers* 235. More concisely, "we are the embryo of a great empire." Hamilton, "The Defense" No. II (1795), 18 *Papers* 498. The economic writings of Alexander Hamilton disguise the tension he elsewhere expressed between the enslavement of the golden chain of acquisitiveness and virtue, patriotism and freedom. In Hamilton's defense it might be urged that he made the best arrangements possible under the actual conditions of a regime that was fundamentally not to his liking.

Thomas L. Pangle has argued that the *Federalist*, the popular exposition of the Constitution, employs Lockean language in alluding to the ultimate questions. Thomas L. Pangle, "The *Federalist Papers'* Vision of Civic Health and the Tradition Out of Which That Vision Emerges," 39 *Western Political Quarterly* 599–600 (December, 1986). See also Pangle, *The Spirit of Modern Republicanism: The Moral Vision of the American Founders and the Philosophy of Locke* (Chicago: University of Chicago Press, 1988), pp. 117–119, 125. True, *Federalist* 2 teaches the indispensability of government and the necessity of the people ceding some of their "natural rights" to endow government with the requisite powers. And *Federalist* 10 does declare that the protection of the diverse, different and unequal faculties for the acquisition of property is the "first object of Government." Certainly both teachings are in the Lockean mold, but what are the implications for our understanding of Hamilton? John Jay and James Madison respectively, not Hamilton, wrote *Federalist* 2 and 10. My understanding of Hamilton's writings other than the *Federalist* disagrees with Pangle's conclusion that "even for men of the highest caliber, virtue is at most a subordinate goal, and perhaps no more than a means to fame." Pangle, 39 *Western Political Quarterly* 592. Jay and Madison in the *Federalist* may have pointed to Locke, but Hamilton's letters to men he respected transcended Locke by advocating ethical or moral, not civic or political virtue, and thus echoed the spirit of the classical teaching. For the argument that the *Federalist* contained Lockean elements, but was not simply Lockean, see David F. Epstein, *The Political Theory of the Federalist* (Chicago: University of Chicago, 1984), p. 5, and Morton White, *Philosophy, the Federalist, and the Constitution* (New York: Oxford University Press, 1987), pp. 9, 227, who emphasizes both Locke and Hume as the most important philosophers to influence Publius.

Locke himself "always thought the actions of men the best interpreters of their thoughts" (Locke, *Essay Concerning Human Understanding*, P. H. Nidditch, ed., Bk. I, ch. 3, para. 7 (New York: Oxford University Press, 1979), p. 69). What do Hamilton's actions tell us of his proximity to or distance from Locke? Compared to Thomas Jefferson, a missionary who named Locke as one of "the three greatest men the world had ever produced," Hamilton did not celebrate Locke's philosophy and couldn't even recognize Locke's portrait at Monticello. Jefferson to Dr. Benjamin Rush, January 16, 1811, in *The Life and Selected Writings of Thomas Jefferson*, Adrienne Koch, William Peden, eds. (New York: Modern Library, 1944), p. 609. Would Alexander Hamilton be considered by Locke as one of the praiseworthy "industrious and rational" accumulators of property? Upon Hamilton's death his friend Gouverneur Morris noted that Hamilton had left his family in "indigent circumstances." 2 *The Diary and Letters of Gouverneur Morris* 458, Anne Cary Morris, ed. (New York: Charles Scribner's Sons, 1888). Morris lamented that "our friend Hamilton... has been suddenly cut off in the midst of embarrassments which would have required several years of professional industry to set straight: a debt of between fifty thousand and sixty thousasnd dollars..., a property which..., if brought to the hammer, would not, in all probability, fetch forty [thousand dollars]; a family of seven young children. We have opened a subscription to provide for these orphans, and his warm-hearted friends, judging of others by themselves, expect more from it than I do." Ibid., p. 459. "Of all the men in American history who have occupied the office of secretary of the treasury, Hamilton, the greatest, was probably the least affluent." Robert A. Hendrickson, *The Rise and Fall of Alexander Hamilton* (New York: Van Nostrand Reinhold, 1981), p. 612; cf. p. 230. It would seem that Hamilton's actions do not imply his attachment to Lockean acquisitiveness.

After finishing the text of this chapter, my attention was drawn to Martin Diamond's suggestion of a "way through which Americans should inquire into, and go about, the ethical enterprise of politics." "Ethics and Politics: The American Way," *The Moral Foundations of the American Republic* Third Edition, Robert Horwitz, ed. (Charlottesville: University of Virginia Press, 1986), p. 108. "We must accept that their [the American Founders'] political order had its foundation in the human interests and passions; but we must appreciate also that their political order presupposes certain enduring qualities that can and should be achieved in the American character." There is considerable agreement between my understanding of Hamilton's principles and Diamond's argument that the American regime is a compound of human interests, passions and character.

16. To Lt. Col. John Laurens, Sept. 12, 1780, 2 *Papers* 428, italics in the original.

17. 5 *Papers* 425.

18. Quoted in George Washington Parke Custis, *Recollections and Private Memoirs of Washington* (Philadelphia: J. W. Bradley, 1861), p. 352, italics added.

19. Hamilton's Pay Book refers to "Aristotle's *Politics* chap. 6 Definition of money." E. P. Panagopoulos, ed., *Alexander Hamilton's Pay Book* (Detroit: Wayne State University, 1961), p. 41. Hamilton also refers to Aristotle on the causes of the duration of the Spartan government. *Pay Book*, p. 54; Hamilton's notes for his Constitutional Convention speech of June 18, 1787, mention Aristotle. 4 *Papers* 185.

20. Samuel E. Morison, *The Ancient Classics in a Modern Democracy* (London: Oxford University Press, 1939), p. 21.

21. Ibid., p. 23.

22. Ibid.

23. Panagopoulos, "The Origin and Background of the Pay Book," *Alexander Hamilton's Pay Book*, p. 10.

24. E. P. Panagopoulos, "Hamilton's Notes in His Pay Book of the New York State Artillery Company," 62 *American Historical Review* 317 (1957).

25. Panagopoulos, "The Origin and Background of the Pay Book," *Alexander Hamilton's Pay Book*, p. 9.

26. Hamilton, "Second Letter from Phocion," 3 *Papers* 553.

27. James Wilson, "A Charge...to the Grand Jury...," in 2 *The Works of James Wilson* 823, Robert McCloskey, ed. (Cambridge: Belknap Press of Harvard University Press, 1967).

28. Stuart Gerry Brown, *Alexander Hamilton* (New York: Washington Square Press, 1967), p. 172; "The delegates to the Constitutional Convention assembled at a time when the influence of the classics was at its height.... No eighteenth century statesman could escape the fine Hellenic hand of Aristotle, the student of politics." Richard M. Gummere, *The American Colonial Mind and the Classical Tradition* (Cambridge: Harvard University Press, 1963), pp. 174–175.

29. Gilbert Lycan, *Alexander Hamilton and American Foreign Policy: A Design for Greatness* (Norman: University of Oklahoma Press, 1970), p. 7.

30. Ibid., p. 9; on the importance of virtue in the *Federalist*, which was written principally by Hamilton, see Garry Wills, *Explaining America: The Federalist* (Garden City, N.Y.: Doubleday, 1981), pp. 185–192, 268–270.

31. Lycan, *Alexander Hamilton*, p. 13.

32. To Lt. Col. John Laurens, May 22, 1779, 2 *Papers* 53, italics supplied.

33. Hamilton, "Publius I," Oct. 19, 1778, 1 *Papers* 563.

34. Helene Johnson Looze, *Alexander Hamilton and the British Orientation of American Foreign Policy, 1788–1803* (The Hague: Mouton, 1969), p. 127.

35. The Earl of Birkenhead, *Contemporary Personalities* (London: Cassell, 1924), p. 115.

36. To James A. Bayard, April 16–21, 1802, 25 *Papers* 606.

37. Hamilton, Undated "Fragment on the French Revolution," 8 *The Works*

of Alexander Hamilton 427, H. C. Lodge, ed. (St. Clair Shores, Mich.: Scholarly Press, 1971).

38. Ibid., p. 426.

39. James A. Hamilton, one of Hamilton's sons, describes the upbringing of the Hamilton children on readings from the Bible and Goldsmith's history of Rome. James A. Hamilton, *Reminiscences* (New York: Scribner's, 1869), pp. 3–4.

40. Henry D. Aiken, "Introduction," David Hume, *Dialogues Concerning Natural Religion* (New York: Hafner, 1948), pp. xiv–xv.

41. Norman Kemp Smith, "Preface," David Hume, *Dialogues Concerning Natural Religion* (Indianapolis: Library of the Liberal Arts, n.d.), p. vi.

42. Kemp Smith, "Introduction," *Dialogues*, p. 43, italics added.

43. To the Comtesse De Boufflers, Jan. 22, 1763, David Hume, 1 *The Letters of David Hume* 374, J.Y.T. Greig, ed. (Oxford: Clarendon Press, 1932), italics added.

44. 2 *The Letters of David Hume* 334, italics added.

45. Kemp Smith, "Introduction," *Dialogues*, p. 57.

46. Ibid., p. 61.

47. Ibid., p. 62.

48. 1 *The Letters of David Hume* 154, italics added.

49. 2 *The Letters of David Hume* 323, italics added.

50. Ibid., pp. 323–324.

51. Ibid., pp. 324 n.1, 334 n.1.

52. Ibid., p. 326.

53. Ibid., Appendix M, pp. 453–454.

54. Hume, *Dialogues Concerning Natural Religion*, Kemp Smith, ed., Part XII, p. 227. See also Kemp Smith, "Introduction," *Dialogues*, pp. 72–73; Henry Aiken, "Introduction," *Dialogues*, pp. xi–xii.

55. Hume, *The Natural History of Religion*, Sect. VIII, p. 335, Sect. XV, p. 363, in Hume, 2 *Essays Moral, Political, and Literary*, T. H. Green and T. H. Grose, eds. (2 vols.; New York: Longmans, Green, 1912), italics in the original.

56. 2 *Essays Moral, Political, and Literary* 399, italics added.

57. Ibid., p. 403, "only," my italics. For Hume's attack on the "religious hypothesis" and his argument that "the state ought to tolerate every principle of philosophy," including the denial of "a divine existence, and consequently a providence and future state," see Hume, *Enquiries Concerning Human Understanding and Concerning the Principles of Morals, Enquiry Concerning Human Understanding*, P. H. Nidditch, ed., Sect. XI, pp. 139, 146, 133 (3rd ed.; Oxford: Clarendon Press, 1975). Hume classes "the belief of a divine Existence" among irrational "prejudices." Ibid., p. 147.

58. Hume, *An Enquiry Concerning Human Understanding*, 3rd ed., P. H. Nidditch, ed., Sect X, Part I, p. 115 n.1.

59. Ibid., p. 114.

60. Ibid., Sect. X, Part II, p. 127, italics added.

61. Ibid., p. 130.

62. Ibid., p. 127.

63. Ibid., p. 131.

64. 1 *The Letters of David Hume* 361.

65. Ibid., p. 237.

66. Ibid., p. 351.

67. *New Letters of David Hume*, R. Klibansky and E. Mossner, eds. (Oxford: Clarendon Press, 1954), p. 11.

68. Ibid., p. 13, italics added.

69. Forrest McDonald, *Alexander Hamilton* (New York: Norton, 1979), p. 374 n.15.

70. Hamilton, "Second Letter from Phocion," 3 *Papers* 549–550.

71. Ibid., p. 548.

72. To Lafayette, Jan. 6, 1799, 22 *Papers* 404, Hamilton's italics.

73. May 26, 1792, 11 *Papers* 443, italics in the original.

74. Ibid., p. 444.

75. Ibid., p. 443, italics in the original.

76. Ibid., p. 444.

77. To G. Morris, May 19, 1777, 1 *Papers* 255.

78. To James Duane, Sept. 3, 1780, 2 *Papers* 404.

79. Ibid., at 405.

80. For the development of the executive in the Convention, see Charles Thach, *The Creation of the Presidency* (Baltimore: Johns Hopkins University Press, 1969 [1923]).

81. 4 *Papers* 185; see the reference to Aristotle.

82. 4 *Papers* 193.

83. Ibid.

84. See Bower Aly, *The Rhetoric of Alexander Hamilton* (New York: Russell and Russell, 1965 [1941]), an Aristotelian study of Hamilton's speaking; see 5 *Papers* 151 on the vigorous executive as a part of a "representative democracy [that] as far as is consistent with its genius has all the features of good government."

85. 5 *Papers* 67.

86. Ibid., p. 81.

87. Ibid., p. 43.

88. Ibid., p. 37.

89. Ibid., p. 68.

90. Ibid., pp. 68–69.

91. Ibid., p. 43.

92. Ibid., p. 48. Thomas Jefferson, the self-styled democrat, actually went much farther than Alexander Hamilton in recommending natural aristocracy: "The natural aristocracy I consider as the most precious gift of nature for the instruction, the trusts, and government of society. . . . May we not even say that that form of government is the best which provides the most effectually for a pure selection of these natural aristoi into the offices of government?" Jefferson to John Adams, Oct. 28, 1813, in Lester J. Cappon, ed., 2 *The Adams–Jefferson Letters* 388 (Chapel Hill: University of North Carolina Press, 1959).

93. 5 *Papers* 42, italics added.

94. 4 *Papers* 187, italics in the original.

95. 5 *Papers* 95.

96. Ibid., pp. 36–37.

97. *Federalist* 1, p. 7.

98. *Federalist* 9, p. 51.

99. Ibid., pp. 51–52.

100. David Hume, *An Enquiry Concerning Human Understanding*, 3rd ed. P. H. Nidditch ed., Sect. VIII, Part 1, p. 90, "Of Liberty and Necessity," italics in the original. For full title citation of volume, see note 57, above.

101. Hamilton, "The Farmer Refuted," 1 *Papers* 100 n.

102. Hume, "That Politics May Be Reduced to a Science," in Hume, 1 *Essays Moral, Politicial, and Literary* 99, italics added.

103. Ibid.; Hamilton's "The Farmer Refuted" quotes Hume's essay on "The Independency of Parliament": "It is therefore a just *political* maxim, that *every man must be supposed a knave*." 1 *Papers* 95, italics in the original.

104. Hume, "That Politics May Be Reduced to a Science," 1 *Essays Moral, Political, and Literary* 105.

105. Ibid., p. 106.

106. Duncan Forbes, *Hume's Philosophical Politics* (Cambridge: University Press, 1975), p. 229.

107. *Federalist* 77, p. 520.

108. *Federalist* 67, p. 452; *Federalist* 69, p. 467.

109. *Federalist* 69, pp. 467–468.

110. *Federalist* 70, p. 471.

111. Aristotle, *The Rhetoric of Aristotle*, R. Jebb, trans. (Cambridge: University Press, 1909), p. 171.

112. 3 *Oxford English Dictionary* 167 (1933).

113. Samuel Johnson, 1 *A Dictionary of the English Language* (London: W. Strahan, 1755), n.p.

114. *Federalist* 70, p. 472.

115. Ibid., pp. 475–476.

116. *Federalist* 73, p. 494.

117. Ibid., pp. 492, 497; *Federalist* 74, p. 500.

118. *Federalist* 68, pp. 457–458.

119. Ibid., p. 461.

120. *Federalist* 75, p. 505.

121. *Federalist* 72, p. 488.

122. *Federalist* 76, p. 510.

123. Franklin and Washington were "good men" of "virtue." 5 *Papers* 176.

124. To George Washington, May 5, 1789, 5 *Papers* 335.

125. 5 *Papers* 337, italics in the original.

126. "We are both of an opinion that there is *no* power in the President to appoint an Envoy Extraordinary, without the concurrence of the Senate." 20 *Papers* 246; see also "Tully No. III" (1794): "A sacred respect for the constitutional law is the vital principle, the sustaining energy of a free government." 17 *Papers* 160. "Second Letter from Phocion" (1784): "... in a doubtful case, the constitution ought never to be hazarded, without extreme necessity." 3 *Papers* 558.

127. Rossiter, *Alexander Hamilton and the Constitution*, pp. 86, 214.

128. Alexander Hamilton and James Madison, *The Letters of Pacificus and Helvidius on the Neutrality Proclamation of 1793 with the Letters of Americanus*, Richard Loss, ed. (Delmar, N.Y.: Scholars' Facsimiles and Reprints, 1976).

129. 15 *Papers* 669.

130. Hamilton, *The Letters of Pacificus*, p. 10, italics in the original. Hamilton's "Opinion on the Constitutionality of an Act to Establish a Bank" (1791) similarly fenced in the power of Congress with limitations derived from, though he does not use the term, political thought. See the requirement that means be "not immoral, or not contrary to the essential ends of political society." 8 *Papers* 98. Thus in interpreting both congressional and presidential power Hamilton summons the aid of political thought in order to enforce extra-constitutional limitations.

131. Rossiter, *Alexander Hamilton and the Constitution*, p. 248; see also Introduction, above, n.5.

132. 15 *Papers* 42.

133. Secretary of State Thomas Jefferson argued that revolutionary France and the United States had "similar principles of government." Jefferson, 6 *The Writings of Thomas Jefferson* 200, P. L. Ford, ed. (New York: Putnam's, 1892–1899).

134. Edward S. Corwin, "Preface," *The President's Control of Foreign Relations* (Princeton, N.J.: Princeton University Press, 1917).

135. In *Alexander Hamilton and the Constitution* Rossiter mentions Helvidius outside the elaboration of Corwin's thesis.

136. By writing that Pacificus is "still" one of the most effective arguments for the strong presidency, Rossiter hints that Hamilton's argument was superior to Madison's. This may be so, but Rossiter does not prove the superiority. He assumes it from the outset. Rossiter, *Alexander Hamilton and the Constitution*, p. 214.

137. Quoted in James Madison, 6 *The Writings of James Madison* 138 n.1, G. Hunt, ed. (New York: Putnam's 1906).

138. Locke, *Second Treatise*, parag. 160, in *Two Treatises of Government*, Peter Laslett, ed. (Cambridge: University Press, 1960).

139. Hamilton, 4 *The Works of Alexander Hamilton* 432 n.1, H.C. Lodge, ed. (New York: Putnam's, 1904).

140. Irving Brant, 3 *James Madison* 379 (Indianapolis: Bobbs-Merrill, 1950).

141. Madison, 6 *The Writings of James Madison* 196.

142. Ibid., pp. 137–138.

143. Ibid., p. 137.

144. Ralph Ketcham, *James Madison* (New York: Macmillan, 1971), p. 346.

145. Ibid., p. 347.

146. Madison, in *The Letters of Pacificus and Helvidius*, Letters IV, V, pp. 87, 96.

147. 4 *The Works of Alexander Hamilton* 489 n.1 (H. C. Lodge, ed., 1904).

148. L. Hacker, *Alexander Hamilton in the American Tradition* (New York: McGraw-Hill, 1957), p. 198.

149. H. Morgenthau, *In Defense of the National Interest* (New York: Knopf, 1951), p. 14.

150. H. J. Ford, *Alexander Hamilton* (New York: Scribner's, 1920), p. 288.

151. F. Oliver, *Alexander Hamilton: An Essay on American Union* (New York: Putnam's, 1906), p. 335.

152. 1 J. Story, "Preface," *Commentaries* viii, T. Cooley, ed. (4th ed.; Boston: Little, Brown, 1873).

153. Douglass Adair, *Fame and the Founding Fathers* (New York: Norton, 1964), p. 73.

154. "Historical Notice," in Hamilton, Jay, and Madison, *The Federalist* xcii, John C. Hamilton, ed. (1892).

155. Ibid., p. ciii.

156. Adair, *Fame and the Founding Fathers*, p. 73.

157. Ibid., pp. 24, 16 n.14.

158. Ibid., p. 24, italics added.

159. Ibid., p. 26.

160. Ibid., p. 16 n.14.

161. Ibid., p. 16.

162. Gerald Stourzh, *Alexander Hamilton and the Idea of Republican Government* (Stanford, Calif.: Stanford University Press, 1970), p. 202.

163. Ibid., p. 203.

164. Washington to the President of the United States, Sept. 25, 1798, John Fitzpatrick, ed., 36 *The Writings of George Washington* 460–461 (Washington, D.C.: Government Printing Office, 1941).

165. Washington to Hamilton, Feb. 2, 1795, 18 *Papers* 248.

166. To William Hamilton, May 2, 1797, 21 *Papers* 78, italics added.

167. To James A. Bayard, Jan. 16, 1801, 25 *Papers* 323.

168. Aristotle, *Nichomachean Ethics*, F. H. Peters, trans. (London: Kegan Paul, 1891), p. 115.

169. Ibid., pp. 116, 118.

170. Stourzh, *Alexander Hamilton*, p. 184.

171. McDonald, *Alexander Hamilton*, p. 35.

172. Wills, *Explaining America: The Federalist*, p. ix.

173. Alex Bein, *Die Staatsidee Alexander Hamiltons in ihrer Entstehung und Entwicklung* Beiheft 12, *Historische Zeitschrift* (Munich: Verlag R. Oldenbourg, 1927), p. 171.

174. Ibid., p. 171.

175. Cooke, Review, Wills, *Explaining America: The Federalist*, 87 *American Historical Review* 532–533 (April, 1982); cf. Jacob Cooke, *Alexander Hamilton* (New York: Scribner's, 1982), pp. 8, 23n.

176. Bein, *Die Staatsidee Alexander Hamiltons*, p. 172.

177. Leslie Stephen, 2 *History of English Thought in the Eighteenth Century* 152 (3rd ed.; Harcourt, Brace and World, 1962 [1902]), italics added.

178. David Hume, *A Treatise of Human Nature*, L. A. Selby-Bigge, ed., Book III, Part I, Sect. 1, 2nd rev. ed., P. H. Nidditch, ed. (Oxford: Clarendon Press, 1978), pp. 469–470.

179. Alasdair MacIntyre, *After Virtue: A Study in Moral Theory* (Notre Dame: University of Notre Dame Press, 1981), p. 54.

180. Hume, *Treatise*, Book III, Part III, Sect. I, p. 574.

181. Ibid., pp. 574–575, italics not in the original.

182. Ibid., p. 591.

183. 1 *The Letters of David Hume* 416.

184. Ibid., pp. 32, 35, italics added.

185. Ibid., p. 33.

186. Hume, *Enquiries Concerning Human Understanding and Concerning the Prin-*

ciples of Morals, Enquiry Concerning the Principles of Morals, Sect. V, Part I, p. 218, italics added to "interest."

187. Ibid., Sect. V, Part II, p. 219.

188. Ibid., p. 229 n1.

189. Ibid., Sect. V, Part I, pp. 215–216, italics added.

190. Ibid., Sect. V, Part II, p. 230, italics added.

191. Ibid., Sect V, Part I, p. 217, italics in the original.

192. Ibid., Sect. I, p. 172.

193. Hume, *Treatise*, Book II, Part III, Sect. III, p. 415, italics added.

194. "Second Letter from Phocion," 3 *Papers* 532.

195. 3 *Papers* 543.

196. Drew McCoy, *The Elusive Republic* (Chapel Hill: University of North Carolina Press, 1980).

197. Ibid., p. 132.

198. Ibid., p. 133.

199. J.G.A. Pocock, *The Machiavellian Moment: Florentine Political Thought and the Atlantic Republican Tradition* (Princeton, N.J.: Princeton University Press, 1975), p. 530.

200. Ibid., p. 521.

201. Ibid., p. 526.

202. Hamilton to William Duer, June 18, 1788, 1 *Papers* 499.

203. To James Duane, Sept. 3, 1780, 2 *Papers* 417; cf. Hume, Essay VII, 1 *Essays Moral, Political, and Literary* 125.

204. Adrienne Koch, *Power, Morals and the Founding Fathers* (Ithaca, N.Y.: Cornell University Press, 1961), p. 79.

205. Ibid., p. 58.

206. Ibid., p. 80.

207. Roland J. Mulford, "The Political Theories of Alexander Hamilton" (Ph.D. Diss., Johns Hopkins University, 1903), p. 24.

208. Herbert J. Storing, "Introduction," 1 *The Complete Anti-Federalist* 74, H. J. Storing, ed. (Chicago: University of Chicago Press, 1981).

209. Plutarch, *The Lives of The Noble Grecians and Romans*, John Dryden and Arthur H. Clough, trans. (New York: Modern Library, 1932), p. 96.

210. Cf. Aristotle on Sparta, *Politics*, Ernest Barker, trans. (Oxford: Clarendon Press, 1948), pp. 73–80.

211. Ames, "A Sketch of the Character of Alexander Hamilton," in Seth Ames, ed., 2 *Works of Fisher Ames* 257 (Boston: Little, Brown, 1854; New York: DaCapo, 1969).

212. Ibid., p. 263.

213. To Rufus King, Oct. 2, 1798, 22 *Papers* 192.

214. To Tobias Lear, Jan. 2, 1800, 24 *Papers* 155.

215. 24 *Papers* 184.

2

The Political Thought and Conduct of President George Washington

This chapter explores the political thought and conduct in office of President George Washington. The scholarship on Washington argues predominantly that he shunned political thought. Three conflicting generalizations emerge from a review of the Washington literature: he did not engage in political thought; although he taught political principles, they were entirely modern republicanism; his principles were entirely ancient republicanism. Part II of this chapter presents Washington's principles and briefly contrasts them with Hamilton's and Jefferson's principles. My thesis is that Washington's political thought mixes modern republicanism (liberty, equality of men, popular sovereignty and majority rule) and classical republicanism (inegalitarian virtue and the formation of character by liberal education). Part III examines President Washington's conduct in office and its theoretical underpinnings.

WASHINGTON'S POLITICAL THOUGHT IN THE LITERATURE

Many of the commentators on George Washington deny that his greatness rests on a theory of politics. In 1851 the French historian Guizot held that Washington was "a man of experience and action" and had "no systematic pretension in his manner of thinking...No principle fixed beforehand governed him."[1] Washington "was a stranger to every theory....his acts...had not a systematic character." Guizot critically concluded that Washington was "uninfluenced by any theory": "he made no show of the principles that were to govern him."[2]

During the twentieth century this opinion of Washington gained in authority. W. E. Woodward, for example, gave the sharpest American expression of Guizot's interpretation of Washington: "One of the most significant facts about Washington's long and distinguished career is that he never formulated any coherent theory of government. Hamilton and Jefferson both worked out distinctly articulated systems of politics.... But there is nothing in the body of American political thought that we can call Washingtonism."[3] Woodward struck a familiar note in the literature by disparaging Washington's intellectual capacity: his observations "lack a fundamental idea" because "a coherent political philosophy is not an impelling necessity to this type of intellect."[4] According to Bernard Faÿ, Washington "made great efforts to keep Americans from dispersing their strength in discussing theories."[5] Writing in 1961, J. A. Carroll drew the familiar dichotomy between the man of thought and the man of action: "Washington was not an architect in ideas; he was essentially a man of deeds."[6]

Although debunking students of Washington, such as Woodward, stress Washington's lack of political thought, this criticism also occurs among writers with a higher estimate of Washington's greatness, such as Carroll. In 1969 Morton Borden asked: "Why...was Washington great? In what did he excel? By common consent his intellectual talents were limited. He knew little of... political theory.... Scholars interested in...the clash of ideas must turn elsewhere."[7] Echoing this common disparagement of Washington's political thought, in 1974 Forrest McDonald wrote that Washington "understood little and thought even less about the fine points of speculative disputation from which Hamiltonians and Jeffersonians derived justification for their conduct."[8] The negativism of these critics unfortunately removes the greatest incentive for studying Washington's thought carefully and seriously.

This rejection of Washington as a political thinker contrasts with early accounts. Thomas Paine, the celebrated political writer who regarded himself as "one of the principal founders of the American republic," enclosed the key to the Bastille with a letter to Washington: "That the principles of America opened the Bastille is not to be doubted; and therefore the key comes to the right place."[9] Entirely apart from the influence of American principles on the French Revolution, clearly Paine implies that Washington made the central contribution in articulating the "principles of America." Paine's eulogy on Washington held that before the American Revolution Washington had reposed "under the groves of fame and philosophy" and that "his principles were the result of... philosophy." Washington could "outride fortune by the foresight of philosophy"; his Farewell Address was "the effort of a mind, whose powers...could...unfold truth without the labor of investigation."[10] This testimony is all the more valuable in coming from a Jeffersonian and a critic of Washington's. Fisher Ames, skillful orator of the Federalists, eulogized Washington's thought: "Others, I hope but few ... will deem it incredible that Washington should think with as much dignity and elevation as he acted.... Such a chief magistrate as Washington, appears like the polestar in a clear sky, to direct the skillful statesman."[11]

John Marshall, who knew Washington personally, wrote that "in speculation, he was a real republican, devoted to the Constitution of his country, and to that system of equal political rights on which it is founded."[12] Clearly, Marshall states that Washington had a political teaching and that it was modern republicanism. Early in the nineteenth century Chateaubriand said that "Washington represented the needs, the ideas, the enlightenment, the opinions of his day; instead of impeding the development of modern ideas, he promoted them."[13] That is, Washington is best understood as a child of the Enlightenment, and his achievement is limited to the promotion of modern republicanism.

In 1832 Daniel Webster held that the question of principle for the United States was identical with the question that Washington had addressed: "whether free states may be stable, as well as free; whether popular power may be trusted, as well as feared; in short, whether wise, regular and virtuous self government is a vision for the contemplation of theorists, or a truth established, illustrated and brought into practice in the country of Washington."[14] Washington's "leading principles," said Webster, "are not left doubtful" but are found in the Constitution, in the measures recommended and approved by Washington, in his speeches to Congress and in the Farewell Address. Summarizing in 1889 the trends in the understanding of Washington, Henry Cabot Lodge concluded that "there is no need to argue the truism that Washington was a great man, for that is universally admitted. But is is very needful that his greatness should be rightly understood, and the right understanding of it is by no means universal. His character has been exalted at the expense of his intellect, and his goodness has been so much insisted upon both by admirers and critics that we are in danger of forgetting that he had a great mind as well as high moral worth."[15]

In 1945 Harold Bradley found that although "the first President seems curiously remote from the realm of abstract ideas," "Washington ... fancied himself as something of an amateur philosopher—at least in the field of political thought. His private correspondence is filled with allusions to the delights of the philosophically minded—a category in which obviously he included himself."[16] But Bradley is unable to develop his understanding of Washington's political teaching from Washington's praise of contemplation over political practice because, for Bradley, Washington "would seem ... miscast as a political philosopher. He was neither a phrase maker nor an original thinker.... One may search the public papers of Washington without finding a concise statement of political philosophy.... He prepared no treatise on government or politics."[17] Yet "through all of his thinking ran the major conviction that government must be strong or it is no government worthy of the name."[18]

According to Bradley, Washington's legacy to his countrymen is a set of "pleasant platitudes reflecting ... his day" and "convictions," that is, dogmas, such as a strong central government, rather than reasoned principles that explain the American regime, that is, political thought.[19] By political thought we mean "the reflection on, or the exposition of, political ideas; and by a political idea we may understand any politically significant 'phantasm, notion, species, or whatever it is about which the mind can be employed in thinking' concerning political fundamentals."[20] "Political thought which is not political philosophy finds its adequate expression in laws and codes, in poems and stories, in tracts and public speeches *inter alia*." Political thought may be briefly contrasted with political philosophy. Political thought is "indifferent to the distinction between opinion and knowledge; but political philosophy is the conscious, coherent and relentless effort to replace opinions about the political fundamentals by knowledge regarding them." Second, political thought "may not be more, and may not even intend to be more, than the expounding or the defense of a firmly held conviction or of an invigorating myth." Third, a non-philosophical political thinker "is primarily interested in, or attached to, a specific order or policy; the political philosopher is primarily interested in, or attached to, the truth." Thus an American political thinker is primarily attached to the United States. Fourth, the proper form of political philosophy is the treatise. Finally, political thought is coeval with the human race, but political philosophy emerged "at a knowable time in the recorded past."[21] It almost goes without saying that a regime's political thought may more closely approach political philosophy at one time than another. American political thought may be understood as a continuum running from the most pedestrian statements to statements that raise, but do not answer, fundamental questions of political philosophy.

Bradley, however, argues in effect that either Washington must be a political philosopher at the level of, say, an Aristotle, or Washington can leave his countrymen only unreasoned and unauthoritative platitudes and dogmas. Bradley overlooks the excluded middle of political thought. Few, if any, American political thinkers would meet Bradley's test of "political philosophy," and knowing this, Bradley applied a more lenient test to Alexander Hamilton, John Adams, James Madison and Thomas Jefferson. Bradley's test for these statesmen was not in any way "political philosophy," but "enduring contributions to political practice and theory," "unusual insights into the problems and institutions of government" and "views upon the nature and function of government and the appropriate relationship between government and the citizen."[22] Bradley

makes Washington's speculation seem unimportant by comparison to
the speculation of Hamilton, Adams, Madison and Jefferson because
Bradley reasonably and appropriately treats the latter quartet as con-
tributors to American political thought, not political philosophy. "These
four men constitute a quartet which has not been surpassed and perhaps
has not been equaled in the history of political thought in the United
States."[23] If Bradley had applied the test of political thought to Washington's teaching, Bradley would necessarily have reached a higher estimate of Washington's importance and service to his countrymen.

In 1955 Saul Padover emphasized Washington's character and disparaged his intellect while admitting nevertheless that principles were
important for Washington: "What . . . accounts for his peculiar greatness
and appeal is not book learning but character."[24] Contrasting Washington's thought with the expectations of "our own 'other directed' society,"
Padover finds that today "George Washington would hardly be a successful leader, if, indeed, he would be considered a leader at all. A society
whose main and overriding concern is with imitation of one another
would probably be disinclined to follow a man of severe moral conduct
. . . who was convinced that moral principles are the foundations of the
universe and that they never change."[25] More generally, the present
currents of opinion make it difficult for twentieth-century scholars to
develop the sympathetic understanding that is indispensable for grasp-
ing Washington's thought. In short, contemporary opinion makes it difficult to comprehend a statesman who, in the language of Henry
Tuckerman, had "the openness to right impressions characteristic of an
intellect . . . whose chief affinity is for absolute truth."[26]

In 1958 Marcus Cunliffe chiefly focused on Washington's temperament and character: "The point is that his age differed profoundly from
ours; that in certain ways he is better understood within a classical framework than as a man of modern times."[27] Cunliffe's approach, suggestive
as to character, takes off from an unacknowledged source, John Adams's
comparison of Washington to Marcus Aurelius.[28] For Cunliffe the classical framework explains Washington as "the disinterested patriot."[29] But
Cunliffe also uses "a classical framework" to explain Washington's beliefs
or thought. This "classical framework" "does at least help us to grasp
why men such as Washington believed that they could create a huge new
nation on the republican model."[30] "The lessons of the classical past,
when the world was young, as America felt itself to be young, suggested
that such a republic was a working possibility, as well as providing a
warning that things might go wrong." In short, Cunliffe implies that
Washington's teaching is best understood within a classical framework.

In 1969 James Morton Smith objected to "the tendency of the twentieth-century to view Washington as a mindless man."[31] That is sound
as far as it goes. In part, over the past twenty-five years, Smith argues,

the "neglect of Washington springs from his failure to write any systematic or theoretical statement of his political and social philosophy until his Farewell Address, in part from the difficulty of classifying him as a liberal or conservative thinker."[32] Smith's assertion about the lack of a theoretical statement until the Farewell Address conflicts with Daniel Webster's understanding, for whom Washington's "leading principles" were "not left doubtful" and were found in Washington's thought as a whole. Smith's other point, the difficulty, nay, impossibility, of classifying Washington as a liberal or conservative thinker, is a more adequate explanation of the resistance of modern liberal and conservative scholars to Washington's thought. Smith is on sound ground in writing that the omission of Washington or giving him brief notice, "as in most intellectual histories," is an "easy out," that is, is indefensible.[33]

In 1972 James Flexner's biography closed with some but, according to Henry Cabot Lodge's requirement, still insufficient recognition of Washington's intellect and political thought. Washington "had found a persuasive formula for self regulation" in Stoicism, "but it did not define effective principles of government."[34] "Washington had to seek in more modern sources for effective principles of government": "many of the philosophical conceptions Washington acted out had originated in France." Washington, Flexner implies, was a classical man in character and an entirely modern political thinker. More precisely, Flexner interprets Washington's teaching as undiluted modern republicanism.

Thus the scholarship discussed above poses in the main three generalizations. These generalizations are, first, that Washington lacked political thought; second, that his political teaching was modern republicanism; third, that his political teaching was classical republicanism. Let us examine Washington's writings with these generalizations in mind.

PRESIDENT WASHINGTON'S POLITICAL THOUGHT

Washington's theory of political education held that the elucidation of principle is an important part of political leadership and that this elucidation would determine the fate of the Federalist party. "If *men*, not *principles*, can influence the choice, on the part of the Federalists, what but fluctuations are to be expected.... If principles, instead of men, are not the steady pursuit of the Federalists," he wrote in 1799, "their cause will soon be at an end."[35] The republican statesman, Washington held, must teach political principle so as to preserve "order, and good government."[36] Washington's concern with political thought is more clearly formulated by Alexander Hamilton: "But is it a recommendation to have *no theory*? Can that man be a systematic or able statesman who has none? I believe not. *No general principles* will hardly work much better than erroneous ones."[37] Washington agreed wholeheartedly with Hamilton's conclusion: the political vocation properly understood involves the statesman in the elucidation of principle.

Washington's political teaching employs, without being limited to, principles of modern republicanism. "I love to indulge the contemplation of human nature in a progressive state of improvement and melioration," confided Washington to Lafayette.[38] Washington drew the consequences of the idea of progress in comparing the founding generation with posterity: "I do not think we are more inspired, have more wisdom, or possess more virtue, than those who will come after us."[39] He also drew the implications of the idea of progress in his comparison of governments in Europe and America. In contrast with Europe, the United States, he taught, has "governments founded on genuine principles of rational liberty, and ... mild and wholesome laws."[40]

Yet Washington confronted his "innocent reveries, that mankind will, one day, grow happier and better" with evidence against the idea of progress, which made him far from being simply a son of the Enlightenment.[41] "But alas! the millennium will not I fear appear in our days. The restless mind of man cannot be at peace; and when there is disorder within, it will appear without, and soon or late show itself in acts. So it is with nations, whose mind is only the aggregate of those of individuals, where the government is representative, and the voice of a despot, where it is not."[42] Discussing the limitations of a philanthropic understanding of progress, Washington held that "while the passions of mankind are under so little restraint as they are among us, and while there are so many motives, and views, to bring them into action, we may wish for, but will *never* see the accomplishment" of such progress.[43] In short, the restless passions that governed Americans postponed the millennium of progress to an indefinite futurity. Washington retained a qualified belief in Providence: "The great Governor of the universe has led us too long and too far on the road to happiness and glory, to forsake us in the midst of it" as long as "there is good sense and virtue enough left to recover the right path."[44]

Washington was strongly interested in federalism. Regarding the Articles of Confederation as almost a complete error in 1787, he argued that "the primary cause of all our disorders lies in the different state governments, and in the tenacity of that power, which pervades the whole of their systems."[45] Washington saw a direct connection between the lack of public virtue and the need for coercion from a national government: "I confess ... that my opinion of public virtue is so far changed that I have my doubts whether any system without the means of coercion in the sovereign, will enforce obedience to the ordinances of a general government; without which, everything else fails."[46] Washington wanted a "well-toned government" from the Philadelphia Convention, the purpose of which was to "determine whether we are to have a government of respectability under which life, liberty, and property will be secured to us" or are to submit to a government that may be the result of chance.[47]

"To complete the American character," Washington held, "it remains for the citizens of the United States to show to the world, that the reproach heretofore cast on republican governments for their want of stability, is without foundation, when that government is the deliberate choice of an enlightened people."[48] Washington saw the need to vindicate American republicanism from the British critique that "without the protection of Great Britain we should be unable to govern ourselves; and would soon be involved in anarchy and confusion."[49] The connection between Washington's emphasis on stability and the property right would appear to arise from the reputation of popular governments as unjust and, hence, unstable associations in which the many poor tried to expropriate the wealthy few.[50] After his tour of 1,887 miles through the southern states, President Washington proclaimed that the people "begin to feel the good effects of equal laws and equal protection"; "equal laws and equal rights prevail"; and to Lafayette Washington termed ours "an equal and good government."[51] To a British correspondent Washington wrote that "liberty, civil and religious, secured on the liberal basis of reason and virtue, are the rich rewards of the past exertions of our citizens."[52]

Washington found the basis of the Constitution in popular sovereignty: "The power under the Constitution will always be in the people."[53] The Farewell Address similarly proclaimed that "the basis of our political systems is the right of the people to make and to alter their constitutions of government."[54] This principle led Washington to find in majority rule the application of popular sovereignty. His Sixth Annual Address to Congress enumerated "the fundamental principle of our Constitution which enjoins that the will of the majority shall prevail."[55] Speaking of the Whiskey Rebellion, Washington held that if minorities are allowed to prostrate laws made by the majority, "there is an end put, at one stroke, to republican government."[56] The result will be anarchy and confusion because other men may dislike another law and oppose it "with equal propriety until all laws are prostrate, and every one (the strongest I presume) will carve for himself."

"The Constitution is the guide, which I never will abandon," Washington informed the Boston Selectmen.[57] "As the Constitution of the United States, and the laws made under it, must mark the line of my official conduct, I could not justify my taking a single step in any matter, which appeared to me to require their agency, without its being first obtained."[58] Despite this ringing defense of the Constitution and constitutionalism, Washington understood the Constitution as a necessary but not sufficient cause of good government. Thus Washington departed from the notion of modern republicanism held by the influential political philosopher Immanuel Kant. Kant subscribed to the view, characteristic of modern republicanism, that emphasized the devising and implementing of the right political institutions as distinct from classical republicanism, which had stressed the formation of character through liberal education. Kant taught that "the problem of organizing a state, however hard it may seem, can be solved *even for a race of devils*, if only they are intelligent," that is, practice enlightened selfishness.[59] "A good constitution," said Kant, "is not to be expected from morality, but, conversely, a good moral condition of a people is to be expected only under a good constitution."[60]

Washington thought beyond the somewhat smug listing of institutions, such as separation of powers, used in Hamilton's *Federalist* 9 to prove the superiority of modern over ancient political science. Washington taught in effect that no constitution can compensate for a decline of America into a nation of devils, even if they are intelligent. Speaking of what lies beyond the Constitution, namely, the character of the people and statesmen, Washington informed Lafayette:

I would not be understood my dear Marquis to speak of consequences which may be produced, in the revolution of ages, by corruption of morals, profligacy of manners, and listlessness for the preservation of the natural and unalienable rights of mankind; nor of the successful usurpations that may be established at such an unpropitious juncture, upon the runs of liberty, however providently guarded and secured, as these are contingencies against which no human prudence can effectually provide.[61]

Washington expressly teaches that institutions such as the constitutional separation of powers can prevent our government from degenerating into despotic or oppressive forms only "so long as there shall remain any virtue in the body of the people." Washington in effect reverses Kant's notion of causality: lasting republican constitutions presuppose the absence of "corruption of morals" or the presence of good character.

Americans have become so accustomed to the received opinion that the idea of progress is identical with the American way of life that it is shocking to see George Washington speak of the decline of the American regime. Yet Washington's scouting of decline was by no means limited to him. He joins four other thinkers of the classic period of American political thought in soberly examining the decline of the regime. Chapter 1 showed that Alexander Hamilton argued that without virtue republican government and freedom would perish. Consider also the arguments of John Adams, Thomas Jefferson and Tom Paine.

John Adams wrote to Jefferson that he once read a book advancing the thesis "that had Brutus and Cassius been conqueror, they would have restored virtue and liberty to Rome.... Have you found in history one single example of a nation thoroughly corrupted, that was afterwards restored to virtue, and *without virtue, there can be no political liberty.*" In what is almost an epitaph for the American commercial republic, Adams fires a volley of penetrating questions at Jefferson: "Will you tell me how to prevent riches from becoming the effects of temperance and industry? Will you tell me how to prevent riches from producing luxury? Will you tell me how to prevent luxury from producing effeminacy, intoxication, extravagance, vice and folly?... Yet all these ought not to discourage us from exertion, for ... I believe no effort in favor of virtue is lost, and all good men ought to struggle both by their counsel and example."[62] Adams reasoned from the existence of temperance and industry in America to the accumulation of riches, from riches to luxury, and from luxury to effeminacy, intoxication, extravagance, vice and folly—the decline of virtue, the regime and political liberty. John Adams's closely reasoned and eloquent argument is fully compatible with the spirit of Hamilton's and Washington's arguments. Adams and Hamilton in particular show that the Lockean formula of the accumulation of property ultimately extinguishes virtue and political liberty.

During the American Revolution Thomas Jefferson's *Notes on the State of Virginia* held that "the spirit of the times may alter, will alter. Our rulers will become corrupt, our people careless.... It can never be too often repeated, that the time for fixing every essential right on a legal basis is while our rulers are honest, and ourselves united. *From the conclusion of this war we shall be going downhill.*" Jefferson said of the people: "They will forget themselves, but in the sole faculty of making money, and will never think of uniting to effect a due respect for their rights."[63] Jefferson's prediction of a "downhill" decline is unaccompanied by Adams's manly insistence on exertion and virtue. In the immediate context of his "downhill" prediction, Jefferson implies that popular jealousy, watchfulness and legislative action will suffice. The lawyer's stock remedy of a written statement in law of "every essential right" will, Jefferson implies, safeguard rights though corruption permeates the rulers and carelessness permeates the people. Jefferson fails to explain how liberty or rights could long coexist, even though laws were passed, with corrupt rulers, who would render judicial decisions and constitutional interpretations, and a careless people, who would render jury verdicts. The written law would seem to be no sufficient remedy for the moral decline of the regime.

Finally, Tom Paine expressed a "melancholy, a little predictive, that I hope is not becoming true too soon."

A thousand years hence ... perhaps in less, America may be what Europe now is.... When we contemplate the fall of empires and the extinction of the nations of the ancient world, we see but little to excite our regret.... but when the empire of America shall fall, the subject for contemplative sorrow will be infinitely greater than crumbling brass and marble can inspire it. It will not then be said, here stood a temple of vast antiquity; here rose a babel of invisible height; or there a palace of sumptuous extravagance; but here, Ah, painful thought; the noblest work of human wisdom, the grandest scene of human glory, the fair cause of Freedom rose and fell.[64]

Paine hints that a decline of character will precede the fall of America and that the original character of America will be incredible to posterity: "The innocence of her character, that won the hearts of all nations in her favor, may sound like a romance and her inimitable virtues as if it [sic; they] had never been." This will apply especially to the "fashionable of that day, enveloped in dissipation." Paine opposes the "dissipation" of the fashionable to America's original "inimitable virtues."

All of these thinkers except Jefferson state the problem of perpetuating the regime more deeply than mere official corruption and popular carelessness. All except Jefferson look to virtue as the energy of republicanism and freedom. Only Jefferson argued that recording essential rights in law would somehow enable the regime to survive. Concerning the character of the people, Jefferson reasoned from a moral cause, though he avoided the term greed, to a legal remedy. Washington, Hamilton, Adams and Paine reason from a moral cause or causes of the decline of the regime to a moral remedy. George Washington, then, spoke for what one might call discriminating political minds when he said that "a good general government, without good morals and good habits, will not make us a happy people."[65]

Washington's reliance upon character and virtue is shown in his description of how the government functioned or was intended to function. "The establishment of our new government seemed to be the last great experiment for promoting human happiness by reasonable compact in civil society. It was to be, in the first instance, in a considerable degree a government of accommodation as well as a government of laws. Much was to be done by *prudence*, much by *conciliation*, much by *firmness*."[66] Thus "much" beyond what the Constitution and laws could do was left to the moral virtue of the statesman. Washington declared in his First Inaugural Address that "the foundations of our national policy will be laid in the pure and immutable principles of private morality."[67]

Two of Washington's writings, the First Inaugural Address and the Farewell Address, underscore the crucial importance of virtue for republican government. As the First Inaugural succinctly put the matter, there is no truth more thoroughly established, than that there exists in the economy and course of nature, an indissoluble union between virtue and happiness.... Since we ought to be no less persuaded that the propitious smiles of Heaven, can never be expected on a nation that disregards the eternal rules of order and right, which Heaven itself has ordained: And since the preservation of the sacred fire of liberty, and the destiny of the republican model of government, are justly considered as *deeply*, perhaps as *finally* staked, on the experiment entrusted to the hands of the American people.[68]

The Farewell Address teaches that " 'tis substantially true, that virtue or morality is a necessary spring of popular government."[69] Washington terms "virtue or morality" the "foundation of the fabric" of popular government.[70] "Can it be," he asks in the Farewell Address, "that Providence has not connected the permanent felicity of a nation with its virtue?"[71] Lafayette revealed how much the American experiment under Washington combined the classical concern for virtue with the modern dispensation of liberty and equality when he wrote of "a doctrine truly American of *virtuous* liberty and legal equality."[72] Virtue in America was to direct the use of liberty to good rather than evil.

What, according to Washington, was to be the source of virtue in the American republic? Clearly, Washington would have disagreed with Tocqueville's conclusion that at best the American regime would be decent and orderly but devoid of poetry and the highest excellence.[73] Washington's thought that education was a means to virtue or moral excellence was an implicit reply to Kant's argument that virtue is irrelevant to the founding of regimes and that only the constitution matters. Washington's thought was also a reply to a classical criticism of democracy.[74] Aristotle taught that democracy was the rule of the many, who are generally the poor.[75] The poor lack leisure for education; hence democracy is the rule of ignorance.[76] As if in reply to this criticism Washington steadfastly supported the liberal arts and liberal education. He based his support for the liberal arts on the precedent of "men of real talents in arms" who "have commonly approved themselves patrons of the liberal arts and friends to the poets of their own as well as former times": Alexander the Great, Caesar, Augustus, Louis XIV and Queen Anne of England.[77] "Although we are yet in our cradle, as a nation, I think the efforts of the human mind with us are sufficient to refute (by incontestable facts) the doctrines of those who have asserted that everything degenerates in America."[78] "To promote literature in this rising empire, and to encourage the arts, have ever been amongst the warmest wishes of my heart."[79]

Washington's principal contribution to education for virtue was his plan to create a national university. Nor was this a routine proposal mechanically supported by Washington: "My solicitude for the establishment of a national university in this country, has been great, and unceasing."[80] "That a national university in *this* country is a thing to be desired, has always been my decided opinion."[81] Washington's First Annual Address left Congress to choose between aiding established universities or creating a national university. Washington's address introduced the idea of a national university under the heading of the "promotion of science and literature." "Knowledge," said Washington, "is in every country the surest basis of public happiness. In one in which the measures of government receive their impression so immediately from the sense of the community as in ours it is proportionably essential."[82] Knowledge, Washington added, contributes to the security of a free Constitution. It convinces the statesman to seek the enlightened confidence of the people. It teaches the people to know and value their rights, to provide against invasions of their rights, to distinguish between oppression and the exercise of lawful authority and to discriminate the spirit of liberty from licentiousness.

Washington best stated his plan for a national university in his Eighth Annual Address to Congress and his last will and testament. His message to Congress of 1796 recommends both a military academy and a national university. Congress, Washington argued, is aware "how much a flourishing state of the arts and sciences, contributes to national prosperity and reputation."[83] He justified the national university with the argument that "the more homogeneous our citizens can be made" in "principles, opinions... manners... [and] common education," "the greater will be our prospect of a permanent union."[84] "A primary object of such a national institution should be, the education of our youth in the science of *government*. In a republic, what species of knowledge can be equally important? and what duty, more pressing on its Legislature, than to patronize a plan for communicating it to those, who are to be the future guardians of the liberties of the country."[85]

Washington's will donated fifty shares of the Potomac Company for the endowment of a national university "under the auspices of the general government" in the District of Columbia.[86] His will stated that a purpose of the national university was to prevent sending American youth to foreign countries for their education "often before their minds were formed, or they had imbibed any adequate ideas of the happiness of their own; contracting, too frequently, not only habits of dissipation and extravagance, but principles unfriendly to republican government and to the true and genuine liberties of mankind; which, thereafter are rarely overcome."[87] A second purpose of the national university was "to do away [with] local attachments and state prejudices, as far as the nature of things would, or indeed ought to admit, from our national councils" by "a plan devised on a liberal scale which would have a tendency to spread systematic ideas through all parts of this rising empire."[88]

Washington's will called for the establishment of a university in a central part of the United States to which "the youth of fortune and talents from all parts thereof might be sent for the completion of their education in all the branches of polite literature; in arts and sciences, in acquiring knowledge in the principles of politics and good government." A draft of Washington's will more closely described the political education as getting the youth "fixed in the principles of the Constitution, [to] understand the laws, and the true interests and policy of their country, as well as the professions they mean to pursue."[89] Washington's last will concluded with "a matter of infinite importance in my judgment": the national university would enable the youth to acquire friendships and to free themselves from "local prejudices and habitual jealousies" that were "pregnant of mischievous consequences to this country."[90]

In a little noticed letter to Jefferson, Washington revealed that he wished to locate the national university in the District of Columbia "because many advantages, I conceive, would result from the jurisdiction which the general government will have over it, which no other spot would possess."[91] Washington's plan for a national university directly involves the national government in selecting the "ablest professors" and in determining a proper liberal education for forming the character of potential statesmen, the trustees of American liberties. The Constitution as drawn up and ratified mentioned nothing of education. Certainly, Washington's teaching is that the Constitution permits, nay, requires, a broad exercise of national governmental power over the American mind, or else republican government and freedom will ultimately perish in the United States. Washington's understanding of the power of the national government may be deduced from his encouragement of its actively forming the human mind and holding aloft the constitutional standards Americans should revere. If the national government could educate the educable potential statesmen, in Washington's reasoned judgment the national government could certainly do such lesser things as passing the Alien and Sedition Acts.[92] Washington, in sum, was not behind Alexander Hamilton in his understanding of the inherent, just, prudent and necessary power of the "general government" of the United States.

Washington's plan for a national university to foster virtue and extirpate sectional and state prejudice differs in important respects from the thought of Alexander Hamilton and Thomas Jefferson, both of whom enjoy a greater reputation than Washington as insightful commentators on the American regime. Hamilton's principal educational plan was semireligious, "The Christian Constitutional Society," whose purposes were the support of the Christian religion and the Constitution.[93] Hamilton agreed with Washington on the primacy of inegalitarian virtue, but Hamilton stopped short of solving nationally and on the level of principle how to inculcate virtue. Washington distinguished between liberal education for potential statesmen and religious education for the people, whereas Hamilton supported a mixture of religious and constitutional education as an electioneering device for Federalism. In short, Washington thought through far more than Hamilton the problem of providing for virtue. For Washington, providing an education for virtue and meeting the threat to the Union from state particularism were different aspects of the same problem.

In 1813 Thomas Jefferson, anxious to exonerate Washington of the charge of having held Federalist principles, argued that "General Washington did not harbor one principle of federalism . . . He sincerely wished the people to have as much self-government as they were competent to exercise themselves. The only point on which he and I ever differed in opinion, was, that I had more confidence than he had in the *natural* integrity and discretion of the people, and in the safety and extent to which they might trust themselves with a control over their government."[94] This implies that Jefferson differed with Washington over the inherent and spontaneous wisdom and virtue of the people, with Jefferson holding that virtue was somehow instinctive in Americans and Washington holding that virtue, while "according to nature," was far from being instinctive in Americans. The educational work of Washington and Jefferson shows that they agreed on the importance of forming character through liberal education. But the national scope of Washington's university, which was to be created and closely supervised by the national government and aimed by that government against state particularism, and the state's rights cast of Jefferson's University of Virginia, suggest that Washington had a deeper grasp of the whole than Jefferson. Washington was directly concerned with the formation of American *national* character, and Jefferson was not, because for Washington the American regime was greater than the sum of its parts. For Jefferson, as in his state's rights manifesto in the Kentucky Resolutions, the parts of the regime, the states, were greater or more important and authoritative than the whole.[95]

Thus Washington's thought on education was more pregnant with consequences than Hamilton's on the problem of virtue and more comprehensive than Jeffersons' thought on the relationship among liberal education, the molding of potential statesman and the formation of American national character. No student of the American regime would dismiss Hamilton's and Jefferson's ideas, but the attention given to the thought of both statesmen has prevented the just consideration of Washington's political teaching. The examination of his teaching suggests that Washington deserves to rank not only "first in the hearts of his countrymen" but, concerning virtue and education, also ahead of Hamilton and Jefferson in the minds of his countrymen.

Now we should consider certain objections likely to be made to my interpretation of Washington's political thought. The first objection might be that I have discussed Washington's political thought somewhat independently of his policies and programs. This objection implies that a statesman's political thought is necessarily only camouflage for his policy goals. In reply, we should avoid projecting our understanding of and cynicism about recent presidents back to Washington, who was not a strongly programmatic president in the sense that, say, Lyndon Johnson was with his Great Society. Some of Washington's political thought was programmatic; for example, I discussed his doctrine of virtue in the context of his legislative proposal for a national university. But a great part of his political thought was not tied to specific programs. Washington thought politically by in effect asking himself, "What does America stand for?" and he answered this question by saying, "This is what I believe it stands for." In his correspondence and state papers he concentrated above all on the explanation and safeguarding of the new regime under the Constitution, and those tasks were President Washington's most important "program." In other words, Washington devoted himself more to the chief of state role than to other activities in which modern presidents typically engage.

A second objection is that Washington did not engage in political philosophy, and hence his thought lacks scholarly interest. Washington attempted to combine ancient virtue and modern rights. This is not a theoretically satisfactory position: Washington compromised on a lower level elements from Aristotle, the philosoper of virtue or excellence and duties, and Locke, the philosopher of natural rights. "Logic admits of no compromise. The essence of politics is compromise." The original positions of Aristotle and Locke are as far apart as the supremacy of virtue, a moral limit on property, censorship and the closed society, on the one hand, and the supremacy of comfortable self-preservation, the lack of a moral limit on property and "toleration" or the semi-open society, on the other hand. Washington proceeded unphilosophically as if to say: "Virtue is good and rights are good. Therefore we can have both in full measure." He emphasized the "natural and unalienable" rights of men as a distinctive theoretical principle, but at best he only alludes to the teaching of philosophers such as Locke. As an active statesman Washington does not demonstrate the soundness of Locke's teaching of corporeal self-interest, nor should we expect him to do so.

If Washington's attempted synthesis was not theoretically sound, what did he contribute on a lower level to American political thought? Jefferson correctly praised Washington for his "judgment," not genius. For Washington principled judgment rather than genius was exactly what the times demanded at the founding of the American republic. As he said in the Circular Letter to the Governors of June 8, 1783:

The foundation of our empire was not laid in the gloomy age of ignorance and superstition; but at an epocha when the rights of mankind were better understood and more clearly defined, than at any other period. The researches of the human mind after social happiness have been carried to a great extent; the treasures of knowledge acquired by the labors of philosophers, sages, and legislators, through a long succession of years, are laid open for our use, and their collected wisdom may be happily applied in the establishment of our forms of government.

The United States came into existence as a nation at an "auspicious period" when practical judgment rather than soaring contemplation was needed. Washington understood that the United States had to assign to the public sector or government the care of the qualities, such as moral character, that the United States required to work well.[96]

Washington's emphasis on the governmental role in forming character differs sharply from the moral vacuum in which Publius-Madison leaves the American regime in *Federalist* 10 and 51. In *Federalist* 10 Publius identified two methods for curing the mischiefs of faction: to remove its causes or to control its effects. The two methods of removing the causes of faction were by destroying the liberty factions need to exist or "by giving to every citizen the same opinions, the same passions, and the same interests."[97] Publius called the second method "impracticable" without proving that Washington's narrowly focused program for giving homogeneous opinions to potential statesmen was "impracticable." In contradistinction to Washington, Publius observed that moral and religious controls were ineffective: "we well know that neither moral nor religious motives can be relied on as an adequate control."[98] Publius resignedly predicts that "enlightened statesmen will not always be at the helm" without exerting himself to improve this situation.[99] Publius thus opposes classically inspired tools of government while he tacitly follows Locke in liberating property from moral control: "The protection of these faculties ["the diversity in the faculties of men from which the rights of property originate"] is the first object of government."[100] Publius's solution for controlling the effects of faction is not moral and religious education, "enlightened statesmen" or homogenizing the opinions of potential leaders but the extended republic: "In the extent and proper structure of the Union, . . . we behold a republican remedy for the diseases most incident to republican government."[101] In *Federalist* 51 Publius describes "this policy of supplying by opposite and rival interests, the defect of better motives," a policy that practically ensures that better motives will always be lacking. Thus I submit that Washington's teaching on virtue and the national university is a necessary corrective to and an improvement upon the institutionalism and moral skepticism of *Federalist*

10 and 51. If Washington's teaching is understood on the statesman's level, his teaching is a solid criticism of our mainstream republican heritage, and this is no small accomplishment. We who have reaped the results of the *Federalists's* exclusion of government from forming character, especially in our age when almost "everything is permitted," can understand the relevance of Washington's ideas to our contemporary concerns about the perpetuation of the regime. Washington's political thought edifies and, compared to Hamilton's and Jefferson's thought on liberal education, is deeper than it has been acceptable to believe. Washington's teaching advises his countrymen how to perpetuate a complicated invention, particularly on the comparative importance of the Constitution and extra-constitutional influences such as virtue. For the above reasons I deny the objection that Washington's political thought lacks scholarly interest.

It may be objected that I paid too much attention to the criticisms of Washington in the literature, but only by stating the difficulties in the ruling interpretations of Washington's political thought can we approach his thought with sympathetic understanding. A thorough canvass of the Washington literature is part of the price we must pay to free our minds from scorn and bias. A final objection might be that Washington's national university proposal would not have promoted national unity and was intended as "indoctrination."[102] Robert E. Lee and Jefferson Davis, the criticism notes, were educated at West Point, but this did not prevent them from serving Virginia and the South when the chips were down; John C. Calhoun received a New England education, but this did not prevent him from becoming a theorist of nullification against national authority. The weakenss of this objection is that it overlooks the express purpose of Washington's university, to foster unity, moderation and virtue; the critic of Washington's plan thus fails to prove that it would not work by drawing an analogy to different types of institutions. As to the objection of indoctrination, Washington in his modest way would have preferred to speak of molding character; " 'academic freedom' was not even an expression" nor did relativism paralyze native resolution.

The weight of evidence favors the interpretation that Washington engaged in political thought. I conclude that his thought mixes classical and modern republicanism. His thought may be understood as a reply to three points in the classical Aristotelian indictment of democracy, that democracy is unjust, unstable and, above all, the rule of ignorance. The classical element of Washington's republicanism is inegalitarian virtue and the formation of character by the liberal education of potential statesmen; virtue sustains republican government, and liberal education can be a means to virtue. The modern elements of Washington's republicanism include liberty, the equality of men, popular sovereignty and majority rule.

Washington paradoxically relied on a classical solution for the perpetuation of modern republican institutions. To state his point in an oversimplified but not misleading form for the sake of clarity, modern republican institutions such as the constitutional separation of powers and popular suffrage at brief intervals are empty boxes unless statesmen of virtue fill the offices of government. But classical virtue and the formation of character in a national university are hierarchical and cannot be justified or accounted for within the egalitarianism and institutionalism of modern republicanism. Washington's advice on virtue and liberal education attempts to enlarge the supply of "enlightened statesmen" and to correct a shortcoming of modern republicanism.

It is appropriate to close this discussion of Washington's political thought by mentioning his belief that not political historians but the "Bards ... hold the keys of the gate by which patriots, sages and heroes are admitted to immortality."[103] The poet Gertrude Stein appraised Washington in a novel or play that asks the question: "What is an American and what makes him different from a citizen of any other country?"[104] She depicts Washington's thought and action as writing a novel beyond the capacity of Napoleon or Lincoln: "he wrote principally what he had as a future."[105] Stein refers to the sinking of Washington's reputation: "Once when they were all older George Washington was not cared for. He was not anxious about that."[106] She notes as well a decline from Washington to later statesmanship: "If it is possible to know that a monkey came down from a man not a man from a monkey.... this is the background of America from George Washington to Bryan."[107] Finally, Stein reflects the debate over the presence or lack of Washington's thought and intellect. On the one hand, "George Washington thought not."[108] On the other hand, "think how George Washington can link. Link this with that."[109] "What has George Washington thought. George Washington is not the cause of everything nor will they manage it just now. But if he is. But if he is."[110] The reappraisal of Washington's political thought need not necessarily lead to the pious conclusion that it is "the cause of everything" in the American regime. That would be to commit the same error as his detractors but in the opposite direction.

PRESIDENT WASHINGTON'S CONDUCT IN OFFICE

Washington characterized his presidency as "an administration which I do not hesitate to pronounce, the infancy of the government, and all other circumstances considered, that has been as delicate, difficult, and trying as may occur again in any future period of our history."[111] John Quincy Adams concluded that "among the felicities of Washington's life is the unity of the two great objects which he had to pursue: first, the war of independence; and secondly, the establishment of the Constitution of the United States. There is a unity of a Grecian drama in both of them.... The Revolutionary age and the Constituent age were the times for great men; the Administrative age is an age of small men and small things."[112]

Upon accepting the office of president, Washington told Henry Lee: "Though I prize, as I ought, the good opinion of my fellow citizens; yet if I know myself, I would not seek or retain popularity at the expense of social duty or moral virtue."[113] Washington's idea of leadership may be understood in part from his description of the intended audience of his statesmanship: "an enlightened public, and the virtuous, and well disposed part of the community."[114] As Washington put it, "the approbation of good and virtuous men, is the most pleasing reward my mind is susceptible of, for any service it has been in my power to render my country."[115] Conceiving of his task as including working "for the good of mankind in general," Washington included in the extended audience of his statesmanship "many of the moderate and virtuous of other countries."[116]

"Washington never formulated a systematic statement of the functions and appropriate qualities of a chief executive," according to Leonard White.[117] "With me," Washington wrote, "it has always been a maxim, rather to let my designs appear from my works than by my expressions."[118] But Washington's letters and state papers are filled with reflections, maxims and decisions that should enable us to understand his main ideas on presidential conduct. Washington was keenly aware of the importance of doing a good job as president. In 1790 he wrote to Jefferson: "I consider the successful administration of the general government as an object of almost infinite consequence to the present and future happiness of the citizens of the United States."[119] Washington was also acutely aware of the importance of setting precedents. "Many things," he wrote, "which appear of little importance in themselves and at the beginning, may have great and durable consequences from their having been established at the commencement of a new general government. It will be much easier to commence the administration, upon a well adjusted system, built on tenable grounds, than to correct errors or alter inconveniences after they shall have been confirmed by habit."[120]

A part of Washington's "well adjusted" system was his prayer in his message establishing Thanksgiving as the first national holiday: "to render our national government a blessing to all the people, by constantly being a government of wise, just and constitutional laws, discreetly and faithfully executed and obeyed."[121] Washington's aims included the establishment of the Constitution as a "confederated government, where due energy will not be incompatible with the unalienable rights of freemen."[122] Washington, in short, sought to establish "enlightened liberty."[123] Another aim of Washington's declared that the "aggregate happiness of the society, which is best promoted by the practice of a virtuous policy, is, or ought to be, the end of all government."[124] President Washington understood his task as including the duty to administer the government of the United States.[125] Finally, his aims included establishing a just medium for the presidency, the "respect which is due to the chair of government" without an excess of pomp or familiarity.[126]

President Washington sought to realize his aims through governmental administration and an ethical and investigative approach to the presidency. His other means included Congress, the people and appointments. Political parties were an undesirable means and obstacle. The nucleus of Washington's administrative theory appears in his letter to the secretary of war: "Before I conclude, let me, in a friendly way, impress the following maxims upon the Executive officers. In all important matters, to deliberate maturely, but to execute promptly and vigorously.... Without an adherence to these rules, business will never be *well* done, or done in an easy manner; but will always in in arrear, with one thing treading upon the heels of another."[127] These rules were supplemented by another rule, made necessary because of the popular character of the regime: "In a government which depends so much in its first stages on public opinion, much circumspection is still necessary for those who are engaged in its administration."[128] Washington disliked being away from the presidential mansion where the streams of information poured in and where he could compare the opinions of his advisers before making a decision. Henry Lee caught the essence of Washington's relations to his advisers when he wrote of Washington "drawing information from all, acting from himself."[129]

Washington's approach to the presidency was intensely ethical and investigative. As he remarked during the crisis over Jay's Treaty: "there is but one straight course, and that is to seek truth and pursue it steadily."[130] Referring to the presidency, he said that "I have found no better guide hitherto than upright intentions, and close investigation, I shall adhere to these maxims while I keep the watch."[131] President Washington described his tenets in politics: "in politics, as in religion my tenets are few and simple: the leading one of which, and indeed that which embraces most others, is to be honest and just ourselves, and to exact it from others; meddling as little as possible in their affairs where our own are not involved."[132]

President Washington was sensitive to the criticisms of his conduct by Jefferson and Madison and argued that contrary to their suspicions, "I could have *no* view in extending the powers of the Executive beyond the limits prescribed by the Constitution."[133] How did Washington understand the constitutional limits upon presidential power in an emergency? He allows us a glimpse of his possible answer in the context of commenting upon events in France. "If there were good grounds to suspect

that the proscribed and banished characters were engaged in a conspiracy against the Constitution of the people's choice, to seize them even
in an irregular manner, might be justified upon the ground of expe-
diency, or self preservation."[134] But, Washington, added, the condemnation of those seized "without a *hearing*" and the assignment of a
punishment more rigorous perhaps than death "is the summit of despotism."[135] Washington's argument is based on the inherent power of a
popular government to preserve itself and is the closest Washington
comes to a parallel with the situation confronting Lincoln during the
Civil War. The limitations of this argument are that Washington is discussing a conspiracy against a *foreign* government and constitution, not
an actual conspiracy against the government and Constitution of the
United States. The precedential value of Washington's argument is,
therefore, small.

James Flexner deduces Washington's understanding of presidential–
congressional relations from a seventy-three-page document, which he
says "was never delivered" and was "discarded," intended as Washington's First Inaugural Address.[136] Flexner reasons somewhat curiously
that "the discarded inaugural is an extremely important document."[137]
If it is "extremely important," why was it "discarded" and never delivered? Flexner says that Washington's letters and the "discarded" document give "a good idea...of the ideas he carried with him to the
Presidency." The discarding of the document, however, is not a proof
that Washington advocated its ideas on all subjects. In this discarded
and unofficial address Washington called Congress "the first wheel of
the government, a wheel which communicates motion to all the rest."[138]
Flexner infers that this statement expresses Washington's understanding
of government as congressionally centered, one in which the president
would "not" be "a prime mover" or an "initiator of policy."[139]

In fact, sometimes Washington routinely submitted measures to Congress and accepted the result or lack of result.[140] On important matters,
such as his proposal for a national university, President Washington was
prepared to go over the head of Congress to the people. Speaking of
his wish to mention the national university measure in his Farewell Address, Washington told Hamilton:

But to be candid, I much question whether a recommendation of this measure
to the Legislature will have a better effect *now* than *formerly*. It may show indeed
my sense of its importance, and that is a sufficient inducement with *me* to bring
the matter before the public in some shape or other, at the closing scenes of my
political exit. My object for preparing to insert it where I did...was to set the
people to ruminating on the importance of the measure, [and the] most likely
means of bringing it to pass.[141]

For President Washington the people were the ultimate tribunal when
Congress stalled a measure of importance for the common good. Con-

trary to Flexner's interpretation, Washington attempted to be both a "prime mover" and an "initiator of policy" concerning the national university.[142]

Moreover, Congress itself gave power and discretion to President Washington and his advisers by passing laws in broad terms and generally staying out of administration.[143] Clearly, Washington's designations of the presidency offer indirect evidence of the importance of the office. Rarely does he use the term *presidency*. Instead he often designates the office as the "chair of state," the "chair of government," the "executive trust" and last, but not least, "the helm of government."[144]

Washington's criteria for appointing to the "great offices" of the government combined geographical situations "sometimes with other considerations," such as "abilities" and the "fitness of *known* characters."[145] Shortly after his Inauguration he wrote that "I anticipate that one of the most difficult and delicate parts of the duty of my office will be that which relates to nominations for appointments."[146] An example of Washington's meticulousness in appointments was his statement of the qualifications of the attorney general. "The office of Attorney General of the United States does not require constant labor, or attention. At times, both must be close and deep."[147] The attorney general was understood as a legal adviser rather than an administrator and was allowed to earn private fees.[148] Washington's qualifications for the attorney general were: "natural endowments," a "friend to the general government," "acquired knowledge" of law, particularly the law of nations, and "depth in the science of politics, or ... acquaintance with history and ... general knowledge."[149] After Randolph's resignation as secretary of state, President Washington lamented to Hamilton: "What am I to do for a Secretary of State?"[150] Washington found "the selection of proper characters an arduous duty."[151] Washington's standards for appointment, wrote Leonard White, "were extraordinarily high, far above the levels which had been developed in Great Britain or France, and far above what his contemporaries and successors were able to maintain in the United States."[152]

Washington's policy on faction and political parties derived from the importance he attached to the rational consent of the governed. His Sixth Annual Address to Congress concluded that "our prosperity rests on solid foundations: ... my fellow citizens understand the true principles of government and liberty."[153] "The *mass* of our citizens require no more than to understand a question to decide it properly," he told John Marshall.[154] Reflecting on the conditions for the rational consent of the governed, Washington remarked: "I am *sure* the mass of our citizens in these United States *mean well*, and I firmly believe they will always *act well*, whenever they can obtain a right understanding of matters; but in some parts of the Union ... it is not easy to accomplish this" because misrepresentation frequently spreads faster than the truth. "To this source *all* our discontents may be traced and from it our embarrassments proceed."[155] Washington mentions the "unhappy differences among ourselves" and his lack of discretion in foreign policy.[156]

In a remarkable letter to Jefferson, leader of the Republican opposition, Washington informs Jefferson that he has learned of Jefferson's description of him as being "under a dangerous influence," namely, Alexander Hamilton. Washington denied the charge. His letter to Jefferson continued that "until within the last year or two ago, I had no conception that parties would, or even could go, the length I have been witness to . . . while I was using my utmost exertions to establish a national character of our own, independent, as far as our obligations, and justice would permit, of every nation of the earth." Washington complained to Jefferson of "most insidious misrepresentations" of his actions in "such exaggerated and indecent terms as could scarcely be applied to a Nero; a notorious defaulter; or even to a common pick-pocket." The purpose of these misrepresentations, which the president laid at Jefferson's door, was to "weaken the confidence of the people." Finally, Washington lectured Jefferson: "I was no party man myself, and the first wish of my heart was, if parties did exist, to reconcile them."[157]

President Washington prescribed two remedies for the spirit of faction or party. The first was the dissemination of the truth, as in Hamilton's Camillus Letters on Jay's Treaty, against the "poison" of the Republicans.[158] The Farewell Address states the second remedy, which was to mitigate and assuage the spirit of party by superior virtue: "of all dispositions and habits which lead to political prosperity, religion and morality are indispensable supports."[159] The remaining steps in the argument of the Farewell Address, as we learned in investigating Washington's political thought, are that "virtue or morality is a necessary spring of popular government" and "institutions for the general diffusion of knowledge" can be a means to virtue. Thus contrary to the *Federalists*'s recipe of the extended republic as the remedy for faction, Washington's deepest response to faction and party spirit is liberal education of the proper kind. This remedy rests on the premise that liberally educated men would be in the main politically moderate men.

Washington's deliberations and crises afford additional insights into his conduct of the presidency. When President Washington contemplated retirement at the end of his first term, he gave Madison as two of his reasons "his unfitness to judge of legal questions, and questions arising out of the Constitution."[160] Washington listed fitness to judge constitutional and legal questions among the "essential qualifications" for being president, and there is no doubt that he gave constitutional interpretation a high place among his duties. His Eighth Annual Address to Congress described the Constitution as an "experiment."[161] One of

Washington's tasks was to judge of Jefferson's complaints that the Constitution was being violated with the "ultimate object" of preparing the way for a change "from the present republican form of government, to that of a monarchy, of which the English constitution is to be the model."[162]

Washington copied Jefferson's charges and sent them to Hamilton for *"explanations."*[163] Hamilton replied to the president with a long document entitled "Objections and Answers Respecting the Administration of the Government."[164] Hamilton denied that violations of the Constitution had occurred and argued that the constitutionality of controversial measures, such as the Bank, had been proved.[165] Hamilton answered Jefferson's "ultimate" objection about a conspiracy to convert the republic into a monarchy. "The project from its absurdity refutes itself.... If it could be done at all, which is utterly incredible, it would require a long series of time, certainly beyond the life of any individual to effect it. Who then would enter into such a plot? For what purpose of interest or ambition?"[166] He continued that "those ... who resist a confirmation of public order, are the true artificers of monarchy.... No popular government," said Hamiliton, "was ever without its Catalines and Caesars. These are its true enemies."[167]

Transcending party, Hamilton held that "both" the Federalists and Republicans "may be equally wrong and their mutual jealousies may be materially causes of the appearances which mutually disturb them, and sharpen them against each other."[168] Recalling his speech in the Constitutional Convention, Hamilton described his argument there: "that the republican theory ought to be adhered to in this country as long as there was any chance of its success ... that hitherto from an incompetent structure of government it had not a fair trial, and that the endeavor ought then to be to secure it a better chance of success by a government more capable of energy and order." Hamilton continued with a predictive observation on the Union: "It is certainly much to be regretted that ... ideas of a severance of the Union are creeping in both North and South."[169] He hoped that "the efforts of wise men will be able to prevent a schism." Finally, Hamilton argued that Southern contributions to the relief of the national debt squared with "all the ancient notions of justice and morality."[170] In sum: on the specific charge of a conspiracy to convert the American republic into a monarchy, Hamilton exposed Jefferson's complaint as assertion without evidence.

President Washington replied to Hamilton's answers: "I persuade myself, from the full manner in which you appear to have taken the matter up, that I shall receive both satisfaction and profit from the perusal."[171] Washington advised Hamilton to follow a "middle course" and hoped that "liberal allowances will be made for the political opinions of one another." Washington ended by saying that he had spoken "in the same *general* terms to other officers of the government."[172] Hamilton's reply maintained that he was the "deeply injured party" by the "uniform opposition from Mr. Jefferson" and that Hamilton had only recently resolved to "draw aside the veil from the principal actors" and resist Jefferson's subversion of his measures. Hamilton frankly admitted that the "continuance of a division . . . must destroy the energy of government, which will be little enough with the strictest union."[173]

President Washington also examined the constitutional requirements of the congressional war power. Referring to a possible "offensive expedition against the refractory part of the Creek nation," Washington wrote: "The Constitution vests the power of declaring war with Congress; therefore no offensive expedition *of importance* can be undertaken until after they shall have deliberated upon the subject, and authorized such a measure."[174] Although Washington deferred to Congress's power to declare war, he implied that offensive expeditions that were not of "importance" could be undertaken without a congressional declaration of war and that the executive would judge the meaning of "importance." In 1796 President Washington refused to give the House of Representatives papers relating to Jay's Treaty. Washington's argument relied on his obligation to "preserve, protect and defend the Constitution."[175] The Constitution, he added, assigns the treaty power to the president and Senate; previous Houses of Representatives had accepted this interpretation. Finally, Washington appealed to the opinion of the state ratifying conventions.[176]

Referring to the United States' prohibition of the sale of prizes brought by armed French vessels into American ports, Washington wrote that "in this case, as in all others, the Executive must be governed by the Constitution and laws."[177] Ever the guardian of the Constitution, Hamilton advised President Washington that it was "necessary to submit the *new* article [of Jay's Treaty] to the Senate." Washington replied that Hamilton's opinion was opposed to the attorney general's and occasioned "some embarrassment with me."[178] In sum, Washington was deeply involved in constitutional interpretation, and he performed quite competently despite his modest confession of unfitness to James Madison. Forrest McDonald criticizes Washington for understanding the Constitution "almost as if it were a manual of instructions."[179] Given the opposite possibility, to ignore the instructions of the Constitution, Washington's fault, if it was one, is certainly defensible. Washington may justly be called the most Constitution respecting of our presidents.

President Washington understood one point about the Constitution that has escaped many of his successors. In a letter to Lafayette he wrote: "when the seeds of happiness which are sown here shall begin to expand themselves, and when every one (under his own vine and fig tree) shall begin to taste the fruits of freedom, then all these blessings (for all these blessings will come) will be referred to the fostering influence of the new government. *Whereas many causes will have conspired to produce them.*"[180] Washington understood that the "seeds of happiness [and the] fruits of freedom" would be mistakenly attributed by the people to the "fostering influence" of the new government and, even more, to the new Constitution. This mistake was the basis of the worship of the Constitution that continued for generations. The popular worship of the Constitution was thus understood by our first president as a salutary myth and source of American unity, sacrifice and patriotism.[181] President Washington's example teaches that understanding the Constitution and defending it vigilantly is much too important for the president to delegate to an attorney general or judges. It is instructive that the president who took the Constitution with a sacred seriousness governed before judicial review had spread its wings under Chief Justice John Marshall. President Washington upheld the Constitution most satisfactorily as a non-lawyer before the Constitution became a "craft mystery" of the legal profession and judiciary.

I shall briefly illustrate Washington's deliberation in foreign policy with the Impartiality Proclamation of 1793, Jay's Treaty and the French Revolution. His rule for action toward foreign countries was to "do justice to all, and never forget that we are Americans; the remembrance of which will convince us, that we ought not to be French or English."[182] The Farewell Address stated this point with greater elevation: "The nation, which indulges towards another an habitual hatred, or an habitual fondness, is in some degree a slave."[183]

Concerning the war between France and Britain, Washington's Farewell Address states that "my [Impartiality] Proclamation of the 22nd of April 1793 is the index of my plan....the spirit of that measure has continually governed me."[184] Washington wrote of the crisis over the ratification of Jay's Treaty that he had "never" in the administration of government seen a crisis that "has been so pregnant of interesting events; nor one from which more is to be apprehended."[185] After he sent the treaty to the Senate, the Senate gave the two-thirds vote for ratification without a vote to spare.[186] Washington pronounced the American Revolution "distinguished for moderation, virtue and humanity."[187] He informed Hamilton that the conduct of the directors of the French Revolution toward the United States "is, according to my ideas of it, outrageous beyond conception."[188] Finally, after leaving office Washington told Lafayette that "it is not to be inferred...that they [Americans] will suffer any nation under the sun (while they retain a proper sense of virtue and independence) to trample upon their rights with impunity, or to direct, or influence the internal concerns of their country."[189]

Certain objections might be made to my discussion of Washington's presidency. One objection concerns the suitability of Washington's teaching and example for today's president. In reply, Washington's care for virtue, the Constitution, moderation and reason is or should be the touchstone for the contemporary presidency and opinion. Some of Washington's techniques of governing, for example his stress on good appointments, could be imitated by today's president. A contemporary president may find it prudent to be more of a molder of legislation than Washington was for routine proposals, but Washington's activity on important measures sets an example for today's president. Another objection is that alliance diplomacy has sounded the death knell for Washington's warning against foreign entanglements. However, Washington's warning in the Farewell Address against foreign entanglements applied "largely" to foreign interference in our domestic affairs, not to cooperation with other nations.[190] Moreover, the Farewell Address left foreign policy somewhat open to prudence. Firm alliances would be unnecessary as long as American strength and temporary alliances could preserve our independence and freedoms. Where that condition is lacking, the attractiveness of a firm alliance increases even though a risk is attached. The prudent adaptations of Washington's idea of executive–legislative relations and of his foreign policy credo do not require a break with his most fundamental teachings.

In conclusion, the scholarship on President Washington contends either that he did not engage in political thought, that he taught entirely modern republicanism or that he taught entirely ancient republicanism. My thesis is that Washington's political thought mixes classical and modern republicanism. The classical element is inegalitarian virtue and the molding of potential statesmen by liberal education. The modern elements of Washington's republicanism include liberty, equality, popular sovereignty and majority rule. I further contend that Washington's political thought, though unsatisfactory as political philosophy, is still worthy of attention. Washington distinctly blended elements of classical and modern republicanism around the idea of a national university, and this constitutes on the statesman's level a plausible criticism of the mainstream solution of the political problem in the *Federalist*. Washington's thought on political education is better conceived than the educational thought of his more respected contemporaries, Hamilton and Jefferson.

One of the distinctions between President Washington and the political animals, such as Lyndon Johnson, among recent presidents is the strong ethical orientation of Washington's understanding of his audience, goals and means. He intended his statesmanship to appeal to good men of virtue here and abroad. His goals included setting a positive precedent, rendering the government a blessing to the people, establishing the Constitution as a confederated government that reconciled due energy with the rights of free men, promoting "the end of all government," the aggregate happiness of society, administering the government and establishing a just medium for the presidency. Washington's means included an administrative theory that combined mature deliberation with prompt and vigorous execution, an ethical and investigative approach to the presidency, special attention in executive–legislative relations for important measures, an appeal to the people when Congress sidetracked an important measure, proper attention to appointments and the dissemination of truth and the mitigation of party spirit by superior virtue. Washington opposed faction and political parties because their misrepresentation undermined the rational consent of the governed. Washington's remedy for faction and partisanship was not the *Federalist's* extended republic, in which he seems to have placed little confidence, but a spirit of moderation instilled by liberal education in a national university. His deliberations and crises reveal that he was both active and skillful in constitutional interpretation. Washington's conduct as president shows that he served as a trans-partisan chief executive, guiding the United States to neutrality in European wars and urging Americans to morality.

What is Washington's legacy? If, as Henry Lee said, Washington is "first in war, first in peace, first in the hearts of his countrymen," he is second to none in his concern for the formation of national character, liberal education and virtue: "virtue always felt his fostering hand."[191] In both political thought and action, said Fisher Ames, "Washington's example is the happiest to show what virtue is."[192] Ames said that a eulogy of Washington "must be addressed to the understanding and . . . would seem to be rather an analysis of moral principles than a recital of a hero's exploits."[193] According to Henry Lee, Washington "laid the foundations of our national policy in the unerring, immutable principles of morality, based on religion."[194]

A further glimpse of Washington's legacy emerges from his attachment to the Roman patriot, Cato the Younger, "Washington's favorite character in history," and Washington's fondness for Joseph Addison's *Cato*, Washington's "favorite play."[195] At Valley Forge "when the morale of the army needed a stimulus, Washington caused *Cato* to be performed and attended the performance." Pope's Prologue to Addison's *Cato* reported that "virtue confessed in human shape he draws, what Plato thought, and godlike Cato was."[196] Addison described the play as a "medley of philosophy and war."[197] Addison held that Cato "fights the cause of honor, virtue, liberty" and country.[198] Plutarch praised Cato as "the only free and only undefeated man" because Cato committed suicide rather than let Caesar completely triumph.[199] Washington's legacy was to follow the "high example of antique virtue."[200] But Washington improved upon Cato by showing that honor, virtue, liberty and patriotism are more likely to be perpetuated by the readiness and capacity to wage war successfully than by Cato's example of impotent suicide. Washington's thought and action corrected Addison's teaching in *Cato* about moral philosophy and war.

NOTES

1. François Guizot, "The Life of Washington," in *Monk and Washington: Historical Studies* (London: Routledge, 1851), p. 145.

2. François Guizot, *Essay on the Character and Influence of Washington* (Boston: J. Monroe, 1840), in Morton Borden, ed., *George Washington* (Englewood Cliffs, N.J.: Prentice-Hall, 1969), p. 119.

3. W. E. Woodward, *George Washington: The Image and the Man* (New York: Boni and Liveright, 1926), p. 428.

4. Ibid., p. 429.

5. Bernard Faÿ, *George Washington: Republican Aristocrat* (Boston: Houghton Mifflin, 1931), p. 273.

6. J. A. Carroll, "George Washington," in Morton Borden, ed., *America's Ten Greatest Presidents* (Chicago: Rand McNally, 1961), p. 8.

7. Morton Borden, "Introduction," in Borden, *George Washington*, p. 1.

8. Forrest McDonald, *The Presidency of George Washington* (Lawrence: University Press of Kansas, 1974), p. 96.

9. Paine to James Monroe, Oct. 20, 1794, Paine to Washington, May 1, 1790, in Thomas Paine 2 *The Complete Writings of Thomas Paine* 1371, 1303, Phillip Foner, ed. (New York: Citadel Press, 1945).

10. Tom Paine, "An Eulogy on the Life of General George Washington," in *Eulogies and Orations on the Life and Death of General George Washington* (Boston: W. P. & L. Blake, 1800), pp. 56, 58, 64–65.

11. Fisher Ames, "Eulogy on Washington," 2 *Works of Fisher Ames* 72–73, 88 (Boston: Little, Brown, 1854; New York: Da Capo, 1969).

12. John Marshall, 5 *The Life of George Washington* 777 (Philadelphia: C. P. Wayne, 1807); cf. David Ramsay, *The Life of George Washington* (2nd ed.; Boston: D. Mallory, 1811), p. 333.

13. Quoted in Faÿ, *George Washington* pp. xii–xiii.

14. Daniel Webster, "The Character of Washington," *The Great Speeches and Orations of Daniel Webster* (Boston: Little, Brown, 1879), p. 342.

15. Henry Cabot Lodge, 2 *George Washington* 326–327 (Boston: Houghton Mifflin, 1889).

16. Harold Bradley, "The Political Thinking of George Washington," 11 *Journal of Southern History* 471 (Nov., 1945).

17. Ibid., pp. 470, 485.

18. Ibid., p. 485.

19. Ibid., pp. 470, 472, 485.

20. Leo Strauss, *What Is Political Philosophy?* (New York: Free Press, 1959), p. 12.

21. Ibid., pp. 12–13.

22. Bradley, 11 *Journal of Southern History* 469.

23. Ibid.

24. Saul Padover, "George Washington—Portrait of a True Conservative," 22 *Social Research* 203 (Summer, 1955).

25. Ibid., pp. 209–10.

26. Henry T. Tuckerman, "The Patriot, George Washington," *Essays, Biographical and Critical* (Boston: Phillips, Sampson, 1857), p. 22.

27. Marcus Cunliffe, *George Washington: Man and Monument* (Boston: Little, Brown, 1958), p. 194.

28. Nathaniel Stephenson and Waldo Dunn, 2 *George Washington* 494 (New York: Oxford University Press, 1940).

29. Cunliffe, *George Washington*, pp. 16–17.

30. Ibid., p. 195.

31. James Morton Smith, "Introduction," in Smith, ed., *George Washington: A Profile* (New York: Hill and Wang, 1969), p. xvi.

32. Ibid., p. xv.

33. Ibid., pp. xv–xvi.

34. James Flexner, *George Washington Anguish and Farewell, 1793–1799* (Boston: Little, Brown, 1972), p. 499. In *Washington and the New Nation, 1783–1793* (Boston: Little, Brown, 1970), p. 412, Flexner held that Washington's "own mind was unconcerned with theoretical speculation."

35. To Governor Jonathan Trumbull, Aug. 30, 1799, 37 *The Writings of George Washington* 349, J. Fitzpatrick, ed. (Washington, D.C.: Government Printing Office, 1940), italics in the original; hereafter cited as *Writings* preceded by the volume number and followed by the page number.

36. To Alexander Hamilton, July 29, 1795, 34 *Writings* 264.

37. Alexander Hamilton to James A. Bayard, Jan. 16, 1801, 25 *The Papers of Alexander Hamilton* 321, H. Syrett, ed. (New York: Columbia University Press, 1977), italics in the original; hereafter cited as *Papers* preceded by the volume number and followed by the page number.

38. Jan. 10, 1788, 29 *Writings*, 375.

39. To Bushrod Washington, Nov. 10, 1787, 29 *Writings* 311.

40. Seventh Annual Address to Congress, Dec. 8, 1795, 34 *Writings* 389.

41. To Comte De Rochambeau, Jan. 29, 1789, 30 *Writings* 189.

42. To Dr. James Anderson, Dec. 24, 1795, 34 *Writings* 407.

43. To Rev. Mason Locke Weems, Aug. 29, 1799, 37 *Writings* 347, italics added.

44. To Benjamin Lincoln, June 29, 1788, 30 *Writings* 11; see also the reference to the "finger of Providence," 29 *Writings* 508.

45. To David Stuart, July 1, 1787, 29 *Writings* 238.

46. To James Madison, March 31, 1787, 29 *Writings* 190–191.

47. To Henry Knox, March 3, 1788, 29 *Writings* 435; to Lafayette, June 6, 1788, 29 *Writings* 229.

48. To the Inhabitants of Alexandria, July 4, 1793, 33 *Writings* 3.

49. To Edmund Pendleton, Jan. 22, 1795, 34 *Writings* 98–99.

50. Aristotle, *Politics*, Ernest Barker, trans. (Oxford: Clarendon Press, 1948), p. 122.

51. To David Humphreys, July 20, 1791, 31 *Writings* 318; to Humphreys, March 23, 1793, 32 *Writings* 399; to Lafayette, July 28, 1791, 31 *Writings* 326.

52. To Sir Edward Newenham, Sept. 5, 1791, 31 *Writings* 357.

53. To Bushrod Washington, Nov. 10, 1787, 29 *Writings* 311.

54. 35 *Writings* 224.

55. 34 *Writings* 30.

56. To Charles Mynn Thruston, Aug. 10, 1794, 33 *Writings* 465.

57. July 28, 1795, 34 *Writings* 253.

58. To the Attorney General, Feb. 11, 1790, 31 *Writings* 9.

59. Kant, *Perpetual Peace*, Lewis White Beck, ed. (Indianapolis: Liberal Arts Press, 1957), p. 30, italics added.

60. Ibid., pp. 30–31.

61. Feb. 7, 1788, 29 *Writings* 410.

62. Adams to Jefferson, Dec. 21, 1819, 2 *The Adams-Jefferson Letters* 550–551, Lester J. Cappon, ed. (Chapel Hill: University of North Carolina Press, 1959), italics added.

63. Jefferson, *The Portable Thomas Jefferson*, Merrill Peterson, ed. (New York: Viking Press, 1975), p. 213, italics added.

64. Paine to James Monroe, Sept. 10, 1794, 2 *The Complete Writings of Thomas Paine* 1348–1349 n.244.

65. To Annis Stockton, Aug. 31, 1788, 30 *Writings* 76.

66. To Catherine Macaulay Graham, Jan. 9, 1790, 30 *Writings* 496, italics in the original.

67. 30 *Writings* 294.

68. 30 *Writings* 294–295, italics in the original.

69. Sept. 19, 1796, 35 *Writings* 229.

70. Ibid., pp. 229–230.

71. Ibid., p. 231.

72. Lafayette to Washington, Aug. 20, 1798, in Louis Gottschalk and Shirley A. Bill, eds., *The Letters of Lafayette to Washington, 1777–1799* (rev. ed.; Philadelphia: The American Philosophical Society, 1976), p. 374, italics added.

73. After praising Pascal's success in rallying "all the powers of his mind to discover the most hidden secrets of the Creator," Tocqueville concludes that "the future will show whether such rare, creative passions come to birth and grow as easily in democracies as in aristocratic communities. For myself, I confess that I can hardly believe it." *Democracy in America*, Vol. II, chap. 10, J. P. Mayer and Max Lerner, eds.; George Lawrence, trans. (New York: Harper and Row, 1966), p. 428; on American poetry, see ibid., Vol. II, chap. 17, pp. 451–455: "I gladly agree that there are no American poets." Ibid., p. 453.

74. Washington rarely refers to the American regime as a democracy, but he does so refer to it. To Henry Knox, March 8, 1787, 29 *Writings* 171.

75. Aristotle, *Politics*, pp. 114–115, 268 (Barker trans.).

76. On the importance of property and leisure for goodness, see ibid., pp. 301–302.

77. To Lafayette, May 28, 1788, 29 *Writings* 506–507.

78. Ibid., p. 507.

79. To the Trustees of Washington Academy, June 17, 1798, 36 *Writings* 293.

80. To St. George Tucker, May 30, 1797, 35 *Writings* 458.

81. To the Vice-President, Nov. 15, 1794, 34 *Writings* 23, italics in the original.

82. First Annual Address to Congress, 30 *Writings* 493.

83. 35 *Writings* 316.

84. Ibid., pp. 316–317.

85. Ibid., p. 317, italics in the original.

86. 37 *Writings* 280.

87. Ibid., pp. 279–280.

88. Ibid., p. 280.

89. 34 *Writings* 60 n.50. The probable spirit of the national university may be deduced from certain of Washington's educational recommendations and insights. He thought that learning Greek was "no bad acquisition . . . Philosophy, moral, natural, etc. I should think a very desirable knowledge for a gentleman." To the Rev. Jonathan Boucher, Jan. 2, 1771, 3 *Writings* 36–37. Washington's catalogue of books for a young charge prescribed an edition of "all Cicero's Works." 2 *Writings* 515. He advised a young charge that "a good moral character is the first essential in a man. . . . It is therefore highly important that you should endeavor not only to be learned but virtuous." To George Steptoe Washington, Dec. 5, 1790, 31 *Writings* 163. He informed another young charge of "the advantages of a finished education, a highly cultivated mind, and a proper sense of your duties to God and man." To George Washington Parke Custis, Dec. 19, 1796, 35 *Writings* 341. Washington distinguished among universities using the criterion of the morals of the student body. To David Stuart, Jan. 22, 1798, 36 *Writings* 136; see also ibid., pp. 169–170, 172. "No college has turned out better scholars, or more estimable characters, than Nassau," later Princeton University. Princeton's president from 1768 to 1794 was John Witherspoon. "More than any other American educator, he made Greek and Latin a functional part of the nation's literary style, as well as a vital element of training for both pulpit and public service." Richard M. Gummere, *The American Colonial Mind and the Classical Tradition* (Cambridge: Harvard University Press, 1963), pp. 71–72. One difference between established universities and Washington's national university would be funding: "our country, much to its honor, contains many seminaries of learning highly respectable and useful; but the funds upon which they rest, are too narrow, to command the ablest professors, in the different departments of liberal knowledge. For the institution contemplated, though, they would be excellent auxiliaries." Eighth Annual Address to Congress, Dec. 7, 1796, 35 *Writings* 316. Washington's proposal would fundamentally shift the center of liberal education in the United States by making all established universities "auxiliaries" of the national university.

90. 37 *Writings* 280.

91. March 15, 1795, 34 *Writings* 147.

92. To Bushrod Washington, Dec. 31, 1798, 37 *Writings* 81; to Judge Alexander Addison, March 4, 1799, 37 *Writings* 145.

93. Alexander Hamilton to James A. Bayard, 1802, 25 *The Papers of Alexander Hamilton* 606.

94. Jefferson to John Melish, Jan. 13, 1813, in 13 *The Writings of Thomas Jefferson* 212, Andrew Lipscomb, ed. (Washington, D.C.: Thomas Jefferson Memorial Association, 1905), italics added. Jefferson considered it "lost time" to attend lectures on moral philosophy because "the moral sense, or conscience, is as much a part of a man as his leg or arm" and "is the true foundation of

morality." To Peter Carr, Aug. 10, 1787, 6 *The Writings of Thomas Jefferson* 257.
Jefferson's understanding of "the moral sense, or conscience" further suggests
that for him virtue was instinctive or innate.

95. Jefferson drafted the Kentucky Resolutions of 1798, which declared that
the Constitution was a compact and that "each party has an equal right to judge
for itself, as well of infractions as of the mode and measure of redress." This
resolution nullified the Alien and Sedition Acts of 1798 in the sense of declaring
them "altogether void and of no force." On March 4, 1825, with Jefferson as
rector, the Board of Visitors of his University of Virginia "resolved, that it is the
opinion of this Board that . . . on the distinctive principles of the government of
our State, and of that of the United States, the best guides are to be found in
. . . The Resolutions of the General Assembly of Virginia in 1799 on the subject
of the alien and sedition laws, which appeared to accord with the predominant
sense of the people of the United States." The Board required the Resolutions
as the "text and documents" of the Law School course on "civil polity." 19 *The
Writings of Thomas Jefferson* 460–461. Although Jefferson also required as texts
and documents the Declaration of Independence, the *Federalist* and Washington's
Farewell Address, his emphasis may have been on the Virginia Resolutions of
1799. By a "previous prescription of the texts to be followed in their discourses"
"of government," Jefferson aimed to "guard against . . . the diffusion of that
poison" of "quondam federalism, now consolidation." 16 *The Writings of Thomas
Jefferson* 104.

Jefferson, in referring to the Virginia Resolutions of 1799, may have intended
Madison's Report on the Virginia Resolutions for the 1799–1800 session of the
legislature. This report upholds the compact theory of the Constitution and
defends the argument of the Virginia Resolutions of 1798 that the states "have
the right, and are in duty bound, to interpose for arresting the progress of the
evil."

Jefferson also drafted the Kentucky Resolutions of 1799. The Kentucky Resolutions of 1799 held that "the several states who formed that instrument being
sovereign and independent, have the unquestionable right to judge of the in-
fraction; and, that a nullification of those sovereignties, of all unauthorized acts
done under color of that instrument is the rightful remedy." In 1832 John C.
Calhoun appealed to the Virginia and Kentucky Resolutions in urging nullification. "We are certainly more united against the Tariff, than we have ever been;
and, I think, better disposed to enhance the old Republican doctrines of [17]98
which ["alone" *canceled* and "only" interlined] can save the Constitution." Calhoun to B. Hall, Feb. 13, 1832, 11 *The Papers of John C. Calhoun* 553 (Columbia:
University of South Carolina Press, 1978); see also Calhoun to James Hamilton,
Jr., Aug. 28, 1832, in ibid., p. 625.

Jefferson's letter of Sept. 5, 1799 contemplates secession as a remedy to be
applied by a state in certain cases:" . . . we should never think of separation *but*
for repeated and enormous violations, so these, when they occur, will be cause
enough of themselves." 7 *The Writings of Thomas Jefferson* 391, Paul L. Ford, ed.
(New York: G. P. Putnam's, 1896), italics added. Jefferson reserves the choice
for the states "rightfully" to separate from the Union "in the future." Ibid.,
p. 390. In 1832 Calhoun wrote that "most fortunately, at this critical moment,
the recorded opinions of Mr. Jefferson, the Republican Patriarch, have come to

light on the all important question of the relation between the States and the general government. There can now be no longer a shadow of doubt, that what is called the Carolina doctrines are [*sic*] also the Jeffersonian... In comparing Mr. Jefferson's views with my own, I feel that such is there [*sic*; "striking" *interlined*] coincidence that, I should have been exposed to the charge of plagiarism, were it supposed possible, that I could have previously known what his were." Calhoun to B. Hall, April 3, 1832, 11 *The Papers of John C. Calhoun* 565. Alexander Hamilton wrote of the Virginia and Kentucky Resolutions: "The late attempt of Virginia and Kentucky to unite the state legislatures in a direct resistance to certain laws of the Union can be considered in no other light than as an attempt to change the government." Quoted in James A. Hamilton, *Reminiscences* (New York: Scribner's, 1869), p. 38; see also To Theodore Sedgwick, Feb. 2, 1799, 22 *The Papers of Alexander Hamilton* 452; to Dayton, 1799 6 *The Works of Alexander Hamilton* 384–388, John C. Hamilton, ed. (New York: Charles Francis, 1851).

96. See Walter Berns's criticism of the Founders in this respect in "Privacy, Liberalism, and the Role of Government," in Robert L. Cunningham, ed., *Liberty and the Rule of Law* (College Station: Texas A. & M University, 1979), p. 210.

97. Alexander Hamilton, John Jay, and James Madison, *The Federalist*, Jacob Cooke, ed. (Middletown, Conn.: Wesleyan University Press, 1961), p. 58.

98. Ibid., p. 61.

99. Ibid., p. 60.

100. Ibid., p. 58.

101. Ibid., p. 65.

102. Albert Castel, "The Founding Fathers and the Vision of a National University," 4 *History of Education Quarterly* 280, 298 (December, 1964).

103. To Lafayette, May 28, 1788, 29 *Writings of George Washington* 506.

104. Thornton Wilder, "Introduction," in Gertrude Stein, *Four in America* (New Haven: Yale University Press, 1947), p. xv.

105. Stein, "George Washington," in *Four in America*, p. 176.

106. Ibid., p. 215.

107. Ibid., p. 206.

108. Ibid., p. 209.

109. Ibid., p. 212.

110. Ibid. After writing this chapter, I came upon Paul K. Longmore, *The Invention of George Washington* (Berkeley: University of California Press, 1988), Appendix, " 'The Foundations of Useful Knowledge,' " which emphasizes Washington's extensive reading and criticizes the received opinions of the mindless Washington and Farmer Washington. Ibid., pp. 213–226. Longmore's interpretation is broadly compatible with my argument.

111. 35 *Writings* 60.

112. Adams, 10 *Memoirs of John Quincy Adams* 117, Charles F. Adams, ed. (Philadelphia: J. B. Lippincott, 1876).

113. Sept. 22, 1788, 30 *Writings* 97.

114. To John Jay, Nov. 1, 1794, 34 *Writings* 16; see also 34 *Writings* 447, 35 *Writings* 452.

115. To John Quincy Adams, June 25, 1797, 35 *Writings* 476.

116. To Lafayette, Oct. 8, 1797, 36 *Writings* 41; to John Luzac, Dec. 2, 1797, 36 *Writings* 84.

117. L. White, "George Washington: Administrator," 24 *Boston University Law Review* 145–156 (June 1944), reprinted in Edward N. Saveth, ed., *Understanding the American Past* (Boston: Little, Brown, 1954), pp. 156–157; see also Leonard White, "George Washington as an Administrator," in *The Federalists* (New York: Macmillan, 1948), pp. 97–115; cf. James Hart, "The President as Administrative Chief," in *The American Presidency in Action 1789* (New York: Macmillan, 1948), pp. 134–143. A brief treatment of Washington is in Edward S. Corwin, *The President: Office and Powers* (4th rev. edn.; New York: New York University Press, 1957), chap. 1 and pp. 318–319 n.40. Forrest McDonald briefly notices Washington as an administrator in his *The Presidency of George Washington* (Lawrence: The University Press of Kansas, 1974), pp. 27, 40–41.

118. 36 *Writings* 113.

119. 30 *Writings* 510.

120. "Queries Upon a Line of Conduct to be Pursued by the President," May 10, 1789, 30 *Writings* 321.

121. 30 *Writings* 428.

122. To Sir Edward Newenham, Aug. 29, 1788, 30 *Writings* 72.

123. Ibid., p. 73.

124. 31 *Writings* 142.

125. 32 *Writings* 47.

126. To David Stuart, June 15, 1790, 31 *Writings* 54.

127. July 13, 1796, 35 *Writings* 138, italics in the original.

128. To Comte De Rochambeau, Aug. 10, 1790, 31 *Writings* 83–84.

129. Major General Henry Lee, "Oration on the Death of General Washington," in George Washington Parke Custis, *Recollections and Private Memoirs of Washington* (Philadelphia: J. W. Bradley, 1861), p. 618.

130. 34 *Writings* 266.

131. Ibid., p. 310.

132. Ibid., p. 407.

133. To Alexander Hamilton, May 15, 1796, 35 *Writings* 49, italics in the original; see also 33 *Writings* 422.

134. To John Marshall, Dec. 4, 1797, 36 *Writings* 94.

135. Ibid., p. 94, italics in the original.

136. Flexner, *Washington and the New Nation*, pp. 162–163.

137. Ibid., p. 163.

138. 30 *Writings* 299–300.

139. Flexner, *Washington and the New Nation*, p. 168.

140. 35 *Writings* 254.

141. Sept. 6, 1796, 35 *Writings* 205, italics in the original.

142. For Washington's continued consideration in retirement of the national university against the "sentiments of the legislature," see To St. George Tucker, May 30, 1797, 35 *Writings* 458.

143. White, *The Federalists*, p. 512.

144. 35 *Writings* 488; 31 *Writings* 54; 31 *Writings* 211; 37 *Writings* 167.

145. 34 *Writings* 331, italics in the original.

146. 30 *Writings* 309.

147. 34 *Writings* 318.

148. White, *The Federalists*, p. 164.

149. 34 *Writings* 317–318.

150. Ibid., p. 348.

151. Ibid., p. 349.

152. White, *The Federalists*, p. 257.

153. 34 *Writings* 34.

154. 36 *Writings* 93, italics in the original.

155. 35 *Writings* 37, italics added in the last sentence.

156. Ibid., p. 40.

157. 35 *Writings* 119–120; cf. Washington's sarcasm against "professed" Democrats and "the Republicans, as they have very erroneously called themselves." 36 *Writings* 474, 37 *Writings* 201.

158. 34 *Writings* 264.

159. 35 *Writings* 229.

160. Madison, "Substance of a Conversation with the President," May 5, 1792, in 6 *The Writings of James Madison* 108 n., Gaillard Hunt, ed. (New York: Putnam's, 1906).

161. 35 *Writings of George Washington* 320.

162. Jefferson to Washington, May 23, 1792 in 6 *The Writings of Thomas Jefferson* 3 (P. L. Ford, ed., 1892–1899).

163. 32 *Writings of George Washington* 95–100, italics in the original.

164. Aug. 18, 1792, 12 *Papers*, 228–258.

165. Ibid., p. 251.

166. Ibid.

167. Ibid., p. 252.

168. Ibid., p. 253; cf. David Hume, "Of the Original Contract," 1 *Essays Moral, Political and Literary* 446 (T. H. Green and T. H. Grose, eds., 1912): "But philosophers, who have embraced a party (if that be not a contradiction in terms)." In transcending party, even while under attack by Jefferson, Hamilton showed a rare quality of disinterestedness.

169. 12 *Papers* 254.

170. Ibid., p. 258.

171. Ibid., p. 276.

172. Ibid., p. 277, italics in the original.

173. Ibid., pp. 347–349.

174. 33 *Writings* 73, italics added.

175. 35 *Writings* 2.

176. Hamilton's draft of a reply to the House relies on the character of foreign negotiations and the separation of powers betwen Congress and the executive. 20 *Papers* 68–69.

177. 35 *Writings* 154.

178. 34 *Writings* 241.

179. McDonald, *The Presidency of George Washington*, p. 27.

180. June 19, 1788, 29 *Writings* 526, italics added.

181. For an attempt at a post mortem on the worship of the Constitution, see Edward S. Corwin, "The Worship of the Constitution," in Richard Loss, ed., 1 *Corwin on the Constitution* 47–55 (Ithaca, N.Y.: Cornell University Press, 1981).

182. 35 *Writings* 154.

183. Ibid., p. 231.

184. Ibid., p. 236; see the discussion of Hamilton's Pacificus and Americanus Letters in Chapter 1, above, and 14 *Papers* 326–328, 367–396, 502–507 ("Defense of the President's Neutrality Proclamation").

185. 34 *Writings* 256.

186. Samuel Flagg Bemis, *Jay's Treaty* (2nd ed.; New Haven: Yale University Press, 1962), p. xii.

187. 35 *Writings* 343; cf. Friedrich von Gentz, *The Origin and Principles of the American Revolution, Compared with the Origin and Principles of the French Revolution*, Richard Loss, ed., John Quincy Adams, trans. (Delmar, N.Y.: Scholars' Facsimiles and Reprints, 1977).

188. 35 *Writings* 372.

189. 37 *Writings* 68–69.

190. Curtis P. Nettels, "The Washington Theme in American History," 68 *Proceedings of the Massachusetts Historical Society* 198 n.2 (1944–1947); see the literature cited.

191. Henry Lee, "Oration on the Death of General Washington," in Custis, *Recollections*, p. 622.

192. Fisher Ames, "Eulogy on Washington," 2 *Works of Fisher Ames* 86.

193. Ibid., p. 72.

194. Lee, "Oration on the Death of General Washington," in Custis, *Recollections*, p. 620.

195. Samuel E. Morison, "The Young Man Washington," in Morison, *By Land and by Sea* (New York: Knopf, 1966), p. 169.

196. 1 *The Works of Joseph Addison* 171, Richard Hurd, ed. (London: H. G. Bohn, 1854–1856).

197. Ibid., p. 200.

198. Ibid., p. 173.

199. Plutarch, "Cato the Younger," *The Lives of the Noble Grecians and Romans*, John Dryden and Arthur Clough, trans. (New York: Modern Library, 1932), p. 959.

200. Morison, *By Land and By Sea*, p. 180.

Part II

REVISIONIST PRESIDENTS AND REVISIONIST SCHOLARS OF THE PRESIDENCY

3

Abraham Lincoln

This chapter discusses Lincoln's thought on the American regime and his understanding of presidential power. Lincoln's concept of presidential power is examined in his administration's arrests of dissidents and his suspension of the writ of habeas corpus. The chapter argues that Lincoln's understanding of the regime and presidential power marked a regrettable departure from Hamilton's teaching.

THE REGIME

Lord Charnwood differs from Harry Jaffa and Glen Thurow in holding that "no political theory stands out from his [Lincoln's] words or actions."[1] Jaffa and Thurow argue more persuasively that Lincoln had a theory of the regime.[2] As Jaffa observed, *Federalist* 51 based our political system on the "policy of supplying, by opposite and rival interests, the defect of better motives."[3] Lincoln's "solution involved . . . an engrafting of the passion of revealed religion upon the body of secular political rationalism."[4] Lincoln exploited the religious theme in his presidential proclamation for a fast day and his pre-presidential address on the preservation of American political institutions. The proclamation accused Americans of forgetting God and of becoming "too proud" to pray to God.[5]

Lincoln's address (1838) called for the rule of law to become a political religion. He distinguished reverence for the law from mob rule and urged the removal of grievances by the passage of better laws. This more or less straightforward rule of law argument makes interesting reading when compared to President Lincoln's conduct. Lincoln also warned of leaders who would be discontented with merely operating the Founders' institutions, raising the question of whether President Lincoln himself was one of those "towering" and ambitious geniuses who were a standing danger to republican government.[6] In this address he recommended reverence for the Constitution and laws and popular rationality. His address implied that the Founders were merely ambitious men and that their advocacy of popular government resulted from the Founders seeking gratification of their "ruling passion" for fame. As Jaffa has said of this address, "there appears to be a systematic process of detraction of the Fathers that borders upon the savage."[7] In 1842 Lincoln continued his criticism of the Founders while comparing the political revolution of 1776 with the Temperance movement. The superiority of moral to political freedom and the higher social costs of the revolution of 1776 made the moral revolution symbolized by the Temperance movement superior to the political revolution of 1776.

Lincoln found in the idea of equality the authoritative meaning of the American political regime. Simplifying matters somewhat compared to Hamilton and Washington, Lincoln identified the equality of men as the "*central idea*" of American political opinion.[8] He also declared that the molder of opinion created the conditions for the enforcement of laws and "decisions" and therefore went "deeper" than legislators and judges.[9] Lincoln's suggestions on equality and public opinion seem to tend toward a militant or coercive equality rather unlike the mildness and moderation of Hamilton and Washington. Not surprisingly, Lincoln found not only a single principle defining the American regime but also a single sacred text: "our old and only standard of free government, that 'all men are created equal,' " came from the Declaration of Independence.[10] He deduced freedom for the slaves from the Declaration.[11] It would seem that Lincoln's version of equality filled for him the central role that virtue played for Hamilton and Washington. Lincoln did try at least once to reconcile his idea of equality with the inequality of virtue. He said to a deputation of Negroes that he was assured that "you should be equals of the best."[12] This was, however, a casual mention, not a demonstration that equality can be reconciled with virtue. Neither does Lincoln show the superiority of his idea of equality to virtue. Lincoln's appeal to the Declaration may be rebutted with his saying in another context, that an appeal to authority is a "thus saith the Lord." An appeal to authority is not necessarily a valid or a demonstrative argument.

In a brief autobiography written in 1858 Lincoln characterized his education as "defective."[13] His early appreciation of the importance of education strongly contrasts with the feebleness of his educational measures as president. He avoided issuing a "plan" on education, though he understood education as the "most important" subject before the American people.[14] He hoped for the universal spread of education at least to enable Americans to read the history of their own and foreign countries, showing the value of free institutions. He understood education to be the means for the diffusion of "morality."

Lincoln recommended education, by which he seems to have meant the teaching of reading, so that men could read Scripture and other moral and religious works. He failed to specify which works he had in mind. Lincoln wondered how to combine education and labor.[15] He thought of education as the "natural companion" of free labor.[16] "As in the case of Jefferson, he associated agricultural activity with democracy."[17] Accordingly, the major piece of education legislation that Lincoln signed was the Morrill Land-Grant-College Act. Passed by Congress in 1862, this statute established colleges to promote agriculture and the mechanical arts with the help of public lands donated by the national government. This bias toward agriculture, the mechanical arts and vocational education departed from the lofty goal of Washington's national university. Lincoln's recommended self-education would not work on a large scale.

Lincoln, it is not too much to say, worshiped at the shrine of Thomas Jefferson, calling him the "most distinguished politician" of American history.[18] Jefferson's principles, Lincoln said, were the "definitions and axioms of free society."[19] Yet there were some Jeffersonian principles, regarding the public abuse of religion, that Lincoln could not accept. Jefferson's Query 17 in *Notes on Virginia* stated that "it does me no injury for my neighbor to say there are twenty gods, or no God. It neither picks my pocket nor breaks my leg." In his 1846 campaign for Congress Lincoln published a handbill replying to charges of infidelity that conceded he was not a member of any Christian church. Lincoln revealed that as a young man he believed in the teaching of necessity: "the human mind is impelled to action, or held in rest by some power, over which the mind itself has no control."[20] Certainly, this is a strange doctrine for one celebrated as a teacher and defender of liberty. He said that he only argued the teaching of necessity "publicly" with "one, two or three." He drew the line at open heterodoxy and refused to support for public office anyone who openly opposed or ridiculed religion. Lincoln artfully steers the reader away from Lincoln's private opinions by reassuring his audience of his public orthodoxy.

Lincoln opposed another Jeffersonian principle, natural aristocracy. Jefferson said that "the natural aristocracy I consider as the most precious gift of nature, for the instruction, the trusts, and government of society."[21] Lincoln also deviated from the teaching of the *Federalist* in recommending a frequent appeal to the people. As Glen Thurow remarked, "in rejecting all aristocratic pretensions, Lincoln enshrines the continuing consent of the people. The people, freed of their competitors, are granted a nobility certainly not granted them by the *Federalist* or even Jefferson."[22] Moreover, Lincoln welcomed and encouraged a frequent recurrence to what he understood as the first principles of the regime. Arguments against the frequent recurrence to first principles may be derived from the warning in *Federalist* 49 against frequent reference of constitutional questions to the people because this would imply a defect in the existing government, deprive the government of the veneration bestowed by time, dissolve the prejudices that can strengthen even the most rational government and weaken respect for, and obedience of, the law. In terms of the *Federalist*, Lincoln overestimated the amount of enlightenment and reason in the political community, wherein a "nation of philosophers" is not to be expected. Whether a frequent appeal to first principles in Lincoln's manner is compatible with civil peace would be denied by those who argue that men of such principle fight civil wars.

Lincoln seemed to appeal to the Declaration of Independence at the expense of the Constitution. In 1861 he said that he had "never had a feeling politically that did not spring from the sentiments embodied in the Declaration of Independence."[23] Invoking Proverbs 25:11 ("A word fitly spoken is like apples of gold in pictures of silver"), Lincoln drew an analogy between the Declaration and an apple of gold.[24] The Declaration's principle of "liberty to all" was the golden apple; the Constitution and the Union framed the golden apple. The frame was made for the apple, not the apple for the frame: the frame protected the apple. Clearly, Lincoln subordinated the Constitution and the Union to his vision of the Declaration, and it may be doubted whether this is warranted. The president of the United States takes an oath to preserve and protect the Constitution, not the Declaration. To escape the limitations of the Declaration, Lincoln said that if the Declaration is untrue, let us "tear it out" of "*the Statute book, in which we find it.*"[25] The editorial insertion of the Declaration in a book of statutes does not, of course, make it a statute passed by the House and the Senate and signed by the president or passed over his veto. The seductiveness and emotional ring of the Declaration, compared to the dry prose of the Constitution, and Lincoln's poetic and missionary zeal led him astray and weakened his constitutionalism.

LINCOLN'S UNDERSTANDING OF THE WAR POWER

Lincoln's early understanding of the war power was cautious. The Constitution gave the "war making power" to Congress so that "*no one man*" could embroil the United States in war.[26] Lincoln's formulation of 1848 recognizes no executive war power. He attributes more power to Congress than simply the power to declare war: this is at odds with his doctrine as president. Lincoln departs from Hamilton's teaching that the Constitution grants concurrent power to the president and Congress.

Several commentators have deftly criticized President Lincoln's doctrine and practice in the war powers area. Herbert Agar, for example held that Lincoln was "to revolutionize the office of the Presidency by his ruthless use of the 'war powers' ."[27] According to J. G. Randall, Lincoln "made the Presidency, to a large extent though not completely, the dominant power, certainly more so than it had normally been."[28] Randall argues that "this question of the dictatorship ... should not be passed over lightly, and some of Lincoln's arguments in his own defense may have gone beyond the limits which sound legal reasoning would recognize."[29] "Lincoln's conception of the executive power was too expansive."[30] Lord Charnwood concluded that "in a strictly legal sense, ... the power which Lincoln exercised must be said to have been usurped. The arguments by which he defended his own legality read now as good arguments on what the law should have been, but bad arguments on what the law was."[31]

Justices of the Supreme Court tackled at least three times the issue of Lincoln's power. In *Ex parte* Merryman a general opposed the execution of the writ of habeas corpus, basing his act on the president's order suspending the writ. Speaking only for himself, Chief Justice Taney held that the courts were open and any suspected treason should be dealt with by the judicial process. The general resisted Taney's writ, and Taney sent a copy of his opinion to Lincoln, who failed to comply. In the Prize Cases shipowners whose vessels had been seized as blockade runners challenged Lincoln's blockade of confederate ports. Justice Grier held that Lincoln had the right to begin a blockade: as to "this greatest of civil wars," "the President was bound to meet it in the shape it presented itself, without waiting for Congress to baptize it with a name."[32]

In *Ex parte* Milligan the Supreme Court read the then dead Lincoln a lecture on the meaning of constitutionalism. A military commission found Milligan guilty of conspiracy against the United States, inciting insurrection, disloyal practices and violations of the laws of war. He was found guilty of specifications under each charge: resisting the draft and conspiracy to seize arms and ammunition stored in arsenals. He was sentenced to hang. In May 1865 Milligan petitioned a circuit court for a writ of habeas corpus, arguing that the military commission had no jurisdiction over him because he was a civilian resident of a state where the courts were still open. He also charged that the military commission's action violated his right to trial by jury guaranteed by the Constitution. Mr. Justice Davis delivered the opinion of the Court and found that the military commission lacked the authority to try and sentence Milligan. Davis concluded that "the Constitution of the United States is a law for rulers and people, equally in war and in peace and covers with the shield of its protection all classes of men, at all times, and under all circumstances."[33] Lincoln's death and the ending of the Civil War the year

before this decision may account for the Court's bravery in defending
the Constitution as universally applicable.

Lincoln tried numerous arguments to defend his suspension of the
writ of habeas corpus. He wondered whether all republican governments
must either suppress liberty or perish through internal weakness.[34] In
his 1861 Special Message to Congress he asked rhetorically whether the
government was to perish or whether one law might be "violated" when
all the other laws were "unexecuted."[35] He stated that the Confederate
military leaders, including Robert E. Lee, could have been arrested as
traitors, but they would have been released on habeas corpus.[36] Lincoln
said that the operative meaning of the Constitution differed in times of
rebellion or invasion and in time of peace.[37] His formulation of the war
power hinted at his idea of the authoritative determiner of the Constitution: "the Commander-in-Chief . . . may order what he pleases."[38] If
and when constitutional interpretation derives from the pleasure or will
of the commander-in-chief, that puts an end to constitutional limitations. Lincoln further maintained that in wartime the Constitution vested
the commander-in-chief with the "law of war."[39]

Lincoln's resort to the commander-in-chief clause abandoned Hamilton's position that the grant of power in the first sentence of Article II
and the "take care" clause provided an adequate basis for action. In the
Whiskey Rebellion of Washington's administration martial law was not
declared. Civil officers made arrests with warrants, and military officers
respected the authority of the federal judge of the district. The government tried certain leaders in regular courts. They were sentenced to
death for treason and pardoned by the president.[40]

Lincoln saw no danger that by military arrests during a rebellion the
American people would grow accustomed to losing their liberties.[41] He
compared the Civil War to a passing illness, arguing that the extreme
measures of the war would not persist or reappear because they would
be unnecessary when the patient was restored to health.[42] This soothing
counsel rested on the optimistic premises that his measures had only a
temporary cost and would not set a bad precedent for lesser presidents.

The foregoing argument of Lincoln's minimizes the costs of his policies. In one set of arguments, however, he more candidly faced the
effects and costs of his measures, wondering whether it was "possible to
lose the nation, and yet preserve the Constitution? . . . . often a limb must
be amputated to save a life; but a life is never wisely given to save a
limb."[43] He demotes the Constitution to the status of a limb, but in his
terms it may be asked whether it is possible to lose the Constitution and
yet preserve the nation, and this question must be answered in the neg-
ative. Lincoln's surgical analogy concedes what some of his critics argued,
namely, that the constitutional amputation is a permanent and irrever-
sible bad effect of his policies. In brief because of Lincoln the Consti-

tution after the war was not the same as the Constitution before the war. He temporarily made the presidency dominant over Congress and the Supreme Court, overrode individual rights and set a precedent for the future.

Lincoln's attorney general, Edward Bates, issued an opinion attempting to justify the arrests and the suspension of habeas corpus. Bates held that the three branches of government are coordinate. Hence the president is not subordinate to Congress and the Supreme Court. Congress, Bates continued, has recognized the president's right to use force in the performance of his legal duties. The president swears an oath to preserve, protect and defend the Constitution. He must be allowed discretion in suppressing insurrection. "In a time like the present when the very existence of the nation is assailed by a great and dangerous insurrection," the president has discretionary power to arrest and hold in custody persons known to have criminal intercourse with the insurgents or persons against whom there is probable cause for suspicion of such activity. No court, said Bates, can take cognizance of the president's political acts. Since the president may arrest on probable cause for suspicion, he may ignore a writ of habeas corpus issued by a judge. The president, Bates concluded, is an independent officer and commander-in-chief.[44]

Sydney Fisher rightly pointed out that Bates "begins by assuming the proposition which has to be proved": he derives the right to suspend habeas corpus from the right to arrest and imprison.[45] The view that the president could suspend the writ of habeas corpus in wartime as an incident of his office as commander-in-chief is "simply a trick to get rid of the odious name of martial law by calling it Commander-in-Chief."[46] Fisher injects a note of realism into the discussion of Lincoln's use of the war power: "Every government, when driven to the wall by a rebellion, will trample down a constitution before it will allow itself to be destroyed. This may not be constitutional law, but it is fact."[47]

James Ford Rhodes, the historian, condemned Lincoln's suspension of habeas corpus, the arrests and detention: "In consideration of our own practice, the decision of our courts, the opinions of our statesmen and jurists, and English precedents for two centuries, it may be affirmed that the right of suspending the privilege of the writ of habeas corpus was vested by the Constitution in Congress and not in the Executive."[48] Rhodes continued that "after careful consideration I do not hesitate to condemn the arbitrary arrests and the arbitrary interference with freedom of the press in states which were not included in the theater of war and in which the courts remained open."[49] Rhodes concluded: "I am convinced that all this extra judicial procedure was inexpedient, unnecessary and wrong and the offenders thus summarily dealt with should have been prosecuted according to law or, if their offenses were not indictable, permitted to go free."[50] Lincoln "stands responsible for the casting into prison of citizens of the United States on orders as arbitrary as the lettres-de-cachet of Louis XIV."[51]

On the suspension of the writ J. G. Randall finds that "the weight of opinion would seem to incline to the view that Congress has the exclusive suspending power."[52] According to Randall, Lincoln's defense of his actions while Congress was out of session was, first, that "national safety imperatively demanded that these vigorous measures be taken;" "(and here is the doubtful part), that as he had not exceeded the power of Congress, he supposed that all would be made right by subsequent legislative approval."[53] This is a "bad practice."[54] Hence we should not attach "too much weight to the Lincoln precedent of 1861." "The arbitrary arrests were unfortunate." Dean Sprague concluded that even if Lincoln was justified, he set a "dangerous precedent" that his successors should not follow.[55] Some may argue that Lincoln's frequent pardons curbed the harshness of the arrest system, but if it was necessary to pardon so often, something was wrong with the arrest system that the pardons could not cure.

CONCLUSIONS

Lincoln had a teaching on the regime before he came to the presidency: he taught political religion based on Scripture and the rule of law, the primacy of moral over political freedom and equality as the master principle. Lincoln disagreed with Hamilton and Washington on the regime, virtue and presidential power. He simplified the goal from inegalitarian virtue to one that was more popular and attainable, equality. He replaced inegalitarian virtue with humanitarian equality partly inspired by the Declaration of Independence. By appealing beyond the Constitution to the Declaration Lincoln canceled Hamilton's and Washington's emphasis on the supremacy of the Constitution. Lincoln was, hence, a revolutionary figure.

President Lincoln offered no challenge to Washington as an upholder of the Constitution. Forsaking Hamilton's teaching that the first sentence of Article II was a generous and adequate grant of presidential power, Lincoln also abandoned Hamilton's crucial limitations that presidential power must be compatible with other parts of the Constitution and with the principles of free government. Lincoln's arrests of dissidents and suspension of the writ of habeas corpus are almost universally acknowledged to have set a dangerous precedent. Compared to Washington's sponsorship of a national university for unity and political education, Lincoln failed to provide for such education on a permanent basis. President Lincoln's goals of equality and union required during the Civil War a nearly unlimited exertion of presidential power to make them prevail. This in turn required a new constitutional understanding; Lincoln found the advantage he sought in the commander-in-chief clause. But Lincoln dealt with the extreme case of a civil war, and it is unlikely that his constitutionalism, such as it was, would be edifying to posterity.

I turn now to Theodore Roosevelt's understanding of presidential power in order to detect Hamiltonian influence or opposition to Hamilton.

NOTES

1. Lord Charnwood, *Abraham Lincoln* (3rd ed.; New York: Henry Holt, 1917), p. 455.

2. Harry Jaffa, *Crisis of the House Divided* (New York: Doubleday, 1959); Glen Thurow, *Abraham Lincoln and American Political Religion* (Albany: State University of New York Press, 1976).

3. Quoted in Jaffa, *Crisis of the House Divided*, pp 237.

4. Ibid, p. 238.

5. 6 *The Collected Works of Abraham Lincoln* 156 Roy Basler, ed. (New Brunswick, N.J.: Rutgers University Press, 1953–1955); hereafter cited as *Collected Works*, preceded by the volume number and followed by the page number. Other multi-volume works will be cited in this order.

6. 1 *Collected Works* 114.

7. Jaffa, *Crisis of the House Divided*, p. 206.

8. 2 *Collected Works* 385, Lincoln's italics.

9. 3 *Collected Works* 27.

10. Ibid., p. 205.

11. Ibid., p. 16.

12. 5 *Collected Works* 374.

13. 2 *Collected Works* 459.

14. 1 *Collected Works* 8.

15. 3 *Collected Works* 479.

16. Ibid., p. 480.

17. J. G. Randall, 3 *Lincoln The President* 144 (4 vols.; New York: Dodd, Mead, 1945–1955).

18. 2 *Collected Works* 249.

19. 3 *Collected Works* 375.

20. 1 *Collected Works* 382.

21. Saul Padover, ed., *The Complete Jefferson* (New York: Duell, Sloan and Pearce, 1943), p. 283.

22. Thurow, *Abraham Lincoln and American Political Religion*, p. 119.

23. 4 *Collected Works* 240.

24. Ibid., p. 169.

25. 2 *Collected Works* 500–501, italics added. For the early limited view of the Declaration as principally a proclamation of independence, see Philip F. Detweiler, "The Changing Reputation of the Declaration of Independence: The First Fifty Years," 19 *William and Mary Quarterly* 3rd Series, 557–574 (October, 1962). Dietrich Gerhard, "Abraham Lincoln, die Verfassung und die Unabhängigkeitserklärung," 11 *Jahrbuch für Amerikastudien* 56 (1966), attributes to Lincoln

the opinion that both the Declaration and the Constitution taught liberty for all (citing Lincoln, 4 *Collected Works* 168 ff. [Basler, ed., 1953]). The cited text does not warrant that interpretation, for Lincoln says "the *expression* of that principle, in our Declaration of Independence, was most happy, and fortunate" (ibid., p, 169, Lincoln's italics); he does not say that the Constitution and the Declaration express the same principle. Gerhard shifts ground by arguing that Lincoln held that in case of a conflict the Constitution was to be interpreted in the sense of the Declaration (11 *Jahrbuch für Amerikastudien* 57). Gerhard's second argument asserts the supremacy of the Declaration, not its identity with the Constitution. This second argument implies, in its interpretation of Lincoln, that Lincoln deconstitutionalized American political thought.

26. 1 *Collected Works* 451–452; italics in the original.

27. Herbert Agar, *Abraham Lincoln* (London: Collins, 1952), p. 42.

28. Randall, 3 *Lincoln The President* 150.

29. J. G. Randall, *Constitutional Problems Under Lincoln* (rev. ed.; Gloucester, Mass.: Peter Smith, 1963), pp. 57–58.

30. Ibid., p. 184.

31. Charnwood, *Abraham Lincoln*, p. 378.

32. The Prize Cases, 67 U.S. 459, 491 (1863).

33. 71 U.S. 281, 295 (1866).

34. 4 *Collected Works* 426.

35. Ibid., p. 430.

36. 6 *Collected Works* 265.

37. Ibid., p. 267.

38. 5 *Collected Works* 176.

39. 6 *Collected Works* 408.

40. Randall, *Constitutional Problems Under Lincoln*, p. 144.

41. 6 *Collected Works* 267.

42. Ibid., p. 267.

43. 7 *Collected Works* 281.

44. *Official Records of the Union and Confederate Armies*, Series II, Vol. II, July 5, 1861, pp. 20–30 (Washington, D.C.: Government Printing Office, 1897).

45. Sydney G. Fisher, "The Suspension of Habeas Corpus During the War of the Rebellion," 3 *Political Science Quarterly* 473 (1888).

46. Ibid., p. 482 n.2.

47. Ibid., p. 485.

48. James Ford Rhodes, *History of the Civil War* (New York: Macmillan, 1917), p. 353.

49. Ibid., P. 354.

50. Ibid., pp. 354—355.

51. Ibid., p. 355.

52. Randall, *Constitutional Problems Under Lincoln*, p. 136.

53. Ibid., p. 58.

54. Ibid., p. 59.

55. Dean Sprague, *Freedom Under Lincoln* (Boston: Houghton Mifflin, 1965), p. 303.

4

Theodore Roosevelt

Clinton Rossiter argued that Theodore Roosevelt's stewardship theory of the presidency "may be traced back *in unbroken line* to Hamiton's teachings."[1] What was the character of Hamilton's influence over Roosevelt, generally and with reference to the stewardship theory? "Thank Heaven," said T.R., "I have never hesitated to criticize Jefferson; he was infinitely below Hamilton; I think the worship of Jefferson a discredit to my country."[2] "It was the work of Washington and Hamilton, accomplished in the teeth of the Jeffersonian resistance after the Revolutionary War, which of course rendered it possible for Lincoln and Grant ... to keep this country a nation."[3] Speaking of a friend, Roosevelt's *Autobiography* records that "he admired Alexander Hamilton as much as I did, being a strong believer in a powerful national government; and ... both of us differed from Alexander Hamilton in being stout adherents of Abraham Lincoln's views wherever the rights of the people were concerned."[4]

For Roosevelt, Hamilton's most important political teaching was "a powerful national government." As we saw in Chapter 1 the power of the national government is only part, and not the most important part, of Hamilton's teaching. Roosevelt's interpretation wrongly implies that Hamilton thought of power in isolation from other, more important ends. Roosevelt implicitly denied Hamilton's moderate doctrine of restraints on power. Moreover, Roosevelt's letters never refer to Hamilton as a personal hero. T.R., however, did call Lincoln "my great hero."[5] Lincoln "was superior to Hamilton just because he was a politician and was a genuine democrat and therefore suited to lead a genuine democracy."[6] Although T.R. was "still calling himself a 'strong Hamiltonian' in 1918," his basic loyalties were to Lincoln rather than Hamilton.[7] Despite calling Washington "even greater" than Lincoln, T.R. drew more inspiration and comfort from Lincoln than from the thought of any other American statesman.[8] "Often," wrote Roosevelt, "when dealing with some puzzling affair I find myself thinking what Lincoln would have done."[9]

Contrary to what we should expect from Rossiter's formulation of Hamilton's influence "in unbroken line," Roosevelt's stewardship theory of the presidency never mentions Hamilton at all. Roosevelt instead names his theory the "Jackson-Lincoln theory of the presidency."[10] The stewardship theory regards the "executive as subject only to the people, and under the Constitution, bound to serve the people affirmatively in cases where the Constitution does not explicitly forbid him to render the service."[11] In one formulation of the stewardship theory Roosevelt holds that "occasionally great national crises arise which call for immediate and vigorous action"; "in such cases it is the duty of the President to act upon the theory that he is the steward of the people."[12] This precedes T.R.'s account of the anthracite coal strike: he felt that settling the Panama Canal "was the best thing I have done, with the exception of settling the anthracite coal strike."[13]

What was the stewardship theory in the context of Roosevelt's illustration of it? The coal strike and Roosevelt's plans "illustrated as well as anything that I did the theory which I have called the Jackson-Lincoln theory of the Presidency."[14] Had the strike not ended, T.R. would have ordered Major General Schofield to "dispossess" the mine operators and run the mines as a receiver. T.R. ordered Schofield "that if I sent him he must act in a purely military capacity under me as commander-in-chief, paying no heed to *any* authority, *judicial or otherwise*, except mine."[15] The constitutional source of T.R.'s theory and his order to Schofield was hardly Hamiltonian or even novel. The power of commander-in-chief gave Roosevelt, in his opinion, the authority to order Schofield to prepare martial law and to disregard judicial and congressional authority.[16] This was Lincolnism, not Hamiltonianism, contrary to Rossiter's interpretation of the stewardship theory. Moreover, William Howard Taft pointed out that T.R. had failed to mention compensation of the mine owners for seizure of their property.[17]

T.R. presents a second version of the stewardship theory in which it is not linked to a crisis, in which the "Constitution" supplies the control and congressional statutes are not mentioned.[18] This version raises the question of whether the president should resort to the stewardship theory as a general rule or only during crises and whether Congress should be entirely left out. T.R.'s letters frankly acknowledge his fondness for power: "While President I have *been* President, emphatically; I have used every ounce of power there was in the office and I have not cared a rap for the criticisms of those who spoke of my 'usurpation of power'; for I knew that the talk was all nonsense and that there was no usurpation.... In showing the strength of, or in giving strength to, the executive, I was establishing a precedent of value."[19] T.R. mentions as limits on the president the custom of the two-term limit, which he ignored in 1912, and "Washington and Lincoln representing the type of leader to which we are true." T.R. overlooks the fact that Washington and Lincoln stood for separate and somewhat incompatible principles. Moreover, Lincoln is scarcely a credible authority on the constitutional limitation of the president. Once these things are seen, the last restraints admitted by T.R. disappear.

According to Edward Wagenknecht, Roosevelt "came closest to going beyond his powers in connection with the great coal strike of 1902."[20] An excellent study concluded that Roosevelt's and Taft's theories of the presidency "were more similar than stated. Roosevelt was not quite so bold as he said he was; Taft was not so deferential to the Constitution as he alleged."[21] This is sound as a warning against confusing theory with presidential action, but Taft was certainly more deferential to the Constitution than T.R. Of T.R.'s plan to mine the coal with the army, Taft said: "It was an advocacy of the higher law and his obligation to execute it which is a little startling in a constitutional republic."[22] "Taft basically was a Hamiltonian in his view of the office."[23] But Rossiter traced the influence of Hamilton's teachings through T.R. rather than through his astute critic, Taft. There appears to be only slight evidence for the Hamilton–Roosevelt connection. In the main Roosevelt's stewardship theory suppresses the extra-constitutional restraints, derived from political thought, that were so important for Hamilton and mentions neither the *Federalist* nor the Pacificus Letters. T.R.'s theory was basically that of a lawyer with none of the breadth or profundity of a comprehensive political mind. Hamilton, we may say, would be proud to leave Roosevelt to Lincoln, dubbed the "arch iconoclast" for his dexterous surgeries on the Constitution.[24]

Not only was T.R.'s stewardship theory post-Hamiltonian, T.R. was guilty, according to John Morton Blum, of palpable abuses of power: "while president he initiated a criminal libel suit—a suit presuming an offense against the United States—against a publisher who had criticized him, and he kept in prison without legal sanction a petty criminal who had violated not a law but his concept of the right. Such lawless uses of power, however meritorious or moral their intent, undermined the traditional principles of restraint upon which American order had been built."[25] Blum notices T.R.'s "lust" to rule: "he let his leadership degenerate to demagoguery, his patriotism to perfervid chauvinism, his viable conservatism to a creed akin to fascism."[26] "The tragedy of Theodore Roosevelt was that this was bound to happen. That passionate tension pursuing power never quite controlled itself."

T.R.'s letters and writings show how he understood the American regime. But first we must treat a prior question: whether he contributed to political thought or merely had a set of intuitions. Lewis Einstein and Edmund Morris maintain that T.R. had a "political philosophy," though Morris virtually retracts this compliment with his criticism of Roosevelt's opinion on Americanism: "Ninety nine percent of the millions of words he . . . poured out are sterile, banal, and so droningly repetitive as to defeat the most dedicated researcher."[27] On the other hand, Lord Charnwood holds that "neither a gospel nor a philosophy can be made out of his words or example."[28] Roosevelt "ultimately made up his mind by a flashing sort of intuitive process." According to William Harbaugh, Roosevelt's preachments "rested on nothing more substantial than his own intuition and intelligence."[29]

Elting Morison concludes that "the Roosevelt administration did not contribute any of the massive formulations, either of intellect or spirit, that appear in the national heritage."[30] "Justice between man and man, group and groups, and the various incompatibles was to be achieved by the authority of a strong executive who apparently knew what justice was."[31] Morison continues that "the limitations in this position—considered as a political philosophy—are disastrously apparent. . . . In vain one scrutinizes the scheme to find a logically constructed system of ideas. . . . The Square Deal rests upon no more substantial ground than the intuitive feelings of the executive."

Pringle provides an example of T.R.'s intuitional basis of political action. The context is T.R.'s 1915 testimony under oath on substantive justice: "*Q*: How did you know that substantive justice was done? *Mr. Roosevelt*: Because I did it. . . . *Q*: You mean to say that when you do a thing thereby substantive justice is done? *Mr. Roosevelt*: I do. . . . I mean just that."[32] According to Pringle, this was "the essence of his philosophy." Given the importance to Roosevelt of his personal intuitions, it scarcely makes sense to say, as Mowry did, that "Roosevelt had a deep reverence for traditional moral law."[33] It makes more sense to argue that Roosevelt failed to resist currents of opinion that subverted traditional politico–ethical ideas: "The new economics and political science, the social gospel, pragmatism, and their tangents had all acted as a solvent for the traditional political and ethical concepts."[34] This is but another way of saying that the Progressive movement of which T.R. was a part was not primarily a liberal movement.[35]

Given the inadequacy of Roosevelt's intuitions, how accurate was he with the truth? Edward Wagenknecht notes that "he certainly made statements about himself that were not accurate. He was never a lawyer.

He was never lightweight champion at Harvard. His naval post did not come to him unsolicited."[36] Consider T.R.'s correction of his earlier position on the lightweight championship: "About six years ago.... I took up the matter, examining the records, and found that I had never been lightweight champion."[37] Wagenknecht saves Roosevelt with the statement that "it is not reasonable to suppose that he deliberately lied about these things."

Given the nature of T.R.'s thought as intuition, we are forced to encounter much hasty and unargued generalization. He understood the American regime as a "democratic republican government" in which "orderly liberty" should prevail.[38] He also described Americans as a "business people."[39] Outside of such unsupported dicta Roosevelt did not display much curiosity about the regime. His personal orientation underwent some change. In 1902 he called himself a "strong conservative," while in 1915 he said "I am a near-Socialist. That is, I want to adopt the many excellent things in the Socialist propaganda without adopting the things that seem to me to be evil."[40] His opinion of virtue is adequately described in the *New Nationalism*: "The thing that is most important is for each of us to apply, in his or her way, the *old humdrum, workaday* virtues."[41] Or as T.R. said to an author about her manuscript, "*personally* I prefer virtue."[42] His description of the "old humdrum, workaday" virtues scarcely paints virtue in alluring colors, as a real supporter would. Second, T.R.'s "personal" vote for virtue betrays his intuitional thinking.

On war with England, Roosevelt held in 1895 that the "clamor of the peace faction has convinced me that this country needs a war."[43] Regarding Hawaii he wrote two years later that "we ought to take Hawaii, in the interests of the White race."[44] On immigration in 1892 Roosevelt wrote "I wish the cholera would result in a permanent quarantine against most immigrants![45] In 1894 he was "very glad the immigration has come to a standstill for the last year. We are getting some very undesirable elements now, and I wish that a check could be put to it."[46] As to Negroes, T.R. found them in 1906 "as a race and in the mass . . . altogether inferior to the whites."[47]

Reviewing his record as chief executive in 1916, Roosevelt modestly found that "my great usefulness as President came in connection with the anthracite coal strike, the voyage of the battle fleet around the world, the taking of Panama, the handling of Germany in the Venezuela business, the irrigation business in the West, and finally, I think, the toning up of the government service generally."[48] As for public opinion, T.R. said that "I did not divine how the people were going to think; I simply made up my mind what they ought to think, and then did my best to get them to think it."[49] In the area of appointments Roosevelt stated that "I regard the position of judge as the most important of any to which I make appointments."[50] What Roosevelt meant by a judicial appointment appears in his mention of appointing Oliver Wendell Holmes, Jr., to the Supreme Court: "he is not in my judgment fitted for the position unless he is a party man."[51] This meant to uphold "the policies of President McKinley and the Republican party in Congress." Four years later T.R. lamented that "Holmes should have been an ideal man on the bench. As a matter of fact he has been a bitter disappointment...because of his general attitude."[52] Holmes left this harsh sketch of T.R.: "a very likeable, a big figure, a rather ordinary intellect, with extraordinary gifts, a shrewd and I think pretty unscrupulous politician."[53]

CONCLUSIONS

This chapter has explored Clinton Rossiter's argument that Theodore Roosevelt's stewardship theory of the presidency "may be traced back in unbroken line to Hamilton's teachings." Roosevelt admired Hamilton's ability and achievement without opening himself to Hamilton's broad influence. T.R. corrupted and narrowed Hamilton's teachings merely to a powerful national government and entirely ignored Hamilton's restraints on presidential power in the Pacificus Letters. He mentioned neither the Letters nor the *Federalist* in his account of Hamilton's teachings. Instead of looking to Hamilton T.R. looked to Lincoln for inspiration and guidance, naming his stewardship theory the Jackson-Lincoln theory and calling Lincoln "my great hero." The stewardship theory rested on the commander-in-chief clause of the Constitution and originated in Lincoln's rather than in Hamilton's teachings. Roosevelt's theory had nothing comparable to Lincoln's early teaching on Scripture and the rule of law.

Both Lincoln and Roosevelt excluded judicial limitations on presidential power during a crisis. The true ground of T.R.'s notion of the presidency was Lincoln's refusal to act according to Chief Justice Taney's opinion in *Ex parte* Merryman. At least Lincoln offered the excuse of the Civil War to justify his grasp of power, but Roosevelt had no such defense for his stewardship theory. Moreover, Roosevelt went beyond Lincoln in ordering Major General Schofield to pay "no heed to *any* authority, *judicial or otherwise*, except mine." Roosevelt's order immunizes the president not only from judicial but also legislative oversight and control. T.R.'s two versions of the stewardship theory show that his idea of the presidency was presidential supremacy with or without a crisis. This idea of presidential supremacy was all the more dangerous because of the intuition that guided his decisions. In short, there was less holding T.R. back from presidential adventuring than had held Lincoln back. In sum, I have shown that Roosevelt's stewardship theory of presidential power cannot be traced "in unbroken line" to Hamilton's teachings; the "unbroken line" stops at Lincoln.

Let us now examine the thought of Woodrow Wilson and Franklin D. Roosevelt for Hamilton's influence or opposition to Hamilton.

NOTES

1. Clinton Rossiter, *Alexander Hamilton and the Constitution* (New York: Harcourt, Brace and World, 1964), p. 248; italics added.

2. Theodore Roosevelt, 5 *The Letters of Theodore Roosevelt* 351, Elting E. Morison, ed. (8 vols; Cambridge: Harvard University Press, 1951–1954). Hereafter cited as *Letters*, preceded by the volume number and followed by the page number. The same method of citation will be used for other multi-volume works.

3. 5 *Letters* 410–411.

4. Theodore Roosevelt, *An Autobiography* (New York: Macmillan, 1913), p. 73.

5. 6 *Letters* 1506.

6. 5 *Letters* 351.

7. Edward Wagenknecht, *The Seven Worlds of Theodore Roosevelt* (New York: Longmans, Green, 1958), p. 208.

8. Theodore Roosevelt, *American Ideals* in Roosevelt, *Citizenship, Politics and the Elemental Virtues*, 15 *The Works of Theodore Roosevelt* 7, Memorial Edition (New York: Scribner's, 1925).

9. 3 *Letters* 392.

10. Roosevelt, *Autobiography*, p. 504.

11. Ibid., p. 395.

12. Ibid., p. 464 (1921 [1913]).

13. 3 *Letters* 665.

14. Roosevelt, *Autobiography*, p. 504 (1913).

15. Ibid., pp. 474–475 (1921 [1913]); italics added.

16. Ibid., p. 514 (1913).

17. W. H. Taft, *Our Chief Magistrate and His Powers* (New York: Columbia University Press, 1916), p. 147.

18. Roosevelt, *Autobiography*, p. 362 (1921 [1913]).

19. 6 *Letters* 1087; italics in the original.

20. Wagenknecht, *The Seven Worlds of Theodore Roosevelt*, p. 206.

21. Donald Anderson, *William Howard Taft: A Conservative's Conception of the Presidency* (Ithaca, N.Y.: Cornell University Press, 1973), p. 292.

22. Taft, *Our Chief Magistrate*, p. 146.

23. Anderson, *William Howard Taft*, p. 294.

24. Edward S. Corwin, "The Worship of the Constitution," 4 *Constitutional Review* 11 (January 1920), reprinted in 1 *Corwin on the Constitution* 55 (R. Loss, ed., 1981).

25. John Morton Blum, *The Republican Roosevelt* (Cambridge: Harvard University Press, 1954), pp. 114–115.

26. Ibid., p. 160.

27. Lewis Einstein, *Roosevelt: His Mind in Action* (Boston: Houghton Mifflin,

1930), p. 95; Edmund Morris, *The Rise of Theodore Roosevelt* (New York: Coward, McCann and Geoghegen, 1979), pp. 27, 467.

28. Lord Charnwood, *Theodore Roosevelt* (Boston: Atlantic Monthly Press, 1923), p. 59.

29. William Harbaugh, *The Life and Times of Theodore Roosevelt* (rev. ed.; New York: Oxford University Press, 1975), p. 491.

30. Morison, "Introduction," 5 *Letters* xiv.

31. Ibid., p. xvii.

32. Henry F. Pringle, *Theodore Roosevelt: A Biography* (rev. ed.; New York: Harcourt, Brace and World, 1956), p. 314.

33. George Mowry, *The Era of Theodore Roosevelt* (New York: Harper and Row, 1958), p. 114.

34. Ibid., p. 209.

35. Arthur Ekirch, Jr., *The Decline of Amerian Liberalism* (new ed.; New York: Atheneum, 1967), pp. 171–194.

36. Wagenknecht, *The Seven Worlds of Theodore Roosevelt*, p. 99.

37. 6 *Letters* 944.

38. 3 *Letters* 675; Roosevelt, *American Ideals*, p. 7.

39. 4 *Letters* 932.

40. 3 *Letters* 345; 8 *Letters* 962.

41. Theodore Roosevelt, *The New Nationalism* (Englewood Cliffs, N.J.: Prentice-Hall, 1961), p. 139, italics added.

42. 4 *Letters* 952; italics added.

43. 1 *Letters* 504.

44. Ibid., p. 672.

45. Ibid., p. 291.

46. Ibid., p. 389.

47. 5 *Letters* 226.

48. 8 *Letters* 1113–1114.

49. Ibid., p. 1114.

50. 5 *Letters* 21.

51. 3 *Letters* 289.

52. 5 *Letters* 396.

53. Quoted in Mowry, *The Era of Theodore Roosevelt*, p. 114.

5

Woodrow Wilson and Franklin D. Roosevelt

I expected the thought of Woodrow Wilson and FDR to reflect the influence of Hamilton's teaching, but neither Wilson nor FDR derived their theories of presidential power from Hamilton. Their theories, however, may help us to identify elements of the modern non- or anti-Hamiltonian theory of presidential power.

WILSON ON HAMILTON

One observer writes that Woodrow Wilson "seemed to be more of a Federalist than a Democrat, more of a Hamiltonian than a Jeffersonian."[1] During Wilson's 1912 campaign for the presidency he called Hamilton a "great man" but "not a great American."[2] In fact, Wilson excluded both Hamilton and Jefferson from his roster of great Americans. The influence of French philosophy disqualified Jefferson.[3] Wilson limited the concept of a great American to those who formed or represented a "distinctively American" greatness.[4] Wilson identified the "typical" American with a western or frontier origin, with the exception of George Washington.[5] John Adams and James Madison were, of course, excluded. Hamilton and Madison were unsuited to frontier life, said Wilson.[6] Arguing that Hamilton and Madison differed in their Americanism from Henry Clay, Andrew Jackson and Abraham Lincoln, Wilson preferred the latter trio without much reasoning to defend his choice.

Wilson described Hamilton as one of the "great Englishmen" reared in America but charged that Hamilton's statesmanship was European rather than American.[7] Another Wilsonian criticism was that Hamilton was an untypical American with "aristocratic" sympathies.[8] Wilson's rea-

soning confuses typicality and greatness, making the spurious argument
that Hamilton was an untypical, hence not a great, American. Nevertheless, it must be admitted that Wilson's criticism, with its echoes of
Jefferson, has influenced perceptions of what Hamilton stood for.

Wilson's private opinion of Hamilton's ability was more favorable than
his public appraisals of Hamilton's principles. President Wilson's confi-
dant, Colonel Edward House, reported that Wilson called Hamilton
"easily the ablest" of the Founding generation.[9] Wilson publicly praised
Hamilton's ability but criticized his alleged teachings in the context of
rallying the party faithful. Wilson told Philadelphia Democrats in 1911
that "most of us" must "dissent" from Hamilton's principles of government.[10] In 1912 Wilson informed a Jackson Day dinner that Hamilton
favored unequal, paternalistic government with greater power going to
the wealthy.[11] In a 1911 commencement address to the University of
North Carolina Wilson stated that he was a Democrat because he opposed
Hamilton's theory.[12]

Wilson made two exceptions to his public denigration of Hamilton,
on the tariff and the form of the Union. In 1909 Wilson described
Hamilton as "the great statesman" who had originated a protective tariff
in the public interest.[13] Discussing American ideals in 1901, Wilson held
that the Union had altered in a Hamiltonian rather than a Jeffersonian
direction.[14] Finally, in 1901 Wilson urged the Princeton University Law
Club to follow Hamilton by seeking "justice," not "popularity."[15] The
above remarks about Hamilton were the only exceptions to Wilson's
dictum that "most" of the "old formulas" of American politics were
exhausted.[16] A 1909 remark about Lincoln illuminates Wilson's parallel
skepticism toward the Founders. He asked in effect if his age could
imitate or be inspired by Lincoln. He replied that each age has its own
tasks.[17] Lincoln could shed no light on these tasks because Americans
cannot "live by recollection."[18] Wilson's theory of the living Constitution
answers the question of whether Americans can emulate the Founders.

WILSON'S LIVING CONSTITUTIONALISM

Wilson's consistent emulation of Hamilton or any of the Founders
would have been unlikely indeed because Wilson helped to popularize
the idea that the organic understanding of the Constitution was superior
to the original understanding. His *Constitutional Government in the United
States* weaves together the ideas of a "living political Constitution," centralization of power and the rejection of the Founders' intention. Wilson
finds that environmental conditions require a centralization of power
under the president.[19] The "makers of the Constitution," he wrote, "were
not making laws [sic] with the expectation that, not the laws themselves,

but their opinions, known by future historians to lie back of them, should govern the country."[20] "The Constitution contains no theories"; "it is a vehicle of life, and its spirit is always the spirit of the age."[21]

Wilson's safeguard against the abuse of presidential power is the president's avoidance of "deeply immoral" actions "destructive of the fundamental understandings of constitutional government and, therefore, of constitutional government itself."[22] How can Wilson's living Constitution contain "no theories" and yet contain the interdictory rules of the "fundamental understandings of constitutional government?" His notion of a living Constitution both demands and rejects a limitation comparable to Hamilton's original understanding of a final, objective and binding law of nature. Lacking such a limitation, Wilson teaches that the "personal force of the President is perfectly constitutional to *any* extent to which he chooses to exercise it."[23] "The President is at liberty, both in law and in conscience, to be as big a man as he can. His capacity will set the limit."[24] Wilson accordingly omits the idea of individual rights: "Our definition of liberty is that it is the best practicable adjustment between the powers of government and the *privileges* of the individual."[25] Liberty for Wilson concerns not rights claimable against the national government, including the president, but withdrawable privileges.

In sum: Wilson's theory of presidential power is even more reckless than Theodore Roosevelt's and is based on statism or a theory of highly centralized power. Moreover, Wilson's theory is incompatible with Hamilton's teaching, just as Wilson's organic theory of the Constitution is incompatible with Hamilton's understanding of the Constitution, not to mention Hamilton's ultimate grounds of right political action. Neither Hamilton's influence nor agreement with Hamilton may be found in Wilson's theory of presidential power, which squints at tyranny.

WILSON'S PREMISES: POSITIVISM AND HISTORICISM

Wilson's methodological premises further distanced him from the Founders and the Founding. "Although Wilson was not a moral relativist, certainly not a consistent one, his thought bears witness to two of its forms . . . positivism and historicism."[26] Wilson's dichotomy between politics and administration, said Paul Eidelberg, "corresponds precisely to the positivistic dichotomy between questions of *fact* and questions of *value*."[27] Science can pronounce on facts but is incapable of discriminating among values.

Wilson also subscribed to historicism, at least when he wrote his famous 1886 article, "The Study of Administration." "Political philosophy," wrote Wilson, "like philosophy of every other kind, has only held up the mirror to contemporary affairs."[28] Wilson quoted Hegel on the cultural shackles of reason: "The philosophy of any time is, as Hegel says, 'nothing but the spirit of that time expressed in abstract thought.' "[29] Our public law, said Wilson, is an "historical growth."[30] "We are farther than most of us realize from the times and policy of the framers of the Constitution."[31] As a result of his historicism, Wilson found himself unable to read the *Federalist* with sympathetic understanding: the *Federalist* now seems "tedious" to us.[32] Wilson tried to turn students of the Constitution away from the object of their study: "We are inclined, oftentimes, to take the laws and constitutions too seriously."[33]

Richard Longaker correctly criticized Wilson's conception of the presidency: "the basic miscalculation that led to all the others was his conviction that 'the President is at liberty both in law and conscience to be as big a man as he can.' "[34] In a related criticism David Cronon finds that "one of the greatest blots on Wilson's wartime leadership" was in civil liberties: "the Espionage and Sedition Acts of 1917 and 1918 gave the government dangerously broad authority to punish unpatriotic and subversive activity."[35] Much scholarship on Wilson fails to perceive in his basic miscalculation concerning the presidency a love of extreme that rules out the moderation associated with the skilled republican executive since Washington.[36]

We now turn to Franklin Roosevelt's understanding of Hamilton.

FDR ON HAMILTON

As a Harvard University senior, FDR wrote a "most adulatory and inaccurate essay on Alexander Hamilton."[37] His essay "did not mention the *Federalist*."[38] Thus FDR overlooked Hamilton's genius in interpreting and in securing the ratification of the Constitution. This surprising omission was characteristic of FDR's later remarks on Hamilton, which tended to ignore Hamilton's constructive statesmanship outside of economics and which resulted in a false picture of Hamilton's teachings.

On December 3, 1925 Roosevelt reviewed Claude Bowers's *Jefferson and Hamilton* for the New York *Evening World*. Hamilton, according to FDR, has the "true character of aristocrat and convinced opponent of popular government." "Hamiltons we have today. Is a Jefferson on the horizon?"[39] This review expressed Roosevelt's complete support for Jefferson over Hamilton, and it showed that FDR "had already matured the present-minded view of history which he would evince so frequently later in the White House."[40] Albert Fried called the early New Deal "neo-Hamiltonian" in "policies."[41] Historian Merrill Peterson wrote of the New Deal that "its administrative theory and practice, its fiscal apparatus, its political economy were Hamiltonian."[42]

FDR's references to Hamilton in the 1932 campaign hardly square with the influence argument made by Fried and Peterson. In his Jefferson Day dinner address of April 18, 1932, for example, Roosevelt remarked: "It is not necessary for us in any way to discredit the great financial genius of Alexander Hamilton or the school of thought of the early Federalists to point out that they were frank in their belief that certain sections of the nation and certain individuals within those sections were more fitted than others to conduct government."[43] Roosevelt discussed a speech by Eugene Meyer, governor of the Federal Reserve Board, in behalf of the creation of a Reconstruction Finance Corporation. Meyer had said that the "strong are afraid of the weak and the main object aimed at is the removal of that fear from the strong institutions, so that they may go ahead and conduct business in a normal way." "This," said FDR, "is spoken in the true Hamiltonian tradition."[44]

In his "Campaign Address on Progressive Government" to the Commonwealth Club, September 23, 1932, Roosevelt held that after the American Revolution some Americans came to believe that "popular government was essentially dangerous and essentially unworkable.... we cannot deny that their experience had warranted some measure of fear. The most brilliant, honest and able exponent of this point of view was Hamilton.... Fundamentally he believed that the safety of the republic lay in the autocratic strength of its government."[45] Out of the "great political duel" between Hamilton and Jefferson "came the two parties, Republican and Democratic, as we know them today."[46] Roosevelt was on shaky ground in depicting Hamilton as the founder of the Republican party, whose first great statesman was Abraham Lincoln.

At the Jackson Day dinner, January 8, 1940, Roosevelt praised Hamilton as a "hero...in spite of his position that the nation would be safer if our leaders were chosen exclusively from persons of higher education and of substantial property ownership; he is a hero because he did the job which then had to be done—to bring stability out of the chaos of currency and banking difficulties."[47] FDR's address of September 20, 1940 at the University of Pennsylvania argued that "with the gaining of our political freedom...there came a conflict between the point of view of Alexander Hamilton, sincerely believing in the superiority of government by a small group of public-spirited and usually wealthy citizens, and...the point of view of Thomas Jefferson."[48] In a departure from his previous statements, FDR showed that Hamilton's position was not entirely unreasonable: "Many of the Jeffersonian school of thought were frank to admit the high motives and disinterestedness of Hamilton and his school. Many Americans of those days were willing to concede that if government could be guaranteed to be kept always on the high level of unselfish service suggested by the Hamiltonians there would be nothing to fear." Hamilton, said FDR, relied on elections every four years, "limited to the votes of the most highly educated and the most successful citizens." FDR endorsed Jefferson's criticism of Hamilton in this controversy: "It was...with rare perspicuity, as time has shown, that Jefferson pointed out that, on the doctrine of sheer human frailty, the Hamilton theory was bound to develop, in the long run, into government by selfishness or government for personal gain or government by class, that would ultimately lead to the abolishment of free elections. For he recognized that it was our system of free unhampered elections which was the surest guarantee of popular government."

FDR ON JEFFERSON

It is instructive to compare FDR's support of Jefferson with his criticism of Hamilton. According to Albert Fried, later in the New Deal Roosevelt "affirmed a philosophy of neo-Jeffersonianism."[49] Actually, FDR's worship of Jefferson antedated the New Deal. In 1927 Roosevelt wrote to his mother that Jefferson "had a better insight into the republican form of government than did G. Washington or A. Hamilton. A century and a quarter have proved this."[50] According to Alfred Jones, "a renewed Jefferson symbol provided a partisan standard for the campaign and election of 1932," whereas the Lincoln image emerged in FDR's second administration.[51] In his Jefferson Day dinner address of 1932, Roosevelt praised Benjamin Franklin, Thomas Jefferson and Theodore Roosevelt because they "chiefly stand out for the universality of their interest and of their knowledge."[52] FDR said that "of the three Jefferson was in many ways the deepest student—the one with the most inquiring and diversified intellect and, above all, the one who at all times looked the farthest into the future."[53]

In 1935 Roosevelt hailed the 400th anniversary of the printing of the first English Bible with a questionable interpretation of Jefferson's religiosity: "Learned as Jefferson was in the best of the ancient philosophers, he turned to the Bible as the source of his higher thinking and reasoning."[54] In his Jackson Day dinner address of January 8, 1940, FDR said that Jefferson remained "a hero to me despite the fact that the theories of the French revolutionists at times overexcited his practical judgment." Jefferson "did the big job that then had to be done—to establish the new republic as a real democracy based on universal suffrage and the inalienable rights of man, instead of a restricted suffrage in the hands of a small oligarchy."[55] The latter opinion is how FDR understood Hamilton. It is Jefferson's understanding of Hamilton without the extremism of Jefferson's language. The foregoing analysis shows that Roosevelt was in fundamental disagreement with Hamilton and that he sympathized with Jefferson.

FDR ON THE PRESIDENCY

Roosevelt's understanding of the presidency may be divided into power and purpose. In his First Inaugural Address of March 4, 1933

FDR said that if Congress failed to act and if the emergency was still critical, "I shall ask Congress for the one remaining instrument to meet the crisis—broad Executive powers to wage a war against the emergency, as great as the power that would be given me if we were in fact invaded by a foreign foe." Referring to FDR's declaration of a national bank holiday and gold embargo on March 6, 1933, Clinton Rossiter concluded that "presidential initiative, *even in defiance of the law and agreed constitutional theory*, remains this country's fundamental emergency instrument."[56] Rossiter concluded that the president may resort to "the *boundless* grant of executive authority found in the Constitution."[57] He spoke of Roosevelt's "self-portrait of a chief executive *endlessly* endowed with emergency authority."[58]

Roosevelt went to a non-Hamiltonian extreme in threatening Congress if Congress refused to repeal immediately a provision of the Emergency Price Control Act. His message to Congress of September 7, 1942 reads in part: "I ask the Congress to take this action by the first of October. Inaction on your part by that date will leave me with an inescapable responsibility to the people of this country to see to it that the war effort is no longer imperiled by threat of economic chaos. In the event that Congress should fail to act, and act adequately, I shall accept the responsibility, and I will act."

Edward S. Corwin concluded that "the message of September 7 can only be interpreted as a claim of power on the part of the President to suspend the Constitution in a situation deemed by him to make such a step necessary. . . . Mr. Roosevelt was proposing to set aside, not a particular clause of the Constitution, but its most fundamental characteristic, its division of power between Congress and President, and thereby to gather into his own hands the combined power of both. He was suggesting, if not threatening, a virtually complete suspension of the Constitution."[59] President Roosevelt went far beyond his predecessors and successors in suggesting the weakening of Congress in a way that would have been inconceivable to Alexander Hamilton.

In addition to the detention of Japanese Americans during World War II, to be discussed in the next chapter, Roosevelt received a mixed verdict on whether he sufficiently used presidential power to promote civil liberties. Despite praise for FDR, sixty-four historians, political scientists, journalists, former White House aides, present and former members of Congress, law professors and civil liberties leaders judged that "every" American president since 1933 "failed in significant ways to give constitutional rights the sustained protection from the White House that our democracy requires."[60] Historians disagree over whether FDR properly supervised the FBI in its investigations of American citizens, with one historian arguing that the FBI itself stretched presidential directives under FDR and another historian arguing that the "sweeping domestic intelligence instructions that Roosevelt had given Hoover" had "eased the way for the development of FBI investigative autonomy."[61] Clearly, the disagreement is over the adequacy of presidential supervision and its impact on civil liberties. Another historian carries the criticism to FDR himself, who "was willing to use the FBI's resources for political as well as national security purposes": "In July 1940, President Roosevelt even ordered the FBI to investigate former President Hoover and his sec- retary."[62] This historian somewhat inconsistently concluded that never- theless "the Roosevelt administration was not insensitive to civil liberties," though the administration had used the FBI for "political" purposes.[63]

Roosevelt's doctrine of presidential power depended in part on his analysis of why dictatorships came to power in other countries: "dicta- torships do not grow out of strong and successful governments, but out of weak and helpless ones," FDR said in a Fireside Chat of April 14, 1938.[64] "Dictatorships," said Roosevelt in his 1940 Annual Message to Congress, "—and the philosophy of force that justifies and accompanies dictatorships—have originated in almost every case in the necessity for drastic action to improve internal conditions in places where democratic action for one reason or another has failed to respond to modern needs and modern demands."[65] The refusal to exercise governmental power, so he argued, "brought us to the brink of disaster in 1932."[66] The ar- gument that democracies may fail from an insufficiency of power, though somewhat plausible, does not establish limits of presidential power. It evades the question, what are the limits of presidential power? As governor of New York in 1929 FDR had attacked centralization with the argument that "every previous great concentration of power has been followed by some form of great disaster."[67] As president FDR abandoned the opinion that "great concentration of power" led to "great disaster." But how much power was the president permitted by the Constitution, according to FDR? He never forthrightly answered that question. Roosevelt sought power case by case, and whether out of cau- tion or incompetence, he failed to articulate the outer limits of presi- dential power. This omission is a defect in Roosevelt's explanation of the presidency.

Roosevelt's doctrine of presidential purpose was to understand the presidency as an office of moral leadership. The presidency, he said in November 1932, "is not merely an administrative office. That is the least of it. It is pre-eminently a place of moral leadership. All of our greatest Presidents were leaders of thought at times when certain historic ideas in the life of the nation had to be clarified. . . . That is what the office is—a superb opportunity for reapplying, applying to new conditions, the simple rules of human conduct to which we always go back."[68] What kind of moral leadership did he exert? His discussion of farm and tariff problems explicitly linked economic well-being and morality: "It is a moral as well as an economic question that we face.... We want the opportunity to live in comfort, reasonable comfort, out of which we may build spiritual values."[69] Roosevelt tended to assume that the desire for material "comfort" was finite and that, once a plateau of comfort had been reached, "spiritual values" would emerge more or less spontaneously. There is no clear subordination of material comfort to the higher claims of the human soul and reason.

Perhaps Roosevelt ought to have perceived that a preference for the well-being of the greater number does not add up to a comprehensive view of the good society or the common good. On a somewhat higher level ..., government would be concerned with creating a certain moral tone and encouraging the development of human excellence. FDR never reached that point, however, for he did not conceive of the function of government as fostering the development of virtue or human excellence. He considered the completion or perfection of the individual to be outside the framework of government as such, and was still guided by a rather limited view of happiness.[70]

FDR's moral leadership, then, excluded the fostering of human excellence.

Roosevelt's major achievement was the deflation of American principles, according to Edgar Kemler.[71] He attempted to trace the movement of opinion from the Progressive period to the New Deal.[72] He intended to "expose" or criticize the "inflation" of American principles in "progressive" or "liberal" history.[73] Kemler proposed to reveal the obstruction created by "inflated" principles for American liberalism.[74] His thesis was that liberalism gained in influence as it rid itself of "excess baggage" or underwent a doctrinal purge and simplification.[75] He identified the "excess" doctrines as "spiritual objectives," which were replaced by more realistic and attainable objectives in economics and politics.[76] To restore national income, FDR linked the New Deal to the business cycle, giving liberalism effectiveness at the price of its "spiritual content."[77]

American principles, including liberal ones, felt the impact of a "worldwide deflation of values."[78] Kemler understood the New Deal to be influenced by the decadence that accompanied the defeat of democracies overseas.[79] Changes in Western political philosophy also shaped the New Deal. Kemler divided political philosophy into the angelic and animalistic traditions, the latter of which shed more light on the present than the former.[80] His heroes among the animalistic thinkers included Machiavelli, Hobbes, Nietzsche and Spengler.[81] The deflation of principles in America reaches the point that in politics "we have even begun to question constitutional government itself."[82] Kemler does not elaborate on this interesting comment. In sum, the deflation of American principles resulted from the shift in the self-understanding of liberalism, FDR, the failure of democracies abroad and the change in Western political philosophy to animalistic teachings.

Kemler finds the deflation of American liberalism "on the whole" to have been "beneficial."[83] He failed to consider Tocqueville's critique of animalism or materialism: "Materialism, among all nations, is a dangerous disease of the human mind; but it is more especially to be dreaded among a democratic people because it readily amalgamates with that vice which is most familiar to the heart under such circumstances. Democracy encourages a taste for physical gratification."[84] "Power has been the crux of conduct" in the moral theory of the New Deal; Kemler asserts without argument that "a government devoted to self-aggrandizement ... is at least a starting point for a satisfactory ethos."[85] The ethos of such a government may well be only further self-aggrandizement. Kemler adds that the deflation of democracy to its "*lowest* terms, appeals to ... tendencies which make for better social living, such as desire for food and well-being."[86]

Kemler recognizes that "something" may be said against the deflation of American liberalism.[87] His criticism of past liberalism accused it of excessive loftiness.[88] New Deal liberalism abandons "ethical–religious" ends in favor of "political–economic" ends.[89] Could American statesmen and the American people somehow erect "spiritual values" on the foundation of corporeal satisfaction, as FDR had promised? Kemler finds "little hope" of spiritual improvement after the satisfaction of corporeal desires and calls this the "*most important*" part of the deflation of American liberalism.[90] He contends that Jefferson's emphasis on citizen activity and self-rule has given way to the New Deal's emphasis on passive reaction to a presidential hero. In short, because no ascent from materialism will occur, citizens are now confined to the worship of a heroic leader. "Under the New Deal we have deflated many American ideals."[91] But "we cannot deflate democracy much further."[92] The lack of a lofty moral end introduces confusion: "Perhaps ... in a future without crises, domestic or foreign, we should be at a loss as to what to do."[93] "What is necessary is that we have some idea of our long-run direction," but under the new liberalism "we are not sure where we are going, whether toward Fascism or socialism or somewhere else."[94] Finally, Kemler admits that "inflation [of moral principles] of itself does not condemn a policy."[95] In sum, FDR's moral leadership did not foster human excellence, but in combination with other causes lowered the goal to animalism. Kemler approves generally of the deflation of liberalism while pointing out certain costs and risks, principally the lack of direction.

I have argued earlier that Roosevelt departed from Hamilton's teaching on the presidency. An implicit recognition of this departure is the scholarly practice of interpreting the presidencies of Roosevelt and his important predecessors with ideas such as "constitutional dictatorship," "presidential prerogative" and "Caesarism." Let us first examine constitutional dictatorship.

CONSTITUTIONAL DICTATORSHIP, PREROGATIVE AND CAESARISM

FDR's broad claims of presidential power called forth reactions from various observers. For example, a widely read text in American history observed that "Roosevelt made clear . . . that the presidential power was pretty much what the President made it."[96] An American historian has argued that "the early Presidency under Roosevelt was a near dictatorial office."[97] Writing in 1938, a contemporary observer predicted that if forced to be a dictator, FDR would practice "constitutional despotism."[98] Frank Freidel, Roosevelt's biographer, assures us that the president wanted neither to imitate Mussolini and Hitler nor to assume a "constitutional dictatorship."[99] What is the meaning of that jarring phrase, constitutional dictatorship? For convenience let us first divide the problem into the meanings of constitution, constitutional, dictator and dictatorship. In the fourteenth century *constitution* meant a decree, ordinance, law or regulation, usually one made by a superior authority, civil or ecclesiastical. In Roman law *constitution* meant an enactment by the emperor.[100] In the seventeenth century *constitution* referred to the mode in which a state was constituted or organized, especially as to the location of sovereign power. First in 1689, *constitution* meant the system or body of fundamental principles according to which a nation, state or body politic is constituted and governed. For Sir William Blackstone (1765) *constitutional* meant in harmony with, or authorized by, the political constitution.[101] *Dictator*, a term of Roman origin, meant a ruler or governor whose word was law, an absolute ruler of a state and, first in the sixteenth century, one who attains such a position in a republic.[102] *Dictatorship*, first in 1586, referred to the office or dignity of a dictator and, first in the seventeenth century, to absolute authority in any sphere. A contemporary pejorative understanding of *dictator* is one who assumes absolute control in a government without hereditary right or the free consent of the people; in ancient Rome *dictator* referred to a person constitutionally invested with supreme authority during a crisis, the regular magistracy being subordinated to him until the crisis was met.[103] *Dictator* and *dictatorship*, then, may have neutral, favorable or unfavorable connotations, depending on when the words were used, and the terms have referred to republican regimes. I found no historical dictionary definitions of *constitutional dictatorship* as a compound term. This suggests that the term is quite specialized and of fairly recent origin.

Carl Friedrich's 1937 discussion of constitutional dictatorship emphasizes the appointment of the dictator according to precise constitutional forms, that the dictator must not be invested with discretion to begin or end the state of emergency, that the dictator's powers must defend the existing constitutional order rather than destroy it and the imposition of a strict time limit for the exercise of concentrated dictatorial power.[104] He criticizes the inadequacy of modern constitutional limitations in the United States, according to the above standards. Writing in 1940 with explicit reference to the United States, Frederick Watkins illustrated a difficulty in defining constitutional dictatorship if constitutionalism is understood as a system of government where law restrains the rulers and absolutism or dictatorship "consists in the absence of such restraints."[105] Thus a constitutional dictatorship would seem to be a contradiction in terms. A regime is either constitutional or a dictatorship, but it cannot be both at the same time.

Watkins gives further evidence of the conflict between constitutionalism and dictatorship in writing that although "the *main function* of constitutional dictatorship is to do positive service in the cause of constitutional government," "the *basic problem* of constitutional dictatorship is to increase the effectiveness of *executive* action"; "the *main task* of constitutional dictatorship is . . . to provide freedom in the realm of administration."[106] Watkins's effort to reconcile constitutionalism and dictatorship tends to gloss over the contradiction in favor of dictatorship while borrowing from the prestige of constitutionalism to make dictatorship palatable. Another difficulty in Watkins's account is that while he often refers to the ethical basis of modernity, "the cause of political liberalism," "liberal institutions," "nineteenth century liberalism," "liberal" judges and "political liberalism," he fails to examine the consistency of constitutional dictatorship with liberal political philosophy and the American Constitution.[107] Thus his conclusion, that "our present day arrangements leave much to be desired" in comparison with emergency institutions of ancient Rome, does not demonstrate that the United States should or could imitate Rome.[108] Watkins is on sounder ground in arguing that the United States has failed to surround executive emergency powers with adequate limitations.[109]

Another question concerning the idea of constitutional dictatorship is its applicability to American presidential history. For example, Clinton Rossiter argued that "it is stretching the point considerably to say that any American government has ever been a constitutional dictatorship."[110] But Rossiter described Lincoln as "the greatest of constitutional dictators."[111] Rossiter continued that "Lincoln's actions form history's most illustrious precedent for constitutional dictatorship," and he characterized FDR's presidency as "America's most recent constitutional dictatorship."[112] Furthermore, Rossiter refers to the Civil War, World War I, the Great Depression and World War II as America's "four experiences in constitutional dictatorship": "executive initiative has come to be the basic technique of constitutional dictatorship in this country."[113] Rossiter, then, unwittingly undermines his conclusion that the United States has never been a constitutional dictatorship when he analyzes the presidencies of Lincoln, Wilson and FDR.

What are some of the problems of constitutional dictatorship in America? First, "executives will usually ask for more power than they really need, and...courts are powerless to obstruct or even mitigate their demands."[114] Second, although "no constitutional dictator should be self-appointed," Lincoln and FDR were both self-appointed constitutional dictators.[115] This violated the prudential rule that the power to begin and terminate a constitutional dictatorship should never be in the hands of the dictator himself. Third, both Lincoln and FDR trespassed the boundaries of the constitutional presidency.[116] Fourth, the threat of impeachment, judicial review of presidential acts and elections have proved to be insufficient checks on the dictators.[117] Fifth, with post-Watergate hindsight it can be seen that the character of the president is an insufficient safeguard against the abuse of power.[118] Sixth, and most important, the idea of constitutional dictatorship is not a value-neutral idea but a plea for a new constitutional understanding. Rossiter, for example, argued that "if successful constitutional dictatorship involves either a union of the ordinarily separated powers or a simple disregard of that hoary principle of constitutionalism, then it would seem axiomatic that the less rigidly a government conforms to the separation of powers, the more easily it can adapt itself to the rigors of any particular crisis."[119] This is nothing less than advice from the foremost student of emergency presidential power to set aside one of the important features of the Constitution.

In sum, Clinton Rossiter is inconsistent on whether the United States has experienced constitutional dictatorship. His account also lacks convincing moral and constitutional limits on presidential power in emergencies. This latter defect is due to his failure to understand constitutional dictatorship in light of liberal political philosophy. As we have seen, Rossiter's constitutional dictatorship is thinly disguised advocacy of presidential supremacy. At first Rossiter appears to give a balanced treatment, concluding that "constitutional dictatorship in the United States must be made more constitutional and more dictatorial."[120] But Rossiter's book offers "two general proposals," one of which is that "the inherent emergency power of the President of the United States ...should be left intact and untrammeled."[121] The clue to Rossiter's final position on constitutional limitations is that "the positive state is here to stay, and from now on the accent will be on *power, not limitations*."[122] Thus he urges his readers to bow before the trend of history. Rossiter's notion of constitutional dictatorship tends to maximize allowable presidential power during emergencies at the expense of constitutional limitations. Yet "constitutional dictatorship" aptly describes the regime of FDR and illuminates the course of presidential power from Lincoln.

Lockean prerogative power refers to the executive's discretion to act without a law or sometimes even against the letter of the law for the public good. According to Rossiter, this "Lockean theory of prerogative has found a notable instrument in the President of the United States."[123] Rossiter implies that grafting Locke's prerogative onto the American presidency poses no constitutional problems. A later student of Locke and the American Constitution, however, has argued that "Lockean prerogative is incompatible with constitutional government: ... in order to claim Lockean prerogative, the President would have to circumvent the Constitution and appeal directly to the people as the legitimate source of his powers. The dangers of allowing the powers of the President to be determined by public opinion rather than by the Constitution should be evident."[124] The inclusion in the Constitution of specific provisions for dealing with emergencies "suggests that there is no general emergency power to act outside the Constitution."[125] Prerogative, then, is completely within the Constitution in the form of provisions such as the habeas corpus suspension, and not in inherent presidential power.[126] Dictatorship by the prerogative powers of the executive, Frederick Watkins reminds us, "has ... been regarded at all times as the most dangerous form" and is far inferior to dictatorship by legislative delegation.[127] In short, Arnhart's argument against a presidential prerogative is more carefully reasoned than Rossiter's celebration of prerogative. Let us turn to the third concept, Caesarism, that is put forward to explain and evaluate the modern presidency.

After trying to prove the compatibility of presidential prerogative and the American Constitution, Richard Pious finally concedes that "no set of standards for the exercise of emergency prerogatives can provide an absolute guarantee against Caesarism."[128] What is presidential Caesarism? Amaury de Riencourt, the foremost interpreter of Caesarism, distinguishes "strong presidents" from Caesars, who combine "personal rule" with permanence.[129] At times Riencourt merely emphasizes the Caesarian *"potential"* of the presidency.[130] More often, however, he stresses the *"inevitable* trend" toward a Caesarian presidency as a "counterpart" of democratic equality.[131] He exonerates FDR and other presidents of Caesarian intentions because Caesarism springs from "circumstances" rather than from personal desires.[132] Riencourt depicted FDR as the "first of the outstanding *pre*-Caesarians" who cast a "lengthening shadow" of Caesarism.[133] The New Deal marked a "decisive step" to Caesarism.[134] Yet this occurred "constitutionally" by stretching America's flexible political institutions: Riencourt implied that American political institutions do not favor limited constitutional government. FDR exercised powers of "truly

Caesarian magnitude"; the shadows of Caesarism appeared in FDR's 1940 campaign and came, "as always," from the "people."[135]

Riencourt leaves unclear how fully FDR's presidency led to Caesarism. On the one hand, he describes FDR's World War II power and authority as only a *"premonition"* of coming Caesarism, and on the other hand, Riencourt concludes that the United States "gradually" passed from being a republic to a "Caesarian monarchy" under FDR.[136] The precise stage of Caesarism during FDR's presidency is left as obscure as the responsibility for Caesarism of the statesman himself, "historical necessity," "historical evolution," or "uncontrollable historical forces."[137] But Riencourt elsewhere argues in effect against historical necessity: he calls freedom of the will "man's greatest human asset."[138] He implies that because Americans are free to act, they can resist Caesarism.

A similar unclarity pervades Riencourt's remarks on ethical principles. He first criticizes American ethical thought as insufficiently historical: he calls "psychological blindness" the American habit of thinking in light of "an absolute and timeless justice that excluded all *historical relativity*."[139] Related to presidential power is what Riencourt laments as the prospect of the "death" of the "Western soul."[140] Here he abandons the historical relativity of ethical principles and advocates a return to classical virtue.[141] He recommends the diffusion of virtue among the "elite."[142] He rejects the "psychological collectivism" of contemporary America.[143] *"If they eventually materialize,"* the future Caesars will be only a reflection of the "death" of the "Western soul."[144] This implies that there is time to act and that historical necessity does not drive America toward Caesarism. Riencourt also departs from his thesis of historical relativity in his praise of America, which "alone" has the "moral ideals" necessary for civilization and stability.[145] "American society comes closer to the utopia men have been dreaming of for thousands of years than any other in the world."[146] Moral principles and regimes, Riencourt concludes, are not historically relative in spite of his apparent attachment to historical relativity.

It remains only to summarize Riencourt's doctrine of the causes of Caesarism and of the false cures he warns against. "Caesarism . . . is a slow, organic growth within a society tending toward democratic equality."[147] "The gradual convergence of historical trends joins ever closer together the unconscious longing for Caesarism and the external emergencies that bring it about."[148] "Wars are the main harbingers of Caesarism."[149] Caesarism in America is "considerably eased" by certain facilitating conditions, among which are, most important, democratic equality with its conformity and psychological standardization, the constitutional status of the presidency, the "almost ripe" psychological climate and the tastes and habits of the American people, including hero worship.[150] Institutional cures, such as checks and balances and legis-lation, cannot curb Caesarism, "a psychological alteration that by-passes specific institutions."[151] Institutional cures deal only with symptoms, "not the profound disease...the death of our Western soul."[152] The true cure is to discover "the ways and means of reviving our moribund Culture while retaining all the good and necessary features of Civilization."[153]

CONCLUSIONS

Woodrow Wilson respected Hamilton's ability but denied that he was a representative or great American and disagreed with most of Hamil-ton's teachings. Wilson proposed a living Constitution and the central-ization of power under the president as an alternative to the Founders' Constitution. Wilson inconsistently favored a relativistic notion of the Constitution and stable, objective moral limits on presidential power. Wilson's genuine teaching is not that presidential power should be con-stitutionally limited but that the president's "capacity will set the limit." Wilson's theory makes constitutional and moral restraints almost mean-ingless. His theory of presidential power is more extreme than Theodore Roosevelt's and derives in no way from Hamilton's *Federalist* papers and Pacificus Letters. Wilson failed to refute Hamilton's teachings but de-toured around them. Neither Hamilton's influence, inspiration nor agreement with Hamilton may be found in Wilson's theories of presi-dential power and the Constitution.

FDR mildly praised Hamilton's intentions while strongly criticizing his principles in a Jeffersonian vein. As a interpreter of presidential power FDR failed either to follow Hamilton's principles or to join the issues in argument with Hamilton. Like Woodrow Wilson, FDR did not refute Hamilton so much as he turned away from the Founding. Instead of reappropriating old republican wisdom for new circumstances, FDR shied away from articulating the outer limits of presidential power. Thus a considerable distance separates Hamilton's legitimizing of presidential power and FDR's contentions about the presidency. I am suggesting not that FDR failed to speak some necessary truths about presidential power for the 1930s and 1940s but that his particular truths did not add up to a coherent understanding of presidential power under the Constitution.

FDR also understood the presidency as a center of moral leadership. Hamilton expected the presidency to deal with the conditions of hap-piness, but FDR aimed at supplying well-being or happiness itself, under-stood as the satiation of material desire or freedom from want. The desire for material comfort does not appear to be finite or easily satisfied. Thus the moral end of the New Deal compounds the difficulty of en-forcing moderation and avoiding an excess of presidential power. The lofty standards of Hamilton and Washington reveal that the modern aggrandizement of presidential power serves a low moral end; the scope of presidential power serving this end exceeds what Hamilton and Washington knew could be safely exercised in a constitutional republic. This would be so even if it could be demonstrated that the moral end of the New Deal was more just than the Founder's regime. In sum, FDR's thought on the presidency failed to establish the limits of presidential power or to exert moral leadership above the level of catering to animal wants.

This chapter also investigated the ideas of constitutional dictatorship, presidential prerogative and Caesarism that are often treated as alternatives to Hamilton's teachings. In general these ideas are not an adequate substitute for Hamilton's understanding of the presidency. First, there is the inconsistency of constitutionalism and dictatorship, the question of the applicability of constitutional dictatorship to American presidential history and the lack of objectivity of Rossiter's formulation of constitutional dictatorship. The idea of presidential prerogative was effectively criticized as incompatible with the Constitution. Contrary to his thesis of historical relativity, Riencourt, the expounder of Caesarism, advocates the recovery of classical virtue as the way to halt the standardization of popular character that promotes Caesarism. The presentation of Caesarism abounds in inconsistencies, but *The Coming Caesars* usefully sounds the alarm for what could happen if the deterioration of popular character remains unchecked. The idea of Caesarism is superior to Rossiter's idea of constitutional dictatorship in describing the consequences and risks of the enlargement of presidential power. Riencourt makes a plausible, if incomplete, case that Caesarism springs from declining individualism and external emergencies, and his advocacy of virtue agrees with his analysis of the genesis of Caesarism.

The next chapter discusses the arguments of Edward S. Corwin, Clinton Rossiter and Richard Neustadt in order better to appraise the scholarly anti-Hamiltonian idea of presidential power.

NOTES

1. Raymond B. Fosdick, "Personal Recollections of Woodrow Wilson," in Earl Latham, ed., *The Philosophy and Politics of Woodrow Wilson* (Chicago: University of Chicago Press, 1958), p. 34.

2. John Wells Davidson, ed., *A Crossroads of Freedom* (New Haven: Yale University Press, 1956), p. 57.

3. "A Calendar of Great Americans," in 8 *Papers of Woodrow Wilson* 373 (1893), Arthur Link, ed. (Princeton, N.J.: Princeton University Press, 1966–1988); hereafter cited as *Papers* preceded by the volume number and followed by the page number.

4. 8 *Papers* 369.

5. Review of Goldwin Smith, *The United States: An Outline of Political History*, 8 *Papers* 354.

6. Ibid., p. 355.

7. 8 *Papers* 369.

8. 12 *Papers* 353.

9. Diary of Colonel House, 1914, 29 *Papers* 448.

10. 22 *Papers* 444.

11. 24 *Papers* 11; see a similar statement in "An Evening Address in Buffalo," 1912, 25 *Papers* 84.

12. 23 *Papers* 108.

13. 19 *Papers* 465.

14. 12 *Papers* 216.

15. 20 *Papers* 229.

16. 19 *Papers* 465.

17. Ibid., p. 44.

18. Ibid., p. 45.

19. Woodrow Wilson, *Constitutional Government in the United States* (New York: Columbia University Press, 1921 [1908]), p. 56.

20. Ibid., p. 70.

21. Ibid., p. 69.

22. Ibid., p. 71.

23. Ibid., pp. 71–72, italics added.

24. Ibid., p. 70. President Richard Nixon repeatedly avowed that "I have always been, and am, a great admirer of Woodrow Wilson." *Public Papers of the President: Richard Nixon, 1972* (Washington, D.C.: Government Printing Office, 1974), p. 679. "I have long been a student of Woodrow Wilson"; "I have read most of what he has written." *Public Papers of the President: Richard Nixon, 1971* (Washington, D.C.: Government Printing Office, 1972), p. 187. Jeffrey Tulis has argued that both the Founders and Wilson wanted an energetic presidency. For the Founders the president draws energy from his authority, which comes from his independent constitutional position, but for Wilson and for succeeding presidents power and authority are conferred directly by the people. Jeffrey Tulis, "The Two Constitutional Presidencies," in Michael Nelson, ed., *The Presidency and the Political System* (Washington, D.C.: Congressional Quarterly Press, 1984), p. 81. Wilson, however, places fewer restraints on presidential power than Alexander Hamilton did in the *Federalist* and Pacificus Letters.

25. Wilson, *Constitutional Government in the United States*, p. 18, italics added.

26. Paul Eidelberg, *A Discourse on Statesmanship* (Urbana: University of Illinois Press, 1974), p. 301.

27. Ibid., p. 300, italics in the original.

28. 5 *Papers* 361.

29. Ibid.

30. Ibid., p. 496.

31. From Wilson, *Congressional Government* (1885), quoted in August Heckscher, ed. *The Politics of Woodrow Wilson* (New York: Harper, 1956), p. 2.

32. 7 *Papers* 367.

33. 5 *Papers* 403.

34. Richard P. Longaker, "Woodrow Wilson and the Presidency," in Latham, *The Philosophy and Policies of Woodrow Wilson*, p. 80.

35. David Cronon, ed. *The Political Thought of Woodrow Wilson* (Indianapolis: Bobbs Merrill, 1965), p. 393; see also Harry Scheiber, *The Wilson Administration and Civil Liberties, 1917–1921* (Ithaca, N.Y.: Cornell University Press, 1960).

36. See Wilson's theoretical preference for Aristotle over Tocqueville for the connection between moderation and wisdom. Tocqueville "too often attempted to explain everything.... This is what Aristotle would not have done. He had too much moderation, too fine sagaciousness. This is the difference between first and second genius." 2 *Papers* 296.

37. James MacGregor Burns, *Roosevelt: The Lion and the Fox* (New York: Harcourt, Brace, 1956), p. 20.

38. Frank Freidel, *Franklin D. Roosevelt: The Apprenticeship* (Boston: Little, Brown, 1952), p. 61 note.

39. Albert Fried, ed., *The Jeffersonian and Hamiltonian Traditions in American Politics* (Garden City, N.Y.: Anchor Doubleday Books, 1968), p. 392.

40. Alfred H. Jones, *Roosevelt's Image Brokers* (Port Washington, N.Y.: Kennikat Press, 1974), p. 27.

41. Fried, *The Jeffersonian and Hamiltonian Traditions in American Politics*, p. 403.

42. Merrill Peterson, *The Jeffersonian Image in the American Mind* (New York: Oxford University Press, 1960), p. 359.

43. 1 *The Public Papers and Addresses of Franklin D. Roosevelt* 628 (New York: Random House, 1938); hereafter cited as *Public Papers*, preceded by the volume number and followed by the page number.

44. Ibid., p. 631.

45. Ibid., p. 745.

46. Ibid., p. 746.

47. 9 *Public Papers* 30 (New York: Macmillan, 1941).

48. Ibid., p. 436; the passage on Jefferson's "rare perspicuity" comes from p. 437.

49. Fried, *The Jeffersonian and Hamiltonian Traditions in American Politics*, p. 406.

50. 2 *FDR: His Personal Letters* 629 (New York: Duell, Sloan and Pearce, 1948).

51. Jones, *Roosevelt's Image Brokers*, p. 29.

52. 1 *Public Papers* 628.

53. Ibid., pp. 628–629.

54. 4 *Public Papers* 419 (New York: Random House, 1938).

55. 9 *Public Papers* 30.

56. Clinton Rossiter, *Constitutional Dictatorship* (Princeton, N.J.: Princeton University Press, 1948), p. 258, italics added.

57. Ibid., p. 286; my italics.

58. Clinton Rossiter, "War, Depression, and the Presidency, 1933–1950," 17 *Social Research* 438 (1950), italics added.

59. Edward S. Corwin, *The President: Office and Powers* (4th rev. ed.; New York: New York University, 1957), p. 252.

60. Alan F. Westin and Trudy Hayden, "Presidents and Civil Liberties from

FDR to Ford: A Rating by 64 Experts," 3 *Civil Liberties Review* 9 (October–November, 1976).

61. Athan G. Theoharis, "The FBI's Stretching of Presidential Directives, 1936–1953," 91 *Political Science Quarterly* 649–672 (1976–1977); Roy Turnbaugh, "The FBI and Harry Elmer Barnes: 1936–1944," 42 *The Historian* 389, 387 (1980).

62. Kenneth O'Reilly, "A New Deal for the FBI: The Roosevelt Administration, Crime Control, and National Security," 69 *Journal of American History* 647, 649 (1982).

63. Ibid., p. 651.

64. 7 *Public Papers* 242 (New York: Macmillan, 1941).

65. 9 *Public Papers* 1.

66. 6 *Public Papers* LXI, Introduction (New York: Macmillan, 1941).

67. Quoted in Thomas H. Greer, *What Roosevelt Thought* (East Lansing: Michigan State University, 1958), p. 79.

68. *New York Times*, November 13, 1932, Sec. 8, p. 1, quoted in Greer, *What Roosevelt Thought*, p. 105.

69. Campaign Address, Sioux City, Iowa, September 29, 1932, quoted in Greer, *What Roosevelt Thought*, p. 10.

70. Morton J. Frisch, *Franklin D. Roosevelt: The Contribution of the New Deal to American Political Thought and Practice* (Boston: Twayne, 1975), p. 116; some examples of Roosevelt's thinking about happiness are "security for the individual and for the family," 3 *Public Papers* 288 (New York: Random House, 1938); "more of the good things of life," "places to go in the summertime—recreation," assurance that one won't starve in his old age, and "a chance to earn a living." 4 *Public Papers* 236–237.

71. Edgar Kemler, *The Deflation of American Ideals: An Ethical Guide for New Dealers* (Washington, D.C.: American Council on Public Affairs, 1941), p. 6.

72. Ibid., p. 29.

73. Ibid., pp. 136, 23.

74. Ibid., p. 166.

75. Ibid., p. 25.

76. Ibid., p. 26.

77. Ibid., p. 45.

78. Ibid., p. 21.

79. Ibid., p. 4.

80. Ibid., p. 14.

81. Ibid., pp. 16–17.

82. Ibid., p. 5.

83. Ibid., p. 5.

84. Tocqueville, *Democracy in America*, II, Bk. 2, xv.

85. Kemler, *Deflation*, p. 8.

86. Ibid., p. 21, italics added; cf. note 70 above.

87. Kemler, *Deflation*, p. 72.

88. Ibid., p. 71.

89. Ibid., p. 29.

90. Ibid., pp. 108–109, italics added.

91. Ibid., p. 151.

92. Ibid., p. 38.

93. Ibid., p. 72.

94. Ibid., pp. 149, 72.

95. Ibid., p. 136.

96. Samuel E. Morison, Henry S. Commager, and William E. Leuchtenburg, 2 *The Growth of the American Republic* 524 (6th ed.; New York: Oxford University, 1969).

97. Paul Conkin, *The New Deal* (New York: Thomas Y. Crowell, 1967), p. 90.

98. Basil Maine, *Franklin Roosevelt His Life and Achievement* (London: John Murray, 1938), p. 239.

99. Frank Freidel, *Franklin D. Roosevelt Launching the New Deal* (Boston: Little, Brown, 1973), pp. 205, 247.

100. 2 *Oxford English Dictionary* 876 (1933); hereafter cited as *OED* preceded by the volume number and followed by the page number.

101. Ibid., p. 877.

102. 3 *OED* 330.

103. *The Random House Dictionary of the English Language* (1967), p. 400.

104. Carl J. Friedrich, *Constitutional Government and Politics* (New York: Harper and Brothers, 1937), pp. 215–219; see also Friedrich, *Constitutional Government and Democracy* (4th ed.; Waltham: Blaisdell, 1968), pp. 557–581.

105. Frederick M. Watkins, "The Problem of Constitutional Dictatorship," *Public Policy* (1940), p. 324.

106. Ibid., pp. 340, 345, Watkins's italics for "executive."

107. Ibid., pp. 379, 346, 350, 375.

108. Ibid., p. 378.

109. Ibid., pp. 378, 354–57.

110. Rossiter, *Constitutional Dictatorship*, p. 209; see also p. 286.

111. Ibid., p. 299.

112. Ibid., pp. 239, 285.

113. Ibid., pp. 285, 218.

114. Ibid., p. 299.

115. Ibid., pp. 299, 219.

116. Ibid., pp. 228, 283.

117. Watkins, *Public Policy* 354–356 (1940); Edgar E. Robinson, *The Roosevelt Leadership, 1933–1945* (Philadelphia: J. B. Lippincott, 1955), pp. 400, 408.

118. See Clinton Rossiter, "Constitutional Dictatorship in the Atomic Age," 11 *Review of Politics* 409 (October, 1949): "I realize that I am wandering somewhat afield from the fundamental traditions of Western democracy in asserting that the character of the chief executive is our most important single safeguard against the dangers of temporary emergency dictatorship.... 160 years, 32 Presidents, and still no despot or profligate or scoundrel has made the grade." In *Constitutional Dictatorship*, p. 212, Rossiter argued that "the Bill of Rights, federalism, and the separation of powers are the three main constitutional barriers to the easy establishment of emergency dictatorship in the United States. These are the principles of the American system which must be in whole or in part suspended if such government is to be inaugurated in a national emergency." At ibid., p. 286, Rossiter identifies the "limitations" on presidential constitutional

dictatorship as "the political sense of the incumbent and the patience of the American people."

119. Rossiter, *Constitutional Dictatorship*, p. 154.

120. Ibid., p. 308.

121. For a contrary view of alleged inherent presidential power, see Lucius Wilmerding, Jr., "The President and the Law," 67 *Political Science Quarterly* 321–338 (September, 1952).

122. Rossiter, *Constitutional Dictatorship*, p. 314, italics added; for a moderate discussion of presidential emergency powers, see A. S. Klieman, "Preparing for the Hour of Need: Emergency Powers in the United States," 41 *Review of Politics* 235–255 (April, 1979).

123. Rossiter, *Constitutional Dictatorship*, p. 218.

124. Larry Arnhart, " 'The God-Like Prince': John Locke, Executive Prerogative, and the American Presidency," 9 *Presidential Studies Quarterly* 125 (1979).

125. Ibid., p. 129.

126. Ibid., p. 130; for a view that the Founders did not foreclose the exercise of Lockean executive prerogative, see Richard Pious, *The American Presidency* (New York: Basic Books, 1979), p. 45; for the argument that the Founders intended to exclude presidential prerogative, see Raoul Berger, *Executive Privilege* (Cambridge: Harvard University, 1974), pp. 57, 59.

127. Frederick M. Watkins, *Public Policy* 375, 374 (1940).

128. Pious, *The American Presidency*, p. 84.

129. Amaury de Riencourt, *The Coming Caesars* (New York: Coward McCann, 1957), p. 198.

130. Ibid., p. 152, italics added; see also p. 356.

131. Ibid., p. 198, italics added.

132. Ibid., p. 245.

133. Ibid., pp. 230, 237, italics added.

134. Ibid., p. 244.

135. Ibid., p. 253.

136. Ibid., pp. 259, 263, italics added.

137. Ibid., pp. 265, 245.

138. Ibid., pp. 277–278.

139. Ibid., p. 247, italics added.

140. Ibid., p. 356.

141. Ibid., p. 273.

142. Ibid., pp. 273–274; see the praise of the Founders in this respect, p. 279.

143. Ibid., p. 277.

144. Ibid., p. 356, italics added.

145. Ibid., p. 313, italics in the original.

146. Ibid., p. 281.

147. Ibid., p. 328.

148. Ibid., p. 332.

149. Ibid., p. 331.

150. Ibid., pp. 340–341, 245.

151. Ibid., pp. 328, 356.

152. Ibid., p. 356.

153. Ibid., p. 356; for the contrast between culture and civilization, see pp. 272–274: "Culture thinks in terms of quality, Civilization in terms of quantity." Ibid., p. 273. On the sources of this distinction, see p. 357 n.1.

6

Scholarly Opinions of Presidential Power
Edward S. Corwin, Clinton Rossiter and Richard E. Neustadt

The purpose of this chapter is to reflect on three classics of enduring interest that are reputed to be definitive, reliable, authoritative and standard: Edward S. Corwin's *The President: Office and Powers*, Clinton Rossiter's *The American Presidency* and Richard E. Neustadt's *Presidential Power: The Politics of Leadership*. This reflection should show how scholars developed the idea of the dominant presidency in contradistinction to Hamilton's teachings. The works under consideration discuss the public law of the presidency as well as its less formal role and power in our political system, usually with the purpose of determining whether presidential power should be increased, stabilized or reduced. In what follows I shall deal primarily with these aspects of the presidency while focusing on the authors' justification for their approach and the principles, explicit and implicit, that undergird their advice for change or reform. In this endeavor I have availed myself of the authors' other writings that bear upon my principal concerns. Presidential studies have traditionally attempted to enlighten citizens, statesmen and the advisers of statesmen. It would be entirely in keeping with this tradition to place on the current agenda a retheorization illuminating the presidency's relationship to the regime's central principles, rather than "mopping up" within accepted paradigms or creating new, more formalized "scientific" paradigms.[1]

I

Corwin's doctoral dissertation, "French Foreign Policy and the American Alliance of 1788," foreshadowed a life-long interest in international politics that accompanied his perhaps better known writings on the Constitution and the Supreme Court.[2] His eminence as a constitutional scholar is attested by his being the only non-lawyer among the ten legal writers cited most frequently by the United States Supreme Court for thirty-two years.[3] He published sixty-two articles in legal and professional journals, twenty-three in journals of opinions and periodicals, and wrote eighteen books as sole author, two as co-author, in addition to editing the 1953 annotated *Constitution: Analysis and Interpretation*.[4] In 1935 he served as constitutional adviser to the Public Works Administration, in 1936 as special assistant and in 1937 as constitutional consultant to the attorney general. Corwin's biography, which he reviewed before publication, stated that "in politics he is an independent."[5]

This interpreter of the Constitution of American democracy appears to have published only one piece whose title either hints at a thematic discussion of democracy or even mentions the word.[6] "The Democratic Dogma and the Future of Political Science" is one of his major methodological writings and, hence, is a fitting introduction to his presidency studies. He proposed that the telic or moral dimension of modern political science is the "belated off-spring of eighteenth century rationalism, and has taken all its ideals from that source."[7] Modern American political science is democratric in spite of its unexamined commitment to the "democratic dogma": the "doctrine that the people should rule" because "men act on reason."[8] Corwin concluded that "the primary task of political science is today one of popular education and that therefore it must still retain its character as a 'normative,' a 'telic' science."[9] This understanding of political science implied that Corwin's constitutional scholarship would also deal with moral or telic questions.

One searches the titles of his books and articles in vain, however, for frequent moral expressions. He published a total of seven writings, including the article mentioned above, whose titles signal a thematic concern with moral questions, which leads one to wonder how his constitutional scholarship expressed his understanding of political science and yet rarely used moral language to describe its themes.[10] Corwin's constitutional scholarship was moral in ultimate intention but set out for the destination from a concrete constitutional controversy. A thorough grasp of a constitutional controversy clarifies the importance of understanding political principles, and in this sense public law is a prologue to political thought. Corwin's scholarship was not only moral but also retrospective: "if the historian is to be wise *qua* historian, it must be after the event."[11]

One of Corwin's most important discussions of the presidency, *The Twilight of the Supreme Court*, arbitrates the dispute between government by legislation and executive power.[12] Certainly by 1934 Corwin had accepted that upholding the New Deal entailed a dominant presidency and a weakened Supreme Court and Congress. His case for the dominant presidency appeared in *The Twilight of the Supreme Court*, which he had

originally titled *The Supreme Court and the New Deal*.[13] The work expressed
his favorable view of the New Deal.[14] He tried to connect the principles
establishing the constitutionality of the New Deal to past constitutional
law and theory. Corwin distinguished two ideas of law: the discovery
and declaration of the intrinsic excellence of principles, which entitles
them to victory in the political process; and law as the *"expression of human
will and power."*[15] Corwin's preference for the latter idea of law may be
inferred from his argument that the idea of higher law, an ethical code
of intrinsic justice discoverable but not made by human reason, "usually
betokens" the "lack of clear distinction between the ethical and the strictly
legal."[16] Corwin's justification of the New Deal thus began by canceling
higher law, ethical and extra-constitutional restraints on presidential
power: this is Corwin's revision of Hamilton's understanding of the presidency. Corwin even applied the idea of law as human will and power
to the Constitution itself, arguing that its legal supremacy derived from
its expression of popular will rather than from the excellence of its
principles.[17]

The New Deal, he continued, recognizes the legislature as the *"supreme"* branch of government.[18] But he urged that Congress be limited
to the allowance or disallowance of executive proposals for expenditures
because of Congress's tendency to yield to corruption.[19] Congress, although the supreme authority in Corwin's account, should be confined
to the broader questions of "principle."[20] Corwin disclosed the fundamentals of the executive–legislative relationship in describing the New
Deal as an attempt to arrive at *"some of the results of dictatorship by a mergence
of legislative power with Presidential leadership."*[21] He concludes that contemporary constitutional law and theory endow the president with "indefinite" inherent powers beyond congressional limitation, with
"indefinite" delegated legislative powers and with "all nonjudicial discretion" available from the Constitution and statutes.[22] This conclusion
illustrates the immense distance separating Corwin's doctrine in 1934
from Hamilton's teachings. Corwin is virtually silent on constitutional
limitation. He said that it "cannot" be required that the executive be
prepared for emergency action and yet be chained to law passed for
"normal" situations.[23]

Theodore Roosevelt's stewardship theory limited presidential power
only by specific provisions in the Constitution or statutes.[24] Roosevelt
taught in effect that whatever wasn't specifically prohibited was permitted, as opposed to the doctrine that whatever wasn't specifically permitted was prohibited. Corwin made an already permissive theory even
more permissive with the inference that, under the stewardship theory,
the executive acquired authority to act in the "public interest" whenever
Congress lacked the constitutional power to do so; "nor, obviously, would
[such] executive action . . . be subject to Congressional control." He cited
no example of the executive abuse of power, from which one infers that

he dismissed the risk as unlikely or extremely hypothetical. The less likely Corwin found the executive abuse of power, the less necessary he found clear and enforceable limitations on executive power. Corwin's 1934 idea of executive power casts doubt on Hans Kelsen's argument that the rejection of moral or higher law "absolutes" in effect makes political autocracy impossible.[25]

Robert Newton defined Corwin's primary interest as "those aspects of constitutional law that deal with the respective powers of the president and Congress in matters of diplomacy and war, and the constitutional implications of United States participation in international organizations."[26] Corwin in fact stated the central problem more broadly than Newton implied. In "Our Constitutional Revolution and How to Round It Out," Corwin argued that constitutional provisions delineate the structures of the national government, define its powers and affirm certain individual rights against the powers of the national government.[27] The idea of individual rights, omitted by Newton, guided Corwin's investigation of the powers and structures of the national government, especially of the presidency. Corwin discerned a "revolutionary reversal of constitutional values" in which "the presidency has reached a position of unhealthy dominance in the system" because he compared presidential power to an explicit standard of political health, the idea of individual rights against the national government.[28] Corwin's later scholarship opposed obscurantism concerning the most important questions.

Corwin's *President: Office and Powers* proposed to show the "reciprocal interplay of human character and legal concepts" in the "development and contemporary status of presidential power and of the presidential office under the Constitution" (vii–viii).[29] He describes his approach as "partly historical, partly analytical and critical." Two introductory chapters sketch conceptions of the office, eligibility, election, tenure, disability and impeachment, and the remaining chapters deal with the president as administrator, chief executive, organ of foreign relations, commander-in-chief in wartime, and legislative leader and "institution." The order implicit in the subject matter requires a discussion of legislative leadership before foreign relations and war; Corwin instead presented the problem of presidential power in his first six chapters and his remedy in his final chapter on legislative leadership, a procedure that subordinated the scientific unfolding of his argument to the dramatic requirements of popular education.

Corwin's thesis has a descriptive and a critical dimension. Executive power is a "term of uncertain content," an "indefinite residuum" of methods peculiarly apt for dealing with emergency conditions that lack sufficient "stability or recurrency" to permit their being dealt with under a rule of law (3). The determination of executive power under Article II therefore leaves "considerable leeway for the future play of political

forces" (3–4). The Constitution accordingly "reflects the struggle between two conceptions of Executive power: that it ought always to be
subordinate to the supreme legislative power, and that it ought to be,
within generous limits, autonomous and self-directing" (307). "On the
whole" the autonomous and self-directing presidency has triumphed.
The history of the presidency is a "cyclical" or discontinuous aggrandizement in which Congress preponderated from 1809 to 1829, from
1865 to 1885 and, with exceptions, to the death of McKinley (29, 307,
309). "Not more than one in three" presidents enlarged presidential
power; under other incumbents presidential power either stabilized or
receded: "what the presidency is at any particular moment depends in
important measure on who is president" (30). Corwin identified the
architects of the "great accession to presidential power in recent decades"
as Theodore Roosevelt, Woodrow Wilson and, above all, "the second
Roosevelt who beyond all twentieth-century presidents put the stamp
both of *personality* and *crisis* on the presidency" (310–311; italics in the
original).

Unlike some critics of the presidency, Corwin avoided sliding into the
role of unreflective defender of Congress. Those who minimize the
presidential contribution to legislation overlook, said Corwin, "that in
our crisis-driven world time is often of the essence," that the president
has a superior vantage point from which to discern impending crisis and
that he can organize the votes necessary for the passage of crucial measures (486 n.76). Corwin tried to distinguish his position from that of a
historically minded congressman who asserts that impeachment, the
power of the purse, the power to declare war and the treaty power have
all been weakened or made empty formalities even as the propaganda
advantages of the president have increased. These assertions are not
necessarily false but are "overdrawn in some . . . details" (293).

Corwin's text holds that the "outcome of [Andrew] Johnson's trial . . .
makes the episode of slight value as a precedent," while his notes praise
former Supreme Court Justice Benjamin Curtis, one of Johnson's counsel, who stated "with great acuteness" the definition of an impeachable
offense: treason, bribery and high crimes and misdemeanors "so high
that they belong in this company with treason and bribery" (65, 352–
353 n.68). Corwin's understanding of impeachment thus differs from
what one may call an early Gerald Ford position (legislative will) or
positions that deny any essential difference in criteria of impeachment
for federal judges and executive officers. The realization of Founder
James Wilson's hope that impeachment would "seldom" be used "is partly
due to the fact that presidents have in the past kept pretty clear of courses
that might make people think seriously of so extreme a discipline"
(293).[30]

Corwin spoke somewhat loosely of the "potential" power of the purse while omitting the power to declare war as a check on presidential adventuring and gambles (293–294). Indeed, "our four great wars—all great for their results, three of them great for the effort they required of the country—were the outcome of presidential policies in the making of which Congress played a distinctly secondary role" (204). The use of executive agreements has attenuated the Senate's power to veto, conditionally or unconditionally, treaties (211–217). The rebuttal to the hypothetical historically minded congressman's objections demonstrates that although they are "overdrawn," they are far from misleading.

Corwin's work culminates in a statement of the phases, trends and stimuli of presidential power. American constitutional law and theory identified five factors producing the contemporary presidency: (1) acceptance of the "idea that government should be active and reformist," "especially in matters affecting the material welfare of the great masses of the people" (294, 311); (2) the breakdown of dual federalism in congressional legislative power; (3) the breakdown of separation of powers defining the relation of president and Congress in lawmaking; (4) the breakdown of the prohibition against delegated legislative powers; (5) the impact of two world wars and the "vastly enlarged" United States role in international politics upon the president as commander-in-chief and organ of foreign relations (311–312).

He omits the importance of the various factors, but we can easily trace the implications of his argument. The "change in popular outlook regarding the purpose and scope of governmental power" is "even more fundamental" than the collapse of dual federalism and separation of powers, the "two great structural principles of the American Constitutional System" (310). If popular government means majority rule, "all the developments named above are the direct consequence of democracy's emergence from the constitutional chrysalis" (312). Not presidential leadership as such but democracy itself and the "change in popular outlook regarding the purpose and scope of governmental power" can be blamed for intrusions on private and personal rights.

Corwin saw a "novelty" in the size, permanence and voting strength of the groups served by the New Deal and a theoretical advance as well (277, 311). In 1934 he called Chapter 5 of Locke's *Second Treatise* "perhaps the most important source of the ideas of 'the Founding Fathers' regarding property."[31] The doctrines of vested rights and due process of law had blended Lockeanism into the American political tradition, but these doctrines were "irrelevant" to the solution of the problem of governmental power posed by the New Deal.[32] "Modern conditions subordinate" the ideas of property behind the doctrines of vested rights and due process of law to "entirely different" ideas, notably those of John Dewey, a critic of natural rights.[33] Omitting for some reason Locke's broad definition of property as lives, liberties and estates, Corwin held that Locke's notion of property "embraced 'only...outward things' " such as houses.[34] Locke's idea of property "did not comprise anything closely analogous to modern investment capital."[35] The New Deal, said Corwin, subordinated wealth to the "social process" and "political democracy."[36] The New Deal is an era "whose primary demand upon government is no longer the protection of rights but the assurance of security."[37]

The New Deal impressed Corwin as a profound break with the Lockeanism of the American political tradition. Perhaps, as Morton Frisch has suggested, it is more accurate to describe the New Deal as both a break with and an extension of the earlier Lockeanism:

The specific New Deal thesis was that the government has the responsibility to provide not merely for the *conditions* of happiness (that's the Lockeanism implicit in the American Founding), but for something approaching happiness itself or what we may call well-being or welfare.... FDR transcended some of the limitations of liberal democracy and even enlarged its horizons.... But FDR did not realize that, in constantly seeking to strengthen economic equality, the human personality could in fact become submerged in the interest of a better regulated economic life with its emphasis on health, welfare and freedom from want. FDR may not have foreseen it, but the humane passion for welfarism could result in what Tocqueville has referred to as a soft despotism. This is perhaps the greatest difficulty underlying the New Deal.[38]

Both the New Deal and the Lockean tradition of property rights understood happiness in material terms, with the important difference that the New Deal broadened the older materialism. The tension between liberty and security, which Corwin saw as the offspring of the New Deal, may have been inherent in the natural rights concept because of its materialistic bent. The specific contribution of the New Deal may have been in making that tension evident.

Corwin gave at least two diagnoses of how enlarged expectations of government and of the executive affected liberty. He asked if the Constitution is "on the way out?" This question "is capable of being put seriously and is deserving of a serious answer. Its evident reference is to the Websterian conception of a 'Constitution of Rights,' featured especially by an elaboration of checks and balances. Obviously, this conception of the Constitution is not only on the way out—it *is* out."[39] Yet speaking of principles underlying the Constitution of Rights, he was "reluctant to see extruded from the Constitution...the most important, the most ancient one, the idea that there are rights of the individual which are anterior to government and set a limit to its just powers."[40] His first formulation concluded that the Constitution of Rights "is out";

his second formulation concludes that the "most important" principle underlying the Constitution of Rights was not "out."

The complexity of Corwin's position on the idea of individual rights relates to his responses to the constitutional revolution in 1937. He favored effective policy and limited government while opposing comprehensive judicial restraints on the government. After 1937 he sought new political means of coping with an increasingly less limited government, especially the presidency and the executive. In Yakus v. U.S. 321 U.S. 414 (1944), for example, the Supreme Court endorsed the withdrawal from persons prosecuted for violation of the Emergency Price Control Act of the right to plead the unconstitutionality of the act or of the orders issued under its supposed authorization.[41] How, Corwin asked, can it be demanded that the executive be kept permanently alerted for emergency action and yet be permanently chained within law devised for normal times?[42] "The simplest answer is that this cannot be demanded."

Corwin urged basing all reforms of the presidency on consensus, compromise and moderation and keeping the legislature active in meeting crises.[43] His concrete proposals relied upon the political branches and popular education: the congressional power of the purse, a Cabinet including congressmen and the disqualification of the president from succeeding himself.[44] The development of the institutionalized presidency, said Corwin, "may have relegated my [Cabinet] proposal . . . to the limbo of happy untried ideas—happy, perhaps, because untried" (312). None of Corwin's solutions perform the "characteristic judicial duty of adjusting the universal and eternal to the local and contingent, the here and now."[45] He predicted in 1941 that the Supreme Court largely would withdraw from the important economic policy field to the limited area of the First Amendment.[46] Accordingly, the idea of individual rights against the national government no longer comprehensively limited the political branches. The idea of individual rights against the national government was "in," however, as far as constitutional commentators such as Corwin compensated for the Supreme Court in adjusting the "universal and eternal" to the "here and now."

Toward the end of his life Corwin criticized Mr. Justice Holmes's rejection of natural rights and spoke of the "debt" of American constitutional law to natural law or natural rights concepts.[47] This criticism, though not executed in any detail, was nevertheless an important step toward reassessing liberty against government and the entire theoretical superstructure of the New Deal presidency. It would be an oversimplification to say that Corwin merely challenged presidential power with the thesis of liberty against government. Corwin was, indeed, in common with John Locke a teacher of liberty; also in common with Locke, he attended to the conditions of the responsible use of liberty, the most important of which for most people was religious instruction. Corwin

opposed the secularization of American education to the extent that this
would be encouraged or required by Supreme Court decisions against
religious instruction in public schools. "Finally," he said of McCollum v.
Board of Education 333 U.S. 203 (1948), "this question may be asked:
Is the decision favorable to democracy? Primarily democracy is a system
of ethical values, and that this system of values so far as the American
people are concerned is grounded in religion will not be denied by
anybody who knows the historical record."[48] Corwin thus favored both
presidential and popular responsibility as conditions of liberty; his inquiry into popular responsibility took him from institutional solutions
to the molding of character. He found plausible Tocqueville's argument
that Americans more ardently pursue equality than liberty, which raised
the possibility of liberty being crowded to the wall.[49]

Our appraisal of Corwin's writings on the presidency has identified
two broad themes in his argument. In 1934 Corwin advocated a presidency distinguished by power and freedom of action, few constitutional
and no ethical limitations; in *The President: Office and Powers* Corwin called
for limits on presidential power. Our conclusion must be that in this
work ultimately he favored a limited presidency without a return to
specifically Hamiltonian teachings.

II

Corwin, Clinton Rossiter's teacher at Princeton University, observed
of Rossiter's *American Presidency* that it rested on the premise that the
presidency would "always be just right" (495 n.106). In contrast to Corwin's stance as a political independent, Rossiter reportedly described
himself as an Adlai Stevenson Democrat.[50] A high percentage of Rossiter's books discussed political thought and the Constitution, enabling
him to see more clearly than subsequent specialist writers that the dispute over presidential power reflected a deeper disagreement over the
"American way of life" and its tendency (257).[51] For Rossiter the political
practice of the presidency requires a political theory, an adequate understanding of the theoretical basis of the American way of life. Whether
Rossiter or his theoretical authority supplied such an understanding is
a point to which we shall return.

Rossiter presented the American presidency as a rare success in man's
long search for "free government" (15). His thesis describes the varieties
and future of presidential activity and also offers a prescriptive diagnosis.
He shows the additions to the president's strictly constitutional activities
as chief of state, chief executive, commander-in-chief, chief diplomat
and chief legislator: chief of party, popular voice, protector of the peace,
manager of prosperity and world leader or president of the West. A
usual objection to Rossiter's role analysis is that he treats the president
as performing one role at a time.[52] In Rossiter's defense, he safeguards

himself by calling the presidency a "seamless unity" (41). Rossiter leaves implicit the character of the adhesive binding all of these roles together. He does, however, praise FDR for "genius" in the political "support of policy" (149). It may be, of course, that Rossiter too hastily abandoned this important subject.

A second aspect of Rossiter's thesis concerned the future of presidential power. He described the presidency's power and prestige as the "outstanding feature" of our constitutional development and deduced from this history the "inevitability" of the presidency's "upward course" (83–84). In short, presidential power will increase. Rossiter must demonstrate that the presidency avoids excessive power and independence in order to reconcile the presidency's "upward course" and free government (46). This task requires him to show the adequacy of restraints upon the president. He judged that pressure groups expressing public opinion are the "most effective" long-run check on the president; such public opinion is most effective when it is felt through "other restraints," such as Congress (68–69).

How effective is Congress as a restraint? Congress, said Rossiter, was the "most reliable single" restraint upon the presidency (56). Yet the increase in presidential power was "greatly" assisted by the "long decline" of Congress, and even the Eisenhower presidency "cuts deeply" into congressional powers (87, 82). Rossiter argued that some evidence showed that Congress had recently strayed farther beyond its constitutional limits than the president (251). He concluded that Congress needs *"external"* or presidential leadership (28, italics in the original). Thus for Rossiter Congress is at the same time limiting and being subordinate to the president.

The baffled reader trying to sort out the limitations on the president will gather the drift of Rossiter's argument from his closing pages. He called upon the president increasingly to define the "national purpose" as Congress falls under the increasing domination of local interests (260). Rossiter finds that "in the end" internal checks, such as the president's "conscience" and "training," are more important limitations than external checks (70). Given the weakness of Congress, Rossiter depends upon a president reared in "the American tradition" who respects moral restraints and whose actions are compatible with "constitutionalism, democracy, personal liberty, and Christian morality" (70).

The moral limits upon presidential power can be no more authoritative than their source, which takes us to the adequacy of Rossiter's account of the theoretical basis of the American way of life. As noted above, he said in 1960 that the president must increasingly define the national purpose (260). Writing the same year in a volume of essays entitled *The National Purpose*, Rossiter observed that the United States in its youth had a "profound sense of purpose [i.e., 'testament to freedom ... personal liberty and popular government'], which we lost over the years of our rise to glory."[53] No return was possible through "commentaries on the Great Books" to an earlier understanding of the national purpose.[54] Although he wrote that "no belief has had more meaning for American democracy and Western civilization than the enlightened assumption that all men are created equal and that what they are equal in is freedom," Rossiter taught his students at Cornell University that American political thought is an ideology, which he defined as faith or philosophy used as accessory after the fact or specious justification.[55]

Rossiter's presentation of American political thought was based upon the theory of Carl Becker, the Cornell historian, according to which,

any significant political philosophy is shaped by three different but closely related influences... the "climate of opinion"—those fundamental presuppositions which in any age so largely determine what men think about the nature of the universe and what can and cannot happen in it, and about the nature of man and what is essential to the good life. The second influence is more specific: it derives from the particular political and social conflicts of the time, which dispose groups and parties to accept a particular interpretation of current ideas as a theoretical support for their practical activities. The third influence... derives from the mind and temperament of the individual who gives to the political philosophy its ordered literary form.... Its value for other times and places will depend upon the extent to which the general presuppositions upon which it rests... express some enduring truth about nature and the life of man.[56]

Becker's *Declaration of Independence* had concluded that "to ask whether the natural rights philosophy of the Declaration of Independence is true or false is essentially a meaningless question."[57] In 1943 Becker apparently, but only apparently, backwatered to the extent of saying that "in respect to fundamentals Jefferson's political philosophy is still valid for us."[58]

Becker's letters will aid us in understanding how Rossiter's authority interpreted an important writing on the American way of life. "I am writing a book," said Becker, "on the Declaration of Independence in which my chief task is to show where the natural rights philosophy came from and where it went to and why. This last takes me into the slavery controversy,"[59] Explaining where the "natural rights philosophy... went to and why," Becker wrote that John C. Calhoun

seems to me... the Moses that led them [pro-slavery advocates] out of the natural rights wilderness. His definition of nature in the *Disquisition* did the business.... This was to identify the natural with the historical and the prescriptive, and the natural rights of the slave were thus the same as his legal rights, which weren't many.... In general it is marvelous how similar the whole pro-slavery philosophy is to that of the historic-rights school on the continent.[60]

Becker, Rossiter's authoritative interpreter of the American political tradition, denied the possibility of enduring and objective political truths and asserted that Jefferson's natural rights doctrine had been "refuted."[61]

Becker allowed for no return to an earlier understanding of national purpose: "the facts may be determined with accuracy; but the 'interpretation' of a [political or moral] doctrine will always be shaped by the prejudices, biases, needs of the individual and these in turn will depend on the age in which he lives."[62] George Sabine ably drew the implications of Becker's position for the American way of life, the American political tradition and liberal democracy: "Liberal democracy, as it turned out, like communism and fascism was an ideology," one available prejudice among others.[63] Lest there be any misunderstanding of what it meant to be "raised in the American tradition" along Beckerian lines, let us conclude this account of Rossiter's theoretical guide with the complaint of "Five Unhappy and Bewildered Freshmen," who had informed the *Cornell Daily Sun* that their first term was ending without their understanding the purpose of college education any better than they had in September.[64] Becker defined the purpose of liberal education in the *Daily Sun*: "I think that a philosophy of life, whether Christian or other, is what a student should mainly seek in his college course."[65] Becker's definition of the meaning of life informs us of the "philosophy of life" that coexisted with his historicism: "Meaning of Life = the meaning of life is that we should be always seeking the meaning of life without ever finding it."[66] In sum, the primary restraints upon Rossiter's president are moral ones. The moral emptiness of these restraints and of Rossiter's concept of the national purpose is possibly related to the moral emptiness of the historicism Rossiter adopted from Carl Becker.

After announcing the exhaustion of America's originally "profound sense of purpose," Rossiter concluded that "as an historian, I am bound to point out that this country stands on shaky historical and cultural ground from which to launch a new search for a national mission and then to pursue it."[67] "Where, then, are we to find this...new sense of national purpose?"[68] "It has now become the destiny of this nation," said Rossiter, "to lead the world...through cooperation to confederacy to federation and at last to a government having power to enforce peace. ...This, surely, is the second American mission" that "will have to be voiced by a line of plain-talking Presidents."[69] The logic behind Rossiter's understanding of the new national purpose would seem to be the following: peace is good because it avoids or minimizes the pain and suffering that accompany war. Pain and suffering are unqualifiedly bad because they are the antithesis of pleasure. If the priority of peace rests on the priority of pleasure over pain and suffering, Rossiter's case for world government is based on hedonism. However that may be, he avoids discussing how a world government with the "power to enforce peace" would or could permit individual nations, such as the United States, to judge of threats to their liberties and to defend them. The possibility that a world government with the "power to enforce peace" also entails far-reaching regimentation is nowhere grasped in Rossiter's essay on the new national purpose.

Rossiter rarely concedes that his portrait of the presidency suffers from excessive optimism (240). Americans may justifiably worry about "occasional abuses of power" because "power that can be used decisively can also be abused grossly" (47). These rare warnings deviate from Rossiter's rose-colored picture of impeachment (53). His argument finally reduces to circular reasoning: presidential power is benevolent and safe for liberty because the people support it; and the people support presidential power because it is benevolent and safe for liberty. To the objection that the United States might fall prey to a Perón or a Batista, Rossiter replies by emphasizing American history, the American people and the American climate of opinion (46). Rossiter's own account shows, as he said in another context, that the American presidency is a source of "indestructible myth" (108).

Rossiter's book is itself a subtreasury of myths, among the most important of which is the Whig theory of history described by Butterfield. Rossiter tended to stress "certain principles of progress in the past and to produce a story which is the ratification if not the glorification of the present."[70] He divided the world "into the friends and enemies of progress," or, more precisely, into the supporters and "the opponents of the strong Presidency."[71] His studies of the "Presidency in History" and the "Modern Presidency" demonstrated the working of an "obvious principle of progress," the "inevitability of the upward course of the Presidency."[72] Rossiter tried to run in the same harness two horses that pulled in opposite directions: the Whig interpretation, based on the trans-historical notion of progress, and historicism, according to which the notion of progress is the historically conditioned offspring of a specific time, place, set of circumstances or "climate of opinion." Progress and historicism are not only logically independent but logically incompatible ideas.

It remains only to refer to the subordinate myths of Rossiter's presidency, what Alfred DeGrazia has called fictions or large exaggerations of the real presidents. The "central myth," from which the derived myths create a "veritable fairyland," is "wrapped up in the fictions of a single heroic leader, which defies the truth of the normalcy of the typical president and the collectivity of his behavior."[73] "Trustee of the Nation," "Freedom Boss," "Advocate of the Public Interest," and "Majority (Minority) Champion" exemplify some myths, which have their parallels in Rossiter's work, that DeGrazia pitilessly exposes. One may quarrel with some of DeGrazia's criticisms and yet applaud his effort to remove tacit assumptions of the "strong presidency" persuasion from the "given" to the realm of discussion.

Rossiter's criteria for evaluating presidents changed from quality to quantity in his chapters "Presidency in History" and the "Modern Presidency." The former discussed six presidents from Washington through Theodore Roosevelt who symbolized some "virtue" revered by Americans (107). The latter chapter compared FDR's, Truman's and Eisenhower's "strength" and the "new dimensions" of strength or power added by these incumbents (109, 114). The publication of Richard Neustadt's *Presidential Power* seemed to go far toward meeting Rossiter's call for "new standards" of presidential performance, especially in its tacit concurrence with Rossiter's edict that the intellectual and political "war . . . over the future of America . . . over the American way of life [was] now pretty well decided" (257). Accordingly, the quest for new standards of presidential performance could begin by taking for granted a liberal understanding of the American way of life and then minutely focusing on presidential technique without the intrusion of ethical questions.

III

As an economist with the Office of Price Administration (1942) and a staffer in the Bureau of the Budget (1946–1950) and the White House (1950–1953), Richard Neustadt is the first of our three experts who filled more than a consultant's role in the civilian national government. A self-identified Democrat, he chaired the Platform Committee of the 1972 Democratic Convention.

The audience of *Presidential Power* includes presidents and future presidents, their assistants, their friends, journalists and academics concerned with presidential leadership. The book implicitly assumes among potential presidents the equally high distribution of decency, moderation and dedication to the Constitution without giving us any reason to accept this assumption. Although Neustadt's work purports to be more realistic than earlier accounts devoted to citizenship education, in this respect the book actually carries us further into fiction than even Rossiter's *American Presidency*. Not surprisingly, Neustadt compares the present situation to Lincoln's presidency (5) and elsewhere expresses high admiration for President Lincoln. Neustadt's case studies, however, are limited to the period after 1932. He ignores the important question of whether his conclusions apply to earlier presidents. The limited time span of his cases prevents him from rebutting the contention that he has studied the presidency and the nation in decline.

The documentation of *Presidential Power* includes case studies described elsewhere or treated in the text, interviews with some members of FDR's family, the memories of Neustadt's father's friends and of

Neustadt's acquaintances who worked in the New Deal and interviews in the Eisenhower administration (Preface). The author leaves unclear how he sifted retrospective justification from these interviews and memories. The reader is unable to retrace all of the chain of evidence leading to Neustadt's conclusions. Moreover, the quality of his documentation is admittedly uneven. When Neustadt wrote, Eisenhower's "motives" were intelligible only through his public statements and the private statements of men in the Eisenhower administration (163). Neustadt conceded the need for "caution" in using such sources for understanding Eisenhower. Neustadt's thesis heavily depends upon the reader's acceptance of his interpretation of Eisenhower's motives and performance, for Neustadt's Eisenhower is the foil to Neustadt's Roosevelt. In *Nixon Agonistes* Garry Wills, who is no friend of modern presidents, found Eisenhower's tenure one marked by skillful craftsmanship, as did Fred Greenstein in his path-blazing *Hidden-Hand Presidency*. Thus it would seem that, contrary to Neustadt's implication, FDR was not the sole example of presidential ability.

Of perhaps equal importance to the documentation of Neustadt's case studies is their relationship to his theory of presidential power: if he extracts his theory partly from the case studies, his theory cannot be independently assessed and verified by those same case studies.[74] Concerning the limitations of Neustadt's theory, historian Jean Holder found, contrary to Neustadt, that the example of President John Adams shows that the Constitution alone or chiefly, not persuasion, can be a source of power. Holder concluded that with an able leader in the early republic the presidency was viable on its constitutional basis. Thus Neustadt's theory would seem to be inapplicable to the presidency in all historical periods. His theory cannot decide the question of whether to attempt to restore the presidency to its basis of constitutional authority.

Presidential Power concedes the existence of many alternative understandings of presidential performance. I focus first on some alternatives that Neustadt rejects. He understands presidential leadership to include an emphasis on "spirit . . . values and . . . purposes" (2). Neustadt, however, drops the president's connection to the regime's spirit, principles and purposes, and his omission of these aspects of presidential leadership may exaggerate presidential weakness.[75]

Neustadt understood *Presidential Power* as a reply to and criticism of Corwin's *President: Office and Powers*, which he earlier had called "*the* indispensable foundation for an understanding of that crucial (and peculiar) institution: The Presidency of the United States."[76] Neustadt's critique of Corwin seems to rest on three arguments. Corwin allegedly paid insufficient attention to the politics of the presidency; he almost ignored how presidents could improve their short-run influence;[77] and Corwin ignored the social science goal of prediction and, presumably, control in his understanding of the presidency.[78] The counterarguments defending Corwin are the following. The most important aspects of the presidency over the long run are not the transient political but the moral and constitutional aspects; an understanding of the morality and constitutionality of presidential conduct may prescribe ends for the guidance of potential and serving presidents. This approach, what Corwin called the "reciprocal interplay of human character and legal concepts," can restore the understanding of power as a means to higher, more important ends, not an end in itself. Second, Corwin did not totally ignore the president's power or influence, for he conceded that the determination of presidential power under Article II leaves "considerable leeway for the future play of political forces." Corwin could have enlarged on the techniques the president might use to acquire power, but he refrained from doing so. He in effect practiced an economy of truth concerning how the president could enlarge his power. Corwin might counterattack Neustadt's naive practice of openly advising scoundrels as well as decent potential presidents how to enlarge their power or influence. In addition, Corwin believed that if we must make a choice between increasing and stabilizing presidential power, the history of the presidency and the conditions of the twentieth century argue in favor of the latter course. Finally, Corwin might counterattack that the prediction that Neustadt advocates is blind to the truly important purpose of political science, which is popular education through ethical inquiry. This inquiry, not prediction and control, is or ought to be the way of political science. In sum, the arguments defending Corwin appear more plausible than Neustadt's objections.

Neustadt assigned public law to the distant background of the presidency by distinguishing powers, the supposed theme of public law, from power in this way: powers: formal constitutional, statutory or customary authority:: power: influence (217 n.1). The text collapses this crisp distinction when Neustadt says in effect that powers are an important source of power. "Presidential 'powers'... always remain relevant as he persuades" (34). The authority and status of a president are "great advantages" as he seeks to persuade other men (35). Neustadt contends that " 'powers' are no guarantee of power" without telling us which major commentators on the presidency, if any, have ever maintained that powers sufficiently guaranteed power (10). As we have seen, he conceded that powers can generate power and some attention to the public law of the presidency is, therefore, in order even in a work restricted to the quest for "personal power" (Preface).

Leadership also refers to the president's effect on governmental policy as distinct from the consequences of governmental action (2). The essence of leadership for Neustadt is the president's influence upon the other men in government (2). His notion of influence implies intended causality and is not explicitly distinguished from considerations of improper, illegal or immoral influence upon the other authorities. *Presidential Power* differentiates itself from Eastern liberalism as it subscribes to the end of ideology thesis (200–201). Ideology, in which Neustadt seems to include moral purposes, obstructed "applied intelligence" and was, hence, to be shunned (201). It is not clear whether Neustadt's presidency rests on anything deeper than the rootless pragmatism then in vogue.

Neustadt's intention may be divided into an overt analytical intention and a less explicit prescriptive intention. The analytical intention is to learn how a president can exert his "will" within his administration (Preface). The analytical argument may be subdivided into how to prepare for office and excelling in office. Dismissing the qualifications of men experienced in political party organization and offices, Neustadt defines "governmental office" as the best preparation for the presidency (181). He avoids a stand on the oft-debated question of whether gubernatorial, senatorial or executive experience is the most adequate preparation for presidential competence (182; cf. 161). Neustadt's term *governmental office*, then, is imprecise. Something resembling a " 'first rate' temperament" turns governmental experience into presidential expertise (183). Temperament is the key, but Neustadt fails to investigate this thoroughly and systematically. His imprecision about the relevant areas and quality of pre-presidential experience weakens his discussion of what prepares a president to excel in office. James Barber's *Presidential Character* attempted to develop the temperament aspect under another label, but Neustadt and Barber are identical in presupposing the constitutional argument for the ascendant presidency.

Excelling in office depends upon presidential influence on the men who formulate and administer governmental policy (179). Power results from the president's governmental "vantage points," his Washington reputation and his public prestige. Four chapters discuss commands, persuasion, reputation and prestige. Commands are the least frequent type of decision. The original 1960 edition of *Presidential Power* omits consideration of rational action in the circumstances and concentrates on the president's effect on policy (2). The 1968 Afterword on JFK and the Cuban missile crisis of October 1962 concluded that when war or the threat of war looms, "judgment" then is the sign of " 'leadership' " (214). The addition of judgment to influence, the earlier key test of performance, implies an abandonment of Neustadt's indifference to rational action in the circumstances. The 1968 Afterword hints at a revised criterion of performance: intended causality and rational action or judgment. If Neustadt had revised his 1960 text accordingly in 1968, his work would have merged presidential operations and the prudential concerns of an enlightened citizen. As it is, however, the 1960 text un-

derstands presidential causality without presidential reason and "responsibility" (208).

Neustadt identifies some elements of the power to persuade: reasoned
argument, charm, status and authority, compromise and bargaining, the
ability to induce men to identify the president's needs with their self-
interest, anticipated reactions to the president, public prestige and
knowledge. He preserves a remarkable silence on what is surely another
element of the power to persuade, coercion, whether "administrative
blackjacking" of private business during World War II or the Kennedy
administration's use of the FBI during the 1962 steel price crisis.[79] Thus
the work that scorns other approaches ("academic images") as unrealistic
shrinks from some uncomfortable facts; perhaps, after all, the analogy
between Neustadt and Machiavelli is overdrawn and strained.[80]

Neustadt's intimacy with President Kennedy has received more notice
than how closely Neustadt's version of being president approached Kennedy's understanding of the office. Kennedy reportedly objected that
Neustadt's characterization of the president "makes everything a president does seem too premeditated."[81] Rejecting criticisms of FDR's evaluation of Soviet–American relations, Neustadt said that FDR's mind was
"unfathomed" by even his close associates, which is apparently a separate
issue from whether the president's mind was confused (234 n.5). Neustadt asserted that we lack "certain" evidence of FDR's thinking on Soviet–American problems later faced by President Truman. It may be,
however, that we possess probable or sufficient knowledge of FDR's
assessment of Stalin. In sum, the search for influence is the excessively
premeditated and, hence, unrealistic aspect of Neustadt's presidency,
and he invokes the obscurantist cover of the president's unfathomed
mind when possibly questionable results challenge the soundness of the
president's judgment in using his influence. In fairness, however, the
Afterword on JFK states that American involvement with Saigon had
been "rashly" enlarged by President Kennedy (209).

Neustadt emphasized the importance of political forecasting and predicted that the conditions of the 1950s would last into the 1960s (61, 3,
191). This turned out to be an excessively optimistic forecast in light of
the erosion of trust in national political institutions. For example, the
University of Michigan's Institute for Social Research reported that in
1964 62 percent of a nationally representative adult sample expressed
a high degree of trust in the national government, but this figure had
declined to 37 percent by 1970.[82] Neustadt's forecast failed to identify
the emerging malaise and so moved against rather than with history
(196). At the Cambodian invasion Neustadt attacked the Nixon administration's policies on Southeast Asia, charging that field commanders,
the U.S. embassy in Saigon and the White House were circumventing
the executive branch in running the war.[83] In a television interview he

called for legislative restraints upon the commander-in-chief! It could be argued, however, that President Nixon merely maximized his influence, as Neustadt had recommended. In 1973 Neustadt, in effect, parried this objection in branding the Nixon "regime...[as] the most corrupt."[84] "Even as the old constraints of prudence slackened, the White House staff fell under the control of senior aides so lacking in propriety as those we saw this summer on our television screens."[85] Influence, then, may be distinguished by 1973 into corrupt and uncorrupt varieties. This hedging is as close as he comes to subordinating influence to political morality; it is far from clear how this prevailing stress on influence essentially differs from the outlook of those "senior aides" he deplored in 1973.[86]

Neustadt's prescriptive intention is to demonstrate the reasonableness of being favorably disposed toward presidential power. He properly demands that maximizing presidential power serve higher ends than presidential "pride or pleasure" and public "sentiment" and "partisanship" (183). The side effects of presidential expertise in power are greater governmental energy, greater viability of policy and some insulation for the president, apparently, from mistakes and confusion in policy appraisals (149, 183). His key argument seems to be the viability of policy and the president interested in preserving his influence as the, by definition, expert on the viability of policy (185). For Neustadt the side effects of a president's search for influence mean that "what is good for the country is good for the President, and *vice-versa*" (185).

Neustadt briefly examines risks and temptations in the search for presidential influence, arguing that a president who is excessively sensitive to his "power stakes and sources" might destroy his objectives and himself (150). Yet Neustadt implies that Harry Truman was less than a model president whose methods impaired his influence because he venerated the presidency for what it represented in "government," the Democratic party and American history apart from his power interests (178). It would seem that, contrary to Neustadt, Truman despite his bluster was a restrained president because he looked up to the presidency for what it embodied "apart from him." Neustadt favors presidential restraint, such as the avoidance of total war against China in 1951, yet he criticizes Truman for failing to maximize his influence because Truman subordinated his power quest to presidential duty. In short, Neustadt commendably favors due restraint by presidents but is against one of the effective means of producing restraint, namely, a lofty conception of presidential duty.

Neustadt cites no actual example of a grasp for excessive power in the context of his hypothetical discussion of unlimited war against the Chinese (150). Hence we may assume that for Neustadt such a risk is low, if not non-existent. Reviewing Roosevelt II's quest for personal power, Neustadt concludes that FDR rarely failed to impose his will (158, 234 n.8). FDR is said to have had the greatest "hunger" for power of any twentieth-century president (161). The metaphor is of more than passing interest, for common sense ordinarily denominates an extreme hunger for food as gluttony, that is, a vice rather than a virtue. Why did Roosevelt have a more extreme hunger for power than any twentieth-century president? Virtually alone among these presidents, Roosevelt lacked any higher notion of office to which he conformed his behavior (162). If this is correct, Neustadt is mistaken in implying that the lack of a standard above a president's will to power can produce no unfortunate results except in foreign policy, narrowly defined. For example, Neustadt's list of FDR's mistakes omits an actual case where the president's power interest and viable policy failed to coincide with a decent policy (234 n.8).

For instance, Neustadt omits the incarceration of Japanese Americans during World War II, an act that energized government and was, indeed, a most viable policy cementing the anti-Japanese consensus. This was no small matter of short duration. According to Dillon Myer, the director of the War Relocation Authority (WRA), the evacuation, continued exclusion from summer 1942 until January 1945, and the detention for "varying periods" of more than 100,000 persons, two-thirds of whom were U.S. citizens by birth, "raised extremely grave questions as to the consistency of such a program with the requirements and prohibitions of the Constitution."[87] Myer, who ran the "relocation" or benevolent concentration camps, concluded that "all four of the major reasons advanced . . . for urging mass evacuations are found to be tenuous, highly arguable, or wholly unfounded."[88] The "evacuees" sustained "costly losses" in property.[89] The WRA property officer estimated that the evacuees owned $200 million worth of property at their evacuation; the United States paid total settlement claims of "$38,474,140, which of course did not cover all losses."[90] "Not more" than six out of ten evacuees returned to their former homes.

Moreover, we find that this treatment of Japanese Americans was urged upon a reluctant Attorney General Francis Biddle by a team of government lawyers outside the Justice Department and luminaries such as Earl Warren, attorney general of California, and Walter Lippmann.[91] Morton Grodzins has remarked that "the presidential review of the mass evacuation program was a very hasty one."[92] Grodzins concluded that "the history of the evacuation policy could be called an episode from the totalitarian handbook."[93] "A true assessment of the policy was possible while it was being made, and a historian's hindsight was not needed to condemn it," even if FDR's preoccupation with the military side of the war somewhat mitigates his acceptance of the Japanese American evacuation.[94] Certainly by any standard the Japanese American evacuation meets the specifications of Neustadt's work: experts disagreed (Biddle versus those government lawyers outside of the Justice Department); the president found a viable policy, but one can scarcely conclude that what benefited the president (e.g., prestige, reinforcement of the domestic consensus against Japan) also benefited the country.

If what benefits the president can harm the country, "there would be no reason except sentiment and partisanship" always to remain favorable toward presidential power and those skilled in maximizing it (183). In sum, *Presidential Power* inadequately links the maximization of presidential power to the benefit of the country partly because Neustadt's burrowing into presidential technique as understood by the White House staff hides the void where a moral understanding of government and the regime should be.

CONCLUSIONS

Edward S. Corwin called the New Deal an effort to merge congressional power with executive leadership so as to "attain some of the results of dictatorship." In the 1930s Corwin understood law as the "expression of human will and power," an idea that was hostile to higher law and all ethical restraints on power. Corwin advocated a dominant presidency freed of ethical limits and characterized by freedom of action, power and few constitutional restraints. This is the scholarly basis of the modern anti-Hamiltonian understanding of presidential power. Corwin's *The President: Office and Powers* later advocated a limit on presidential power, but without criticizing his 1934 argument for a dominant presidency and without formally reinstating the ethical limitation. Nevertheless of the three experts Corwin alone in *The President: Office and Powers* called for a limit on presidential power, though in so doing he neglected Hamilton's teachings.

Corwin's thought exemplified somewhat Nietzsche's parable of the three metamorphoses in *Zarathustra*: how the spirit becomes a camel; the camel, a lion; the lion, a child. With the camel's endurance his later thought conveyed much of American constitutionalism. With the lion's freedom his thought struggled with its "last god," the dominant presidency, in the hour of its triumph and created freedom for rediscovery in presidential studies. With the child's innocence his thought heralded a new beginning in the limitation of presidential power.

Clinton Rossiter's *American Presidency* is a transitional work between Corwin's *President: Office and Powers* and Neustadt's *Presidential Power*. Rossiter's book showed the additions to the president's strictly constitutional activities as chief of state, chief executive, commander-in-chief, chief diplomat and chief legislator. Rossiter's discussion of the president's major roles carefully noted that the presidency is a "seamless unity" and insisted that any one of the president's roles "feeds upon and into all the others." Deducing the presidency's future from its past, Rossiter held that presidential power would increase. He tried to reconcile presidential power and free government, but was inconsistent on Congress as a restraint upon the president. He placed greater faith in conscience and moral training as checks upon the president, but Carl Becker, Rossiter's theoretical authority, taught a historicism that left Rossiter with morally empty limits on presidential power. Rossiter's "strong presidency" was, in fact, the paramount presidency because he failed to articulate objective limits on the president's power.

In *Presidential Power: The Politics of Leadership* Richard Neustadt defines presidential leadership as "effective influence upon the other men involved in governing the country." Neustadt's analytical intention is to discover "what a president can do to make his own *will* felt within his own Administration" [italics added]. Thus *Presidential Power* worked within the will and power approach used by Corwin in order to save the New Deal. Neustadt teaches that a " 'first rate' temperament" turns governmental experience into presidential expertise, but he fails to explore "temperament" thoroughly and systematically. His imprecision about pre-presidential experience weakens his argument on what prepares a president to excel in office.

An omission in Neustadt's argument is his general indifference to whether the president combined influence and prudent judgment in domestic politics. According to President Kennedy, Neustadt's argument on effective influence "makes everything a president does seem too premeditated"; in the case of FDR's evaluation of Soviet–American relations, Neustadt invokes the president's "unfathomed" mind when debatable results challenged the prudence of the president's "effective influence." He injected an unusual, for him, moral note into his evaluation of the Nixon administration as the "most corrupt." Inconsistently with his stress on effective influence to the neglect of the constitutional aspects of the presidency, Neustadt appealed for congressional restraints upon President Nixon during the Vietnam War.

Neustadt's theory suffers from a blindness to ethical and constitutional questions and to the need to limit presidential power in light of more important principles. The insensitivity of FDR, Neustadt's model president, to the incarceration of Japanese Americans during World War II shows that what is good for the president in Neustadt's sense is not necessarily good for the regime. Neustadt romanticizes presidential power and FDR in particular, and he is less clear than Corwin was in the 1930s about the ethical price of the dominant presidency. In sum, presidential influence may be a necessary, but is not a sufficient, condition of presidential ability.

Neustadt's infatuation with power is hardly novel but resembles the spirit of the modern philosopher Thomas Hobbes, who taught that "power irresistible justifieth all actions really and properly, in whomsoever it be found. Less power does not."[95] Neustadt's power orientation impressed the impressionable as bold, new and even shocking at the time, but he teaches a decayed, academic Hobbesianism that is unclear about the premises, consequences and implications of that position. In short, Neustadt tried unsuccessfully to graft American liberalism onto Hobbesianism. The greatest service of Neustadt's book would be to reopen the question of the truth of Hobbes's teaching. Looking at our three experts on the presidency, I conclude that neither Corwin, Rossiter nor Neustadt were directly or indirectly inspired or influenced by Hamilton's teachings. The dominant presidency advocated by Corwin in 1934, Rossiter and Neustadt is post-Hamiltonian.

NOTES

1. Alexander George made the latter suggestion in "Assessing Presidential Character," 26 *World Politics* 234–282 (January 1974); see especially pp. 279–280. His review of James Barber's *Presidential Character: Predicting Performance in the White House* (1972) observes that: "Post-Watergate hindsight makes more noticeable the importance of old-fashioned moral character and the difficulty of incorporating this concept into character typologies such as Barber's." George, "Assessing Presidential Character," p. 249 n.21.

2. Edward Corwin, *French Policy and the American Alliance of 1788* (Princeton, N.J.: Princeton University, 1916).

3. Robert Newton, "Edward S. Corwin and American Constitutional Law," 14 *Journal of Public Law* 199 (1965); see the literature cited.

4. See the bibliography in Alpheus T. Mason and Gerald Garvey, eds., *American Constitutional History: Essays by Edward S. Corwin* (New York: Harper, 1964), pp. 216–223.

5. *National Cyclopedia of American Biography, Current Volume G* (New York: James White, 1946), p. 511.

6. Mason and Garvey, *American Constitutional History*, pp. 216–223.

7. Edward S. Corwin, "The Democratic Dogma and the Future of Political Science," 23 *American Political Science Review* 570 (August, 1929).

8. Ibid., p. 571.

9. Ibid., p. 591.

10. Mason and Garvey, *American Constitutional History*, pp. 216–223.

11. Corwin, *French Policy*, p. 367.

12. Edward S. Corwin, *The Twilight of the Supreme Court: A History of Our Constitutional Theory* (New Haven: Yale University Press, 1934), p. 122, italics in the original.

13. Letter from Charles Clark to Corwin, Oct. 2, 1934, Category 1, Carton 1, Corwin Papers, Princeton University Library, Princeton, N.J.

14. Corwin, *Twilight of the Supreme Court*, p. xxvii.

15. Ibid., pp. 103, 105, italics in the original.

16. Ibid., pp. 146, 56.

17. Ibid., pp. 106–107.

18. Ibid., p. 148, italics in the original.

19. Ibid., p. 178.

20. Ibid., p. 148.

21. Ibid., p. 140, italics in the original.

22. Ibid., p. 147.

23. Ibid., p. 133.

24. T. Roosevelt, *An Autobiography* (1913), pp. 388–389, quoted in Corwin, *Twilight of the Supreme Court*, p. 139.

25. H. Kelsen, *Vom Wesen und Wert der Demokratie* (2nd ed.; Aalen: Scientia Verlag, 1963 [1929]), pp. 101–102.

26. Newton, "Edward S. Corwin," pp. 199–200.

27. Edward S. Corwin, "Our Constitutional Revolution and How to Round It Out," 19 *Pennsylvania Bar Association Quarterly* 261–284 (April 1948).

28. Ibid., pp. 261, 284.

29. Page references in the text are to Corwin, *The President: Office and Powers* (4th rev. ed.; New York: New York University Press, 1957), the last revision by Corwin himself.

30. Jonathan Elliot, ed., 2 *The Debates in the State Ratifying Conventions on the Adoption of the Federal Convention* 513 (5 vols.; Philadelphia: Lippincott, 1836).

31. Corwin, *Twilight of the Supreme Court*, p. 197 n.7.

32. Ibid., p. 97.

33. Ibid., p. 98.

34. See John Locke, *Second Treatise*, in *Two Treatises of Government*, Peter Laslett, ed. (Cambridge: University Press, 1960), par. 123, p. 368; Corwin, *Twilight of the Supreme Court*, p. 197 n.7, quoting Locke, *Letter Concerning Toleration*, in Locke, 2 *Works* 239 (1727).

35. Corwin, *Twilight of the Supreme Court*, p. 197 n.7.

36. Ibid., p. 98.

37. Edward S. Corwin, *Total War and the Constitution* (New York: Knopf, 1947), p. 172.

38. Morton Frisch, "Franklin Delano Roosevelt," in Frisch and Richard G. Stevens, eds., *American Political Thought: The Philosophic Dimension of American Statesmanship* (New York: Scribner's, 1971), pp. 233–234, italics in the original.

39. Corwin, *Total War*, p. 180, italics in the original.

40. Edward S. Corwin, "Our Expendable Constitution," 52 *University of Illinois Bulletin* 20 (January, 1955).

41. Corwin, *Total War*, p. 178.

42. Corwin, *Twilight of the Supreme Court*, p. 133.

43. Edward S. Corwin, *A Constitution of Powers in a Secular State* (Charlottesville, Va.: Michie, 1951), p. 87.

44. 19 *Pennsylvania Bar Association Quarterly* 278–282 (April, 1948); Corwin, *President: Office and Powers*, pp. 38, 297 ff.

45. Edward S. Corwin, "The Debt of American Constitutional Law to Natural Law Concepts," 25 *Notre Dame Lawyer* 282 (Winter, 1950).

46. Edward S. Corwin, *Constitutional Revolution, Ltd.* (Claremont, Calif.: Claremont Colleges, 1941), p. 115.

47. 25 *Notre Dame Lawyer* 258–284 (Winter, 1950).

48. Corwin, *Constitution of Powers in a Secular State*, p. 116.

49. Edward S. Corwin, *Liberty Against Government* (Baton Rouge: Louisiana State University, 1948), pp. 182–183.

50. William G. Andrews, "The Presidency, Congress and Constitutional Theory" (Paper presented for delivery to the Annual Meeting of the American Political Science Association, 1971), p. 17.

51. Parenthetical page references to Rossiter in the text are to: Clinton Rossiter, *The American Presidency* (rev. ed.; New York: Harcourt, Brace and World, 1960).

52. Richard Neustadt, *Presidential Power: The Politics of Leadership* (New York: Wiley, 1968), Preface. Because the analytic argument of Chapters 1 through 8 "remains the heart of the book," the section below on Neustadt stays with the 1968 edition. Preface to the 1980 edition, p. xiv. Parenthetical page references to Neustadt in the text below are to the 1968 edition.

53. Clinton Rossiter, "We Must Show the Way to Enduring Peace," in *The National Purpose* (New York: Holt, Rhinehart, 1960), p. 83; Rossiter was also a writer for the President's Commission on National Goals. See his "The Democratic Process" in the President's Commission on National Goals, *Goals for Americans* (Englewood Cliffs, N.J.: Prentice-Hall, 1960), pp. 61–78.

54. Clinton Rossiter, "The Pattern of Liberty," in Milton Konvitz, ed., *Aspects of Liberty* (Ithaca, N.Y.: Cornell University Press, 1958), p. 16.

55. Ibid., p. 19; Introductory Lecture, Government 355, Cornell University, 1964.

56. "Patterns of Study for American Political Thought," handout in Government 355, Cornell University, quoting Becker, "What Is Still Living in the Political Philosophy of Thomas Jefferson," 48 *American Historical Review* 692–693 (July, 1943).

57. Carl Becker, *The Declaration of Independence* (New York: Vintage, 1942), p. 277.

58. "What Is Still Living in the Political Philosophy of Thomas Jefferson," in Phil L. Snyder, ed., *Detachment and the Writing of History: Essays and Letters of Carl Becker* (Ithaca, N.Y.: Cornell University Press, 1958), p. 232.

59. Carl Becker, *"What Is the Good of History?" Selected Letters of Carl L. Becker, 1900–1945*, Michael Kammen, ed. (Ithaca, N.Y.: Cornell University Press, 1973), p. 79.

60. Ibid., p. 80.

61. Becker, *Declaration of Independence*, p. 265.

62. Becker, *"What Is the Good of History?,"* p. 157.

63. George Sabine, "Carl Lotus Becker," in Becker, *Freedom and Responsibility in the American Way of Life* (New York: Random, 1945), pp. xxxvi–xxxvii.

64. Becker, *"What Is the Good of History?"* p. 112 n.2.

65. Ibid., p. 113.

66. Ibid., p. 123.

67. Rossiter, "We Must Show the Way to Enduring Peace," *The National Purpose*, pp. 82–83.

68. Ibid., p. 85.

69. Ibid., pp. 84–85, 92.

70. H. Butterfield, *The Whig Interpretation of History* (London: G. Bell, 1950 [1931]), p. v.

71. Ibid., p. 5; cf. Rossiter, *American Presidency*, p. 256.

72. Butterfield, *Whig Interpretation*, p. 12; cf. Rossiter, *American Presidency*, p. 84.

73. Alfred DeGrazia, *Republic in Crisis* (New York: Federal Legal Publications, 1965), chap. v.

74. See George, 26 *World Politics* 252, n. 22; the study of John Adams is Jean S. Holder, "The Sources of Presidential Power: John Adams and the Challenge to Executive Primacy," 101 *Political Science Quarterly* 601–616 (1986).

75. Peter Sperlich, "Bargaining and Overload: An Essay on *Presidential Power*," in Aaron Wildavsky, ed., *The Presidency* (Boston: Little, Brown, 1969), pp. 186–187.

76. Richard Neustadt, "What Did I Think I Was Doing?" *Presidency Research*, 7, no. 2 (Spring 1985), pp. 4, 8–9; Neustadt, Review of Corwin, *The President: Office and Powers*, 47 *Cornell Law Quarterly* 735 (1958), italics in the original.

77. Neustadt, "What Did I Think I Was Doing?" *Presidency Research*, 7, No. 2 (Spring 1985), p. 6.

78. Neustadt, Review, 43 *Cornell Law Quarterly* 736–737 (1958). Neustadt largely approves of examples of behavioral political science such as the works of David Truman, "most" of Robert Dahl's books and the "potentials" (for what?) of opinion research. Neustadt, "What Did I Think I Was Doing?," *Presidency Research*, 7, No. 2 (Spring 1985), p. 13.

79. Corwin, *President: Office and Powers*, pp. 248–250; Grant McConnell, *Steel and the Presidency 1962* (New York: Norton, 1963), pp. 89–90.

80. William T. Bluhm, *Theories of the Political System* (Englewood Cliffs, N.J.: Prentice-Hall, 1965), pp. 246–259.

81. Quoted in Arthur Schlesinger, Jr., *A Thousand Days* (Boston: Houghton Mifflin, 1965), p. 679.

82. *New York Times*, November 5, 1971, p. 48.

83. *New York Times*, May 17, 1970, p. 7; May 8, 1970, p. 1.

84. Richard Neustadt, "The Constraining of the President," *New York Times Magazine*, October 14, 1973, p. 116.

85. Ibid., pp. 115–116.

86. Summing up the presidency after Watergate, in 1974 Neustadt predicted that "I think it possible that twenty years from now collegial constraints upon a President will be at least as strong as twenty years ago." Neustadt, "The Constraining of the President: The Presidency After Watergate," 4 *British Journal of Political Science* 397 (October, 1974). It is important to appreciate the feeble limits that Neustadt recognizes. Other than collegial constraints "we have little to depend on...except constraints...of operating style....*All is subjective*, turning on him [the president], much as it was until lately with Nixon." Italics added.

87. Dillon Myer, *Uprooted Americans: The Japanese Americans and the War Relocation Authority During World War II* (Tucson: University of Arizona, 1971), p. 257.

88. Ibid., p. 285.

89. Ibid., p. 251.

90. Ibid., p. 255.

91. Ibid., pp. 19, 22.

92. Morton Grodzins, *Americans Betrayed: Politics and the Japanese Evacuation* (Chicago: University of Chicago, 1969 [1949]), p. 272 n.88.

93. Ibid., p. 373.

94. Ibid., p. 366.

95. Thomas Hobbes, *The Questions Concerning Liberty, Necessity, and Chance* in 5 *The English Works of Thomas Hobbes* 116, Sir William Molesworth, ed. (London: John Bohn, 1841).

Epilogue

This study has appraised Edward S. Corwin's thesis that "the modern theory of presidential power" is "the contribution primarily of Alexander Hamilton." Now we can gather up the argument and look briefly at the Reagan presidency to discover where the presidency may be tending. Hamilton's understanding of American republicanism rests on natural law, Christianity, honesty, justice, liberality, moderation and virtue. But the teachings of Hamilton and President Washington show that American republicanism is no seamless coat. There are at least two republican teachings. Washington's teaching emphasizes virtue or morality as the "foundation of the fabric" of popular government. Hamilton diagnosed republicanism with moral virtue but decline to vest the shaping of moral character in the national government or to expect or require conspicuous virtue in American presidents. To Hamilton's credit his teaching on the presidency stressed the restraints of safety and responsibility as well as presidential "energy" and the compatibility of presidential "power" with other parts of the Constitution and with the principles of free government. Hamilton would never simply maximize either presidential energy or power and let it go at that. For Washington restraints on presidential power must flow from both presidential and popular virtue and the Constitution, whereas Hamilton's *Federalist* 67–77 place mainly institutional restraints on the presidency. Hamilton, in fine, relied on virtue in his analysis of republicanism without providing for the diffusion of virtue. In spite of this disagreement, both Hamilton and Washington had a loftier understanding of republicanism, the Constitution, political power and the presidency than the revisionist presidents and scholars. Washington and Hamilton held that the presidency must be more than a powerful institution in order to be republican, that it must be active yet limited. The good intentions of the president and public opinion were no justification for a permissive presidency.

The revisionist presidents championed equality and constitutional innovation (Lincoln), power simply (Theodore Roosevelt), statism and a living Constitution opposed to the Founders' understanding (Wilson) and comfort or welfare defined as the satiation of corporeal craving (FDR). The American regime thus changed from primary emphasis on political freedom at the Founding to economic security. Nor was this change entirely unfortunate: men in dire need cannot be free men. The exercise of political freedom, not to mention virtue, presupposes a certain amount of equipment or property. It remains true, however, that the New Deal deepened the corporealism inherent in the American regime from its outset because of the overriding importance of acquisitiveness. The grander, more diffuse and more difficult to accomplish the presidential objectives became, the more presidential power was required. The rise of presidential aggrandizement from Lincoln to FDR accompanied a revolution in the ends of the regime.

The revisionist scholars' works on the presidency generally undermined the authority and abandoned the guidance of Hamilton and Washington concerning republicanism, political power, constitutionalism and virtue. These scholars attempted to replace Hamilton and Washington's teachings with a masked version of the will to power, a relativism of moral, political and constitutional ends based on historicism and an "inside dopester's" emphasis on presidential technique that is anti-constitutional in fact, if not in intention. The culpability of the scholars, with the partial exception of Corwin, is far graver than that of the revisionist presidents, who were besieged with the importunate questions of what to do now, what to do next. However these circumstances may extenuate, they do not justify the severance of constitutional understanding from the Founding accomplished by the revisionist presidents. The revisionist scholars had the leisure to investigate, a luxury often denied to active statesmen. The revisionist scholars therefore deserve more severe censure than presidents such as Lincoln and FDR. Posterity may condemn the revisionist scholars as the forgetful heirs of successful revolutionaries and constitutional Founders. In sum, the modern theory of presidential power assumes or advocates highly centralized power under the president and a presidency paramount over Congress and the Supreme Court. Although superficially the revisionist presidents and scholars appear to hold a variety of theories of presidential power, these theories culminate in the dominant presidency.

Thus American constitutional and political development since Hamilton and Washington has two results of interest for our present purpose: the decline and disappearance of virtue as a shaping principle and, over the long run, the aggrandizement of presidential power. Contrary to Corwin's continuity thesis, we have seen that Hamilton's understanding of the American regime, his *Federalist* papers and Pacificus Letters on the presidency, and his advice to President Washington neither are nor can be the principal sources of the modern theory of presidential power disseminated by major revisionist presidents and scholars. Corwin's prodigious learning and rank at the forefront of American political scientists make it unlikely that his Hamilton thesis was a historical error or misunderstanding, but we have nevertheless seen that there is more discontinuity than continuity between Hamilton and modernity.

How can we account for this? By 1953, when he published his Hamilton thesis, Corwin had seen the pendulum of constitutional interpretation and presidential action swing to an excess of presidential power, some of this, sad to say, justified by the Supreme Court of the United States.[1] Corwin seems to have believed that anchoring the modern presidency in Hamilton's teachings might retard the trend toward excess or at least restore some moderation, safety and responsibility to interpretation and action. His prescription for the modern presidency was the teachings of Alexander Hamilton, which Corwin invoked, to paraphrase Lord Macaulay, to ensure that the Constitution and the presidency weren't all sail and no anchor. Without comment or elaboration Corwin inserted a "noble lie" in what would surely be a widely used and semi-official interpretation of the Constitution for many years. In other words, Corwin "trimmed" the ship of constitutional interpretation and presidential action to rescue it from leaning to extremes.[2] As he remarked, if judges make law, so do commentators; only Corwin did not act arbitrarily. The prudent commentator "trims" the constitutional ship of state in one way at one time and in another way at another time to avoid capsizing. The commentator thus alters the emphasis of certain principles depending in part on the character and abilities of the president and on the danger to be met.

When the danger was insufficient governmental power during the 1920s and, especially, during the Depression, Corwin prescribed principles favoring a powerful Congress led by an ascendant presidency. These principles included his tacit rejection of a higher law limitation on governmental power, his criticism of constitutional worship, his rejection of the Founders' political science and his advocacy of the ideas of progress, unqualified majority rule, an instrumental, not symbolic, Constitution and a dominant presidency.[3] Elsewhere I have suggested the importance of recovering the idea of natural law as a challenge to unlimited human authority.[4] The dogma of progress, and the corollary of the presidency as a necessary agent of progress, also need scrutiny. The doctrine of an inevitable political and moral progress of the United States from the Founding to the present is a consequence of the limitation of our historical understanding to "the recent past" and of our failure to reenact the experience of the Founding and the birth of the presidency in our minds.[5] Either there is no overall moral trend in American political history, or if there is such a trend, decline or decadence is as likely a possibility as an unbroken ascent.

My larger point, however, is that Corwin's effort to justify increased governmental power succeeded so thoroughly that his later and more thoughtful work, *The President: Office and Powers*, failed to revive constitutional limitations. Despite his gifts and learning, Corwin could not repeal the overstatement of national governmental power of which he was guilty in the 1920s and the Depression. Moreover, as far as I am aware, he never systematically confronted his former teachings. One important lesson and requirement for constitutional scholarship, then, is moderation in stating what the American Constitution will permit in presidential power. All of the strongest arguments for presidential power need not be indiscriminately stated for all audiences and occasions. The scholarly effort to avoid feebleness in government and ensure adequate power must go together with keeping alive constitutional limitations. Some liberals must become more concerned with constitutional limitations outside of the First Amendment than they have been historically, and some conservatives must acknowledge that the adaptation of fundamentals is sometimes necessary.

The importance of Corwin's Hamilton thesis is that it virtually compelled students of the presidency to return from the familiar one-dimensional theory of presidential power to the comprehensive teachings of Alexander Hamilton. The most fundamental long-run limitation on the presidency may well be what Corwin called popular demand and expectation.[6] For example, Hamilton wrote: "The time may ere long arrive when the minds of men will be prepared . . . to *recover* the Constitution, but the many cannot now be brought to make a stand for its preservation. We must await awhile."[7] In advising the American mind to recapture the presidency as Hamilton understood it, Corwin shouldered some of the burden of recovering the Constitution that was torn from Hamilton by Aaron Burr's pistol. Corwin's Hamilton and Washington theses suggest the benefit of political scientists, law teachers and historians discussing the American presidency with a more pronounced Hamiltonian–Washingtonian emphasis than they have been in the habit of doing.

If we accept Corwin's understanding of constitutional advice, in which direction should we "trim" interpretation after the Reagan presidency? An answer to this question requires a brief look at his understanding of his goals and achievements and his notion of the presidency. Any appraisal at this time, however, can be only tentative and exploratory. Denying that he emulated FDR's presidency, Reagan asserted on the eve of his retirement that "I came here with a pretty set program in my mind of what government should be and what it was intended to be by the Founding Fathers and where it had violated those precepts, and my determination to change it."[8] This implies that Reagan also had a "pretty set program" of what the presidency should be as a part of "what government should be," a point to which I shall turn below. The president named a "spiritual revival in America" or a resurgence of pride in America that he called " 'the new patriotism' " and "a rediscovery of our values and our common sense" among his major achievements. The president correctly said that this revival "won't count for much, and it won't last unless it's grounded in thoughtfulness and knowledge."[9] What degree of thoughtfulness and knowledge did President Reagan deploy in explaining the office of president? Fred I. Greenstein, a scholar of the presidency, regretted "how unrevealing Reagan himself is: . . . There was never a discussion on his part of what it means to be President."[10] Thus Reagan differed from our most thoughtful presidents by failing publicly to explain what the presidency should be—a surprising omission from one who was called the "Great Communicator." In spite of Reagan's assertion in his Farewell Address to the American people that his speeches were rooted in "our experience, our wisdom, and our belief in the principles that have guided us for two centuries," he failed to draw his understanding of the presidency from the resources of American constitutional and political thought.

President Reagan contended that "when I came to office, I found in the presidency a weakened institution," and he declared that his framing of the policy debate had compensated "for *some* of the weakening of the office. I found a Congress that was trying to transform our government into a quasi-parliamentary system." Reagan concluded: "But we have not restored the constitutional balance, at least not fully—and I believe it must be restored."[11] This implied that he did not redress some, perhaps much, of the weakening of the presidency. In foreign policy Reagan stated that "sometimes attempts are made to weaken my hand."[12] He argued that the requirement to preserve, protect and defend the Constitution means "for a president . . . protecting his office, and its place in our constitutional framework."[13]

How did President Reagan see the protection of his office in his farewell remarks? He reflected on the modern presidency: "you're always somewhat apart. You spent a lot of time going by too fast in a car *someone else* is driving."[14] Although focused on the president's relationship to the people, this comment generally suggests a passive conception of the presidency in which the president is a passenger, a somewhat unwilling passenger at that, rather than the driver or the navigator. Reagan scarcely will go down in American history as either an assertive or dutiful president. For example, he remarked in his domestic policy farewell address to administration officials: "As soon as I go home to California, I plan to lean back, kick up my feet, and take a long nap. (*Laughter.*) Now, come to think of it, things won't be all that different after all. (*Laughter and applause.*)"[15] Future scholars of the presidency may find President Reagan's jocular confession of laziness in office deserving of something other than laughter and applause.

A clue to President Reagan's more sober assessment of his stewardship was his farewell reference to "a recent article in Commentary Magazine" by "legal commentator L. Gordon Crovitz."[16] Crovitz is actually the assistant editorial page editor of the *Wall Street Journal* and the author, most surprisingly, of a *Commentary* article entitled, "How Ronald Reagan Weakened the Presidency!"[17] The president's speech supplemented Crovitz's article but, most important, did not disagree with or criticize his thesis. Crovitz argued that "the next President will inherit an office whose powers under the Constitution have been steadily eroded by various forms of congressional usurpation," that "an aggressive assertion of executive power" is in a president's self-interest and that Reagan "never actually demanded and consequently never enjoyed" the proper authority without which "the job is hardly worth having:" "after two landslide victories and eight years in office, Reagan will leave the presidency even weaker than he found it."[18]

The erosion of presidential power, Crovitz stated, arose in part from "Reagan's acquiescence in the post-Watergate system of prosecutorial politics."[19] The president and his advisers in the Justice Department failed to safeguard presidential power from the whittling away of the power to impound funds in the Budget and Impoundment Control Act of 1974.[20] Nor did Reagan limit the effects of the War Powers Resolution of 1973. Moreover, he signed the third Boland Amendment removing the usual intelligence agencies from the Central American policy "loop."[21] He failed to make a convincing public case, based on presidential history, for unilateral executive branch power to help the *Contras*. The president committed a "great political blunder" in pleading ignorance of the diversion of Iran arms sale funds to the *Contras* because this plea conceded congressional authority over executive-branch aid despite a two hundred year history of unilateral presidential acts more serious than "a few million dollars for the *Contras*."[22] Finally, Crovitz mentioned "White House passivity" in the "brutalization" of Robert Bork, Reagan's unsuccessful nominee to the Supreme Court.[23] In sum, Crovitz indicted Reagan's indifference to the presidency as an institution with arguments to which Reagan took only minor exception—in effect conceding the charges against him. The *Wall Street Journal* editorialized that his institutional disloyalty was "the greatest failing of his tenure."[24] If Reagan's farewell remarks adequately reflect his notion of the presidency and his sober response to Crovitz's arguments, we may conclude that the president, his speech writers and their authorities were unable to refute these criticisms.

What direction should the understanding of presidential power take in the light of President Reagan's possibly insufficient approach? Let us assume that presidential power may be understood as a series of possibilities ranging from impotence to aggression against the Constitution. A presidential striving for greater vigor and discretion, consistent with the other parts of the Constitution and the principles of free government and without the doctrinal excesses of the past, would seem to be called for in the aftermath of the Reagan presidency. Let us ponder the words of the unusually experienced United States Supreme Court Justice Robert Jackson, who had served as assistant attorney general, solicitor general, United States attorney general and chief of counsel for the United States during the prosecution of certain Axis war criminals. Justice Jackson said: "If not good law, there was worldly wisdom in the maxim attributed to Napoleon that 'The tools belong to the man who can use them.' "[25] To paraphrase Jackson speaking in another context, only the president himself can prevent power from slipping through his fingers. The president has a duty to hand over the presidency unimpaired to his successor. Second, it is helpful to recall, in the words of a disciple of Hamilton's, that America has "a constitution intended to endure for ages to come, and, consequently, to be adapted to the various *crises* of human affairs."[26] Third, presidents and students of the presidency may profit from the instruction of Alexander Hamilton because, as Edmund Burke said in comparing the results of the French Revolution to proper government, "to form a *free government*, that is, to temper together these opposite elements of liberty and restraint in one consistent work, requires much thought, deep reflection, a sagacious, powerful, and combining mind."[27] Hamilton is one of the few such minds to have reflected comprehensively on the presidency. If a choice must be made between the arguments of academics (such as Rossiter and Neustadt) and of statesmen (such as Hamilton and Washington) in understanding the presidency, I conclude that the weight of evidence favors the latter. Such academic authors should yield to the spirit and teachings of our thoughtful statesmen and should be kept "on tap," not "on top."

Hamilton and Washington in effect replied to a part of Burke's challenge to the defenders of mere freedom: "But what is liberty without wisdom and without virtue? It is the greatest of all possible evils; for it is folly, vice, and madness, without tuition or restraint."[28] Hamilton and Washington agreed that under the best circumstances virtue should guide popular liberty and political power to reasonable ends, though they disagreed over what the actual circumstances permitted. But the American republicans no longer honor virtue either in deed or speech: they "continue every day to show by new proofs, that no people can be

great who have ceased to be virtuous." Liberty faces a greater peril than
either an excess or the abuse of presidential power because liberty lacks
the guidance of virtue found in the classic moment of American statesmanship.

NOTES

1. For example, see the upholding as constitutional of the evacuation from
a West Coast military area and detention of all persons of Japanese ancestry in
Korematsu v. United States, 323 U.S. 214 (1944), Opinion of the Court by Justice
Hugo Black. Justice Robert Jackson said in dissent: "Once a judicial opinion
rationalizes such an order to show that it conforms to the Constitution, or rather
rationalizes the Constitution to show that the Constitution sanctions such an
order, the Court *for all time* has validated the principle of racial discrimination
in criminal procedure and of transplanting American citizens. The principle
then lies about like a loaded weapon ready for the hand of any authority that
can bring forward a plausible claim of an urgent need." Ibid., p. 246, italics
added. "But I would not lead people to rely on this Court for a review that seems
to me wholly delusive. The military reasonableness of these orders can only be
determined by military superiors. If the people ever let command of the war
power fall into irresponsible and unscrupulous hands, the courts wield no power
equal to its restraint." Ibid., p. 248. Former Supreme Court Justice Benjamin
Robbins Curtis criticized Lincoln's Emancipation Proclamation, suspension of
the writ of habeas corpus and the military arrests of disloyal persons in 1862:
"Are the great principles of free government to be used and consumed as means
of war? Are we not wise enough and strong enough to carry on this war to a
successful military end, without submitting to the loss of any one great principle
of liberty? We are strong enough. We are wise enough, if the people and their
servants will but understand and observe the just limits of military power." Curtis
wrote of the president: "He is not the military commander of the citizens of the
United States, but of its soldiers." Curtis, "Executive Power" (1862), in Benjamin
R. Curtis, ed., 2 *A Memoir of Benjamin Robbins Curtis with Some of His Professional
and Miscellaneous Writings* 324, 328 (2 vols.; Boston: Little Brown, 1879).

2. George Savile, Marquess of Halifax, "The Character of a Trimmer," in
Complete Works, J. P. Kenyon, ed. (Harmondsworth, Eng.: Penguin Books, 1969),
p. 102.

3. Richard Loss, "Introduction," in Edward S. Corwin, 1 *Corwin on the Constitution* 42 (Ithaca, N.Y.: Cornell University Press, 1981).

4. The idea of natural law has been expelled from legal and constitutional
discourse without necessarily achieving beneficial results. See the article in the
Zeitschrift der Akademie für deutsches Recht by former Reich Commisar for Justice
and Minister without portfolio Dr. Hans Frank speaking of the Academy "def-
initely doing away with former schools" of law, the first named of which were
"the schools of natural law." Excerpted in C. H. McIlwain, *Constitutionalism and
the Changing World* (New York: Macmillan, 1939), p. 272. See also Hermann
Weinkauff, "Die deutsche Justiz und der Nationalsozialismus Ein Überblick,"

"Die Herrschaft des Rechtspositivismus," 1 *Die Deutsche Justiz und der National-sozialismus* 28–31 (Stuttgart: Deutsche Verlags-Anstalt, 1968).

5. I have adapted this argument from R. G. Collingwood, *The Idea of History* (New York: Oxford University Press, 1956), pp. 328–329.

6. As an alternative to the suggestion offered in the text, the following works discuss proposals for constitutional change and for strengthening Congress against the presidency: Arthur M. Schlesinger, Jr., "Leave the Constitution Alone (1982)," in *Reforming American Government: The Bicentennial Papers of the Committee on the Constitutional System*, Donald L. Robinson, ed. (1985), pp. 50–54; Lloyd N. Cutler and C. Douglas Dillon, "A Rebuttal to Arthur Schlesinger, Jr. (1983)," in ibid., pp. 55–58; Charles M. Hardin, *Presidential Power and Accountability: Toward a New Constitution* (1974); James A. Sundquist, *Constitutional Reform and Effective Government* (1986); for plausible arguments that the problem transcends change in the written Constitution, see Don K. Price, *America's Unwritten Constitution* (1983) and Louis Fisher, *Constitutional Conflicts between Congress and the President* (1985). See Donald L. Horowitz, "Is the Presidency Failing," 88 *The Public Interest* 3–27 (Summer, 1987) for a criticism of proposals for parliamentary style changes and a defense of the Founders' fixed term presidency. The following are helpful for an appreciation of the potential and limitations of Congress: Arthur M. Schlesinger, Jr., and Alfred DeGrazia, *Congress and the Presidency: Their Role in Modern Times* (1967); Alton Frye, *A Responsible Congress: The Politics of National Security* (1975); Harvey G. Zeidenstein, "The Reassertion of Congressional Power: New Curbs on the President," 93 *Political Science Quarterly* 393–409 (Fall, 1978); Thomas M. Franck and Edward Weisband, *Foreign Policy by Congress* (1979); Thomas E. Cronin, "A Resurgent Congress and the Imperial Presidency," 95 *Political Science Quarterly* 209–237 (1980); James L. Sundquist, *The Decline and Resurgence of Congress* (1981); Louis Koenig, "Historical Perspective: The Swings and Roundabouts of Presidential Power," in *The Tethered Presidency: Congressional Restraints on Executive Power*, Thomas M. Franck, ed. (1981), pp. 38–63; Allen Schick, "Politics through Law: Congressional Limitations on Executive Discretion," in *Both Ends of the Avenue The Presidency, the Executive Branch, and Congress in the 1980s*, Anthony King, ed. (1983), pp. 154–184; Arthur Maass, *Congress and the Common Good* (1983); George Szamuely, "The Imperial Congress," 84 *Commentary* 27–32 (September, 1987).

7. A. Hamilton to G. Morris, Feb. 29, 1802, 25 *Papers of Alexander Hamilton* 545, italics in the original.

8. Interview with the President, *New York Times*, January 19, 1989, p. 12.

9. Remarks by the President in Question and Answer Session with University of Virginia Students, Office of the White House Press Secretary, December 16, 1988, p. 3; President's Farewell Address to the American People, *New York Times*, January 12, 1989, p. 8.

10. *New York Times*, December 12, 1988, p. 10.

11. Remarks by the President in Domestic Policy Farewell Address, Office of the White House Press Secretary, December 13, 1988, p. 6, italics added.

12. Remarks by the President on Foreign Policy to University of Virginia Students and Guests, Office of the White House Press Secretary, December 16, 1988, p. 7.

13. Ibid.

14. President's Farewell Address to the American People, *New York Times*, January 12, 1989, p. 8, italics added.

15. Remarks by the President in Domestic Policy Farewell Address, Office of the White House Press Secretary, December 13, 1988, p. 1.

16. Ibid., p. 6.

17. 86 *Commentary* 25–29 (September, 1988).

18. Ibid., pp. 29, 25.

19. Ibid., p. 29.

20. Ibid., pp. 25–26.

21. Ibid., p. 27.

22. Ibid., pp. 28–29.

23. Ibid., p. 29.

24. "The Reagan Legacy," *Wall Street Journal*, January 19, 1989, p. A10.

25. Youngstown v. Sawyer, 343 U.S. 579, 654 (1952), concurring opinion.

26. Chief Justice John Marshall, McCulloch v. Maryland, 4 Wheat. (U.S.) 316, 415 (1819), italics in the original; see Samuel J. Konefsky, *John Marshall and Alexander Hamilton* (New York: Macmillan, 1964).

27. *Reflections on the Revolution in France*, 3 *Works of the Right Honorable Edmund Burke* 559–560 (Boston: Little Brown, 1899), italics in the original.

28. Burke, *Reflections on the Revolution in France*, 3 *Works of the Right Honorable Edmund Burke* 559.

Selected Bibliography

This bibliography lists most books and monographs used, not all works consulted. The textual footnotes refer to some of the articles related to the theme of this study. Occasionally, I have listed informative sources alluded to in the text but not cited in the footnotes, such as Chancellor James Kent's memoir of Alexander Hamilton.

Adair, Douglass. *Fame and the Founding Fathers*. New York: Norton, 1964.
Adams, John, and Thomas Jefferson. *The Adams-Jefferson Letters*. Lester J. Cappon, ed. 2 vols.; Chapel Hill: University of North Carolina Press, 1959.
Aly, Bower. *The Rhetoric of Alexander Hamilton*. New York: Russell and Russell, 1965 (1941).
Ames, Fisher. *Works of Fisher Ames*. Seth Ames, ed. 2 vols.; Boston: Little Brown, 1854; New York: DaCapo, 1969.
Anderson, Donald. *William Howard Taft: A Conservative's Conception of the Presidency*. Ithaca, N.Y.: Cornell University Press, 1973.
Aristotle. *Nichomachean Ethics*. F. H. Peters, trans. London: Kegan Paul, 1891.
———. *Politics*. Ernest Barker, trans. Oxford: Clarendon Press, 1948.
———. *The Rhetoric of Aristotle*. R. Jebb, trans. Cambridge: University Press, 1909.
Becker, Carl. *The Declaration of Independence*. New York: Vintage, 1942.
———. *"What Is the Good of History?" Selected Letters of Carl L. Becker, 1900–1945*. Michael Kammen, ed. Ithaca, N.Y.: Cornell University Press, 1973.
Bein, Alex. "Die Staatsidee Alexander Hamiltons in ihrer Enstehung und Entwicklung." Beiheft 12, *Historische Zeitschrift*. Munich: Verlag R. Oldenbourg, 1927.
Bemis, Samuel Flagg. *Jay's Treaty*. 2nd ed.; New Haven: Yale University Press, 1962.
Berger, Raoul. *Executive Privilege*. Cambridge: Harvard University Press, 1974.
Birkenhead, The Earl of. *Contemporary Personalities*. London: Cassell, 1924.

Bluhm, William T. *Theories of the Political System.* Englewood Cliffs, N.J.: Prentice-Hall, 1965.

Blum, John Morton. *The Republican Roosevelt.* Cambridge: Harvard University Press, 1954.

Borden, Morton, ed. *George Washington.* Englewood Cliffs, N.J.: Prentice-Hall, 1969.

Brown, Stuart Gerry. *Alexander Hamilton.* New York: Washington Square Press, 1967.

Burns, James MacGregor. *Presidential Government: The Crucible of Leadership.* Boston: Houghton Mifflin, 1965.

———. *Roosevelt: The Lion and the Fox.* New York: Harcourt Brace, 1956.

Butterfield, Herbert. *The Whig Interpretation of History.* London: G. Bell, 1950 (1931).

Charnwood, Lord. *Abraham Lincoln.* 3rd ed.; New York: Henry Holt, 1917.

———. *Theodore Roosevelt.* Boston: Atlantic Monthly Press, 1923.

Collingwood, R. G. *The Idea of History.* New York: Oxford University Press, 1956.

Conkin, Paul. *The New Deal.* New York: Thomas Y. Crowell, 1967.

Cooke, Jacob E. *Alexander Hamilton.* New York: Charles Scribner's Sons, 1982.

Corwin, Edward S. *American Constitutional History: Essays by Edward S. Corwin.* Alpheus T. Mason and Gerald Garvey, eds. New York: Harper, 1964.

———. *A Constitution of Powers in a Secular State.* Charlottesville, Va.: Michie, 1951.

———. *Constitutional Revolution, Ltd.* Claremont, Calif.: Claremont Colleges, 1941.

———. *Corwin on the Constitution. Volume I: The Foundations of American Constitutional and Political Thought, the Powers of Congress, and the President's Power of Removal.* Richard Loss, ed. Ithaca, N.Y.: Cornell University Press, 1981.

———. *Corwin on the Constitution. Volume II: The Judiciary.* Richard Loss, ed. Ithaca, N.Y.: Cornell University Press, 1987.

———. *Corwin on the Constitution. Volume III: On Liberty against Government.* Richard Loss, ed. Ithaca, N.Y.: Cornell University Press, 1988.

———. *French Policy and the American Alliance of 1788.* Princeton, N.J.: Princeton University Press, 1916.

———. *Liberty against Government.* Baton Rouge: Louisiana State University, 1948.

———. *The President: Office and Powers.* 4th rev. ed.; New York: New York University Press, 1957.

———. *Presidential Power and the Constitution: Essays, by Edward S. Corwin.* Richard Loss, ed. Ithaca, N.Y.: Cornell University Press, 1976.

———. *The President's Control of Foreign Relations.* Princeton, N.J.: Princeton University Press, 1917.

———. *Total War and the Constitution.* New York: Knopf, 1947.

———. *The Twilight of the Supreme Court: A History of our Constitutional Theory.* New Haven: Yale University Press, 1934.

———., ed. *The Constitution of the United States of America: Analysis and Interpretation.* Senate Document 170, 82nd Congress, 2nd Session, 1953.

Cronon, David, ed. *The Political Thought of Woodrow Wilson.* Indianapolis: Bobbs Merrill, 1965.

Cunliffe, Marcus. *George Washington: Man and Monument*. Boston: Little, Brown, 1958.

DeGrazia, Alfred. *Republic in Crisis*. New York: Federal Legal Publications, 1965.

Eidelberg, Paul. *A Discourse on Statesmanship*. Urbana: University of Illinois Press, 1974.

Einstein, Lewis. *Roosevelt: His Mind in Action*. Boston: Houghton Mifflin, 1930.

Ekirch, Arthur, Jr. *The Decline of American Liberalism*. New ed.; New York: Atheneum, 1967.

Elliot, Jonathan, ed. *The Debates in the State Ratifying Conventions on the Adoption of the Federal Convention*. 5 vols.; Philadelphia: Lippincott, 1836.

Epstein, David F. *The Political Theory of the Federalist*. Chicago: University of Chicago Press, 1984.

Faÿ, Bernard. *George Washington: Republican Aristocrat*. Boston: Houghton Mifflin, 1931.

Flexner, James. *George Washington Anguish and Farewell, 1793–1799*. Boston: Little, Brown, 1972.

———. *Washington and the New Nation, 1783–1793*. Boston: Little, Brown, 1970.

Freidel, Frank. *Franklin D. Roosevelt: The Apprenticeship*. Boston: Little, Brown, 1952.

———. *Franklin D. Roosevelt: Launching the New Deal*. Boston: Little, Brown, 1973.

Fried, Albert, ed. *The Jeffersonian and Hamiltonian Traditions in American Politics*. Garden City, N.Y.: Anchor Doubleday Books, 1968.

Friedrich, Carl J. *Constitutional Government and Democracy*. 4th ed. Waltham: Blaisdell, 1968.

———. *Constitutional Government and Politics*. New York: Harper and Brothers, 1937.

Frisch, Morton J. *Franklin D. Roosevelt: The Contribution of the New Deal to American Political Thought and Practice*. Boston: Twayne, 1975.

Greer, Thomas H. *What Roosevelt Thought*. East Lansing: Michigan State University Press, 1958.

Grodzins, Morton. *Americans Betrayed: Politics and the Japanese Evacuation*. Chicago: University of Chicago, 1969 (1949).

Guizot, François. *Monk and Washington: Historical Studies*. London: Routledge, 1851.

Gummere, Richard M. *The American Colonial Mind and the Classical Tradition*. Cambridge: Harvard University Press, 1963.

Hamilton, Alexander. *Alexander Hamilton's Paybook*. E. P. Panagopoulos, ed. Detroit: Wayne State University Press, 1961.

———. *The Papers of Alexander Hamilton*. Harold Syrett, ed. New York: Columbia University Press, 1961–1987.

———. *The Works of Alexander Hamilton*. John C. Hamilton, ed. New York: Charles Francis, 1851.

———. *The Works of Alexander Hamilton*. H. C. Lodge, ed. St. Clair Shores, Mich.: Scholarly Press, 1971.

Hamilton, Alexander, John Jay, and James Madison. *The Federalist*. Jacob Cooke, ed. Middletown: Wesleyan University Press, 1961.

———. *The Federalist*. John C. Hamilton, ed. Philadelphia: J. B. Lippincott, 1892.

Hamilton, Alexander, and James Madison. *The Letters of Pacificus and Helvidius*

on the Neutrality Proclamation of 1793 with the Letters of Americanus. Richard
    Loss, ed. Delmar, N.Y.: Scholars' Facsimiles and Reprints, 1976.

Hamilton, James A. *Reminiscences.* New York: Scribner's, 1869.

Harbaugh, William. *The Life and Times of Theodore Roosevelt.* rev. ed.; New York:
    Oxford University Press, 1975.

Hart, James. *The American Presidency in Action 1789.* New York: Macmillan, 1948.

Heckscher, August, ed. *The Politics of Woodrow Wilson.* New York: Harper, 1956.

Hobbes, Thomas. *The Questions Concerning Liberty, Necessity, and Chance. The Eng-
    lish Works of Thomas Hobbes.* Sir William Molesworth, ed. Vol. 5; London:
    John Bohn, 1841.

Hume, David. *Dialogues Concerning Natural Religion.* Henry D. Aiken, ed. New
    York: Hafner, 1948.

————. *Dialogues Concerning Natural Religion.* Norman Kemp Smith, ed. Indi-
    anapolis: Library of the Liberal Arts, n.d.

————. *Enquiries Concerning Human Understanding and Concerning the Principles of
    Morals.* P. H. Nidditch, ed. 3rd ed.; Oxford: Clarendon Press, 1975.

————. *Essays Moral, Political, and Literary.* T. H. Green and T. H. Grose, eds. 2
    vols.; New York: Longmans, Green, 1912.

————. *The Letters of David Hume.* J.Y.T. Greig, ed. 2 vols.; Oxford: Clarendon
    Press, 1932.

————. *New Letters of David Hume.* R. Klibansky and E. Mossner, eds. Oxford:
    Clarendon Press, 1954.

————. *A Treatise of Human Nature.* P. H. Nidditch, ed. 2nd rev. ed.; Oxford:
    Clarendon Press, 1978.

Jaffa, Harry. *Crisis of the House Divided.* New York: Doubleday, 1959.

Jones, Alfred H. *Roosevelt's Image Brokers.* Port Washington, N.Y.: Kennikat Press,
    1974.

Kant, Immanuel. *Perpetual Peace.* Lewis White Beck, ed. Indianapolis: Liberal
    Arts Press, 1957.

Kelsen, Hans. *Vom Wesen und Wert der Demokratie.* 2nd ed.; Aalen: Scientia Verlag,
    1963 (1929).

Kemler, Edgar. *The Deflation of American Ideals: An Ethical Guide for New Dealers.*
    Washington, D.C.: American Council on Public Affairs, 1941.

Kent, James. "Chancellor Kent's Memories of Alexander Hamilton," in William
    Kent. *Memoirs and Letters of James Kent.* Boston: Little Brown, 1869,
    pp. 281–331.

Ketcham, Ralph. *James Madison.* New York: Macmillan, 1971.

Koch, Adrienne. *Power, Morals and the Founding Fathers.* Ithaca, N.Y.: Cornell
    University Press, 1961.

Latham, Earl, ed. *The Philosophy and Politics of Woodrow Wilson.* Chicago: Uni-
    versity of Chicago Press, 1958.

Lincoln, Abraham. *The Collected Works of Abraham Lincoln.* Roy Basler, ed. New
    Brunswick, N.J.: Rutgers University Press, 1953–1955.

Locke, John. *Two Treatises of Government.* Peter Laslett, ed. Cambridge: University
    Press, 1960.

Lodge, Henry Cabot. *George Washington.* 2 vols.; Boston: Houghton Mifflin, 1889.

Looze, Helene Johnson. *Alexander Hamilton and the British Orientation of American
    Foreign Policy, 1788–1803.* The Hague: Mouton, 1969.

Lycan, Gilbert. *Alexander Hamilton and American Foreign Policy: A Design for Greatness*. Norman: University of Oklahoma Press, 1970.

McConnell, Grant. *Steel and the Presidency, 1962*. New York: Norton, 1963.

McCoy, Drew. *The Elusive Republic*. Chapel Hill: University of North Carolina Press, 1980.

McDonald, Forrest. *Alexander Hamilton*. New York: Norton, 1979.

————. *The Presidency of George Washington*. Lawrence: University Press of Kansas, 1974.

McIlwain, C. H. *Constitutionalism and the Changing World*. New York: Macmillan, 1939.

MacIntyre, Alasdair. *After Virtue: A Study in Moral Theory*. Notre Dame, Ind.: University of Notre Dame Press, 1981.

Morison, Samuel E. *The Ancient Classics in a Modern Democracy*. London: Oxford University Press, 1939.

Morris, Edmund. *The Rise of Theodore Roosevelt*. New York: Coward, McCann and Geoghegen, 1979.

Mowry, George. *The Era of Theodore Roosevelt*. New York: Harper and Row, 1958.

Myer, Dillon. *Uprooted Americans: The Japanese Americans and the War Relocation Authority During World War II*. Tuscon: University of Arizona Press, 1971.

Nelson, Michael, ed. *The Presidency in the Political System*. Washington, D.C.: Congressional Quarterly Press, 1984.

Neustadt, Richard E. *Presidential Power: The Politics of Leadership*. New York: Wiley, 1968, 1980.

Paine, Thomas. *The Complete Writings of Thomas Paine*. Phillip Foner, ed. 2 vols.; New York: Citadel Press, 1945.

Patterson, C. Perry. *Presidential Government in the United States: The Unwritten Constitution*. Chapel Hill: University of North Carolina, 1947.

Peterson, Merrill. *The Jeffersonian Image in the American Mind*. New York: Oxford University Press, 1960.

Pious, Richard. *The American Presidency*. New York: Basic Books, 1979.

Plutarch. *The Lives of the Noble Grecians and Romans*. John Dryden and Arthur H. Clough, trans. New York: Modern Library 1932.

Pocock, J.G.A. *The Machiavellian Moment: Florentine Political Thought and the Atlantic Republican Tradition*. Princeton, N.J.: Princeton University Press, 1975.

Pringle, Henry F. *Theodore Roosevelt: A Biography*. rev. ed.; New York: Harcourt, Brace and World, 1956.

Randall, J. G. *Constitutional Problems Under Lincoln*. rev. ed.; Gloucester: Peter Smith, 1963.

————. *Lincoln the President*. 4 vols.; New York: Dodd, Mead, 1954–1955.

Riencourt, Amaury de. *The Coming Caesars*. New York: Coward McCann, 1957.

Robinson, Edgar E. *The Roosevelt Leadership, 1933–1945*. Philadelphia: J. B. Lippincott, 1955.

Roosevelt, Franklin D. *FDR: His Personal Letters*. Elliott Roosevelt, ed. 4 vols.; New York: Duell, Sloan and Pearce, 1948.

————. *The Public Papers and Addresses of Franklin D. Roosevelt*. 13 vols.; Random House, Harper and Brothers, Macmillan, 1938–1950.

Roosevelt, Theodore. *An Autobiography*. New York: Macmillan, 1913.

————. *The Letters of Theodore Roosevelt*. Elting E. Morison, ed. 8 vols.; Cambridge: Harvard University Press, 1951–1954.

————. *The New Nationalism*. Englewood Cliffs, N.J.: Prentice-Hall, 1961.

Rossiter, Clinton. *Alexander Hamilton and the Constitution*. New York: Harcourt, Brace and World, 1964.

————. *The American Presidency*. rev. ed.; New York: Harcourt, Brace and World, 1960.

————. *Constitutional Dictatorship*. Princeton, N.J.: Princeton University Press, 1948.

Savile, George, Marquess of Halifax. *Complete Works*. J. P. Kenyon, ed. Harmondsworth, Eng.: Penguin Books, 1969.

Scheiber, Harry. *The Wilson Administration and Civil Liberties, 1917–1921*. Ithaca, N.Y.: Cornell University Press, 1960.

Schlesinger, Arthur, Jr. *A Thousand Days*. Boston: Houghton Mifflin, 1965.

Small, Norman J. *Some Presidential Interpretations of the Presidency*. Baltimore: Johns Hopkins University Press, 1932.

Smith, James Morton, ed. *George Washington: A Profile*. New York: Hill and Wang, 1969.

Stourzh, Gerald. *Alexander Hamilton and the Idea of Republican Government*. Stanford, Calif.: Stanford University Press, 1970.

Strauss, Leo. *What Is Political Philosophy?* New York: Free Press, 1959.

Taft, William Howard. *Our Chief Magistrate and His Powers*. New York: Columbia University Press, 1916.

Thach, Charles. *The Creation of the Presidency*. Baltimore: Johns Hopkins University Press, 1969 (1923).

Thurow, Glen. *Abraham Lincoln and American Political Religion*. Albany: State University of New York Press, 1976.

Tocqueville, Alexis de. *Democracy in America*. J. P. Mayer and Max Lerner, eds. George Lawrence, trans. New York: Harper and Row, 1966.

Tourtellot, Arthur B., ed. *The Presidents on the Presidency*. New York: Russell and Russell, 1970 (1964).

Wagenknecht, Edward. *The Seven Worlds of Theodore Roosevelt*. New York: Longmans, Green, 1958.

Washington, George. *The Writings of George Washington*. John Fitzpatrick, ed. Washington, D.C.: Government Printing Office, 1931–1944.

Webster, Daniel. *The Great Speeches and Orations of Daniel Webster*. Boston: Little, Brown, 1879.

White, Leonard. *The Federalists*. New York: Macmillan, 1948.

White, Morton. *Philosophy, the Federalist, and the Constitution*. New York: Oxford University Press, 1987.

Wills, Garry. *Explaining America: The Federalist*. Garden City, N.Y.: Doubleday, 1981.

Wilson, Woodrow. *Constitutional Government in the United States*. New York: Columbia University Press, 1921 (1908).

————. *The Papers of Woodrow Wilson*. Arthur Link, ed. Princeton, N.J.: Princeton University Press, 1966–1988.

Woodward, W. E. *George Washington: The Image and the Man*. New York: Boni and Liveright, 1926.

Index

About the Author

RICHARD LOSS is an independent political scientist who has edited and written introductions to *Presidential Power and the Constitution: Essays, by Edward S. Corwin*, Alexander Hamilton and James Madison's *The Letters of Pacificus and Helvidius on the Proclamation of Neutrality of 1793 with the Letters of Americanus*, Friedrich von Gentz's *The Origin and Principles of the American Revolution, Compared with the Origin and Principles of the French Revolution* and *Corwin on the Constitution*, Volumes I through III. His essays on the Constitution, the presidency and the executive branch have appeared in *Encyclopedia of the American Constitution, Presidential Studies Quarterly* and *Public Administration Review*.